All Summer in a Day

SACHEVERELL SITWELL

All Summer in a Day

An Autobiographical Fantasia

by

Sacheverell Sitwell

Author of "Southern Barque Art," "The Thirteenth Cæsar,"
"The Hundred and One Harlequins," etc., etc.

New York
George H. Doran Company

To
GEORGIA

Preface

"Come, I will sing you some low, sleepy tune,
Not cheerful, nor yet sad; some dull old thing,
Some outworn and unused monotony.
. . . Have I forgot the words?
Faith! They are sadder than I thought they were.

Listen to the passing bell!
It says thou and I must part,
With a light and a heavy heart."

THESE words seem to me to epitomise all that I
have tried to express in this book. I have called
it an Autobiographical Fantasia, and such is the spirit
in which it should be read.

Without undue flattery to my twenty years of conscious experience I may say that I am sure these have
yielded tangible and personal memories enough for
more than one volume, did I wish to write a conventional Autobiography replete with little anecdotes and
every kind of malice that I could arrive at. Of possessing such ambition I hope I am acquitted in this
book. I have chosen but one or two ghosts from my
cupboard, brightly glittering ones by preference, whom
I have dangled in the light for a few moments before
I put them back in their dark corner. Some day, perhaps, I may open both cupboard-doors, dusting and
brushing at least a few of the ghosts, before it is time
to put them away. Here, in these pages, it has been
naturally the oldest and most ragged that have required attention, lest they came to pieces and were
useless, and so I have stretched into distant corners to
see what I could bring to light.

It is noticeable how very little most people can remember who have not had their memory specially trained, or, if you like, distorted, by drawing or writing. "Oh! your uncle remembered Lord Byron. What could he tell you about him?" "He had very curly hair and used to limp." Or—"So you often used to meet Oscar Wilde. What was he like?" "He was very fat, he was wearing one of those green carnations, and he spoke in a loud, affected tone." And this is about all. Indeed, I do not suppose that even Trelawney, a man of considerable intelligence, could have filled his mind consecutively for more than five minutes with his authentic memories of Byron and Shelley. Such is oral, and visual, tradition.

To fortify such meagre material there comes the still more tenuous blood-inheritance, heredity. "I want to know what Napoleon III really looked like. Can't I make enquiries as to whether he has any surviving illegitimate son, get into touch with him, and see what he's like!" But it diminishes, does this physical inheritance, by fifty per cent., on the law of natural averages, at the first impact; and it goes quicker and quicker down the descending scale of probability with each successive generation. Yet Nature is sometimes kind to the historian, and may out of a family of twelve produce one child who is really like his grandfather.

Human beings have for so short a time possessed the patience to stand perfectly still, or the painters' is such a novel and modern profession that it is scarcely possible to follow the physical appearance of any one family in its different digressions and modifications for more than a few generations at the most. I suppose the one exception to this, and the one family who possess an almost complete documentation, are the Hapsburgs, whose peculiar features can be traced down in every generation from the early fifteenth century to the present day. In fact, the ruler of a certain country who is now engaged in that apparently traditional and hereditary war against the Moors is almost the precise counterpart in appearance to Charles V or to the Emperor Leopold I, that rather casual and disinterested flail of the Turks. But of course with the Hapsburgs the task of the historian has been assisted by their continual intermarriages, and so many alliances between cousins, or between uncle and niece, have made that peculiar appearance ineradicable.

To revert to oral and visual memory, I suppose the reason for the apparent scantiness of material on the part of most people is due to their not having set their ideas in order and tried to recall details while the events in question were still comparatively of recent happening. It is surely, therefore, of more value to set forth your memories when you are twenty-five than after you have reached seventy-five. More especially is this so with regard to the older order of shades, the ghosts of a generation or two before our own, who will so soon go and leave but the merest spark of light behind them. They will be standing, that is to say, in a sunlit window, coming through the door into a room, or met and passed by on the stairs; and that may well be all that is left of them, in fact, it amounts to the verdict of posterity, for this fickle and indiscriminate goddess has only a very few worshippers, and when we say that William Blake or Luca Signorelli are safe in the verdict of posterity, we mean that a few people of discerning minds are continually shouting about them. That is all the noise there is; and, for the rest, the great masses of humanity are silent—not in tolerance, but in ignorance.

ix

PREFACE

With regard, then, to one's private mythology, for in this way one might describe the arsenal of memory, those who know anything of interest had better say it; for such little flashes and flickers of light are one's own property and visible to no one else. They get further and further away, and will soon be beyond recall; and this explains why I have seized these short and intangible moments in preference to more durable and concrete meetings. The recording of a few moments has been some two years' work, and it would never have been undertaken but for my brother's encouragement and advice, and that of two friends whom I may apostrophise here as A. D. W. and B. D. Z.

In the only other prose work that I have written I found myself from an excess of poetry driven towards Museum-research and guide-books, old and new; here I have thrown overboard that ballast and narcotic of the senses and am trying to live without it in a world with which the things that really interest me have no contact. In fact they are dead, as dead as the things I describe in these pages; but from these latter I part with a light and a heavy heart, which means that at one time they were of my flesh and blood, however cold they may be now.

14*th July,* 1926.

Contents

Part I: All Summer in a Day

I

Blackberrying

IT must have been early in September. I know this because my sister's birthday used to come at the end of the first week in that saddening month. For some years before we had celebrated this day in the same manner, but those were times when one week, even, was a huge arc from the wheel of time and I had but a faint memory and no precise knowledge of the summers before this. Time had halted by my side for a second, and I became suddenly drenched and wet for evermore in the waters of memory. This, indeed, is how memory is formed, by a succession of these sudden facings of reality, and each one of them becomes registered in mind like one of those blind spots in your knowledge of geography—Madagascar, say, or the Philippines—which you can only relieve by looking in a map and letting the form and position of the island fix itself for a permanency in the mind's eye. I was filled, of a sudden, with this double-consciousness, both realising the moment and wondering how long I should be able to remember it, for these scenes of early childhood which one recalls with so minute a vision on the rare occasions that they come swimming to the surface seem to set up an anniversary each time they appear, which, like your birthday, leaves you older every time it fades back. All the sooner, then, should they be written down, before it is too late and the details have dissolved away, never to return again till one is too old to make use of them.

15

We all of us get older by quick, and ever quicker, turns of the wheel. While we are very young time will move slow and even halt at our side, so that out of the silence we may remember what is happening in that moment; but these pauses come seldom, even in childhood, and soon the wheel has begun to revolve so rapidly that one cannot hope for it to stop. Life becomes irrevocable, and one can no more really alter its course than one could stop an express train by putting a hand among its whirling spokes. There are a certain number of years during which the character inherited and born with one can be expanded and developed; sometimes the direction of development becomes manifest later than in other—more precocious, perhaps more Oriental—lives, but in all cases it is the inevitable that one pursues, and therefore it is the years before certainty comes that are the most interesting, for they show some flicker of doubt, and sometimes a sign of rebellion, upon the path one is driven along. It is the painter's early pictures, his first efforts at expression, that are often more interesting than his mature and inevitable works of middle-age, and in the same way the first dawn of consciousness with the musician, the painter, or the poet, is a more dramatic dawn than any of those winter sunrises that can wake him every twenty-four hours. It is precisely these first glimmerings of light that I am now trying to catch, and with no more energy now than then, because childhood is the real and authentic dark tunnel down which we creep painfully, and no one can ever have hoped more fervently than I did for the traditional lighter spot to appear among these shadows and draw one towards it out of the long vaults and passages.

This particular halting-space of Time took place, as I have said, early in September. It seems misty and cloud-bound all the year among the Derbyshire hills, and this actual month is the dimmest and most distance-hiding of the seasons. No statue can be seen, let alone a passing human figure—gardener or woodsman—at a further distance than ten yards before you. There are the few remaining trees of a lime and elm avenue, in front and to the right of the house; and their old and splintered masts still towered a dizzying height into the air, too far for the eye to follow them, these autumn mornings. You could just see a little way among the furled and reefed sails, and indeed the leaves that lay low enough to touch were still wet and glistening, as though, when the winds blew on which these sails are fed, the whole tree had leaned to one side with the speed, uncovering its pale bosom and flanks to that cold, quick breath, while the branches on the other side were drawn along gurgling and refreshed in the flood. But now these winds had long ago died down and there was not even a whisper or a stir of air to disturb the thick mist among the branches. We came out from these trees soon enough on to the road or drive, and this led through a level meadow to the brink of a wide, sweeping slope leading to the country beyond and out of the park. This descent, as to the road, was closed in by a long, leafy tunnel of trees, that looked shimmering and rather ghostly in the half-light, until another gate was reached and we were out into the countryside, though not in fact, for there was one more gate to be passed through before the drive joined the highroad.

As one opened this last gate, and then turned round to shut it so that none of the sheep wandering in the field could escape on to the public road, one looked invariably a little to the right down the slope, where the lake should have showed blue and shimmering beyond the fields. But it was not there to-day: or, at any rate, not yet. Instead, the hollow that those sparkling waters should have filled lay absolutely hidden under the fleeces of mist. It looked stark and despairing down the meadows, sopping wet to the feet, and cold as ice when one's hand touched the iron of a gate. And indeed the clanging and cold of the metal brought one quickly out of these reveries across the public road to another gate on the far side. Coming down the road there were a whole straggling convoy of miners, carrying their bundles, and showing faces of an intensified blackness against the hedges. They had been released out of the bowels of the earth and were on their way home for a few hours' sleep and another few hours which they would spend sitting on their heels, Zulu fashion, outside the public-houses till those celestial doors opened and they could while away another hour or so, standing behind the engraved walls of glass— and so to work again. Hard, dark lives are their lot, but I will not pretend, to engage sympathy, that my home was a miner's cottage.

Soon, like smuts in the air, they had drifted away with their curious hob-nailed, lumbering walk, and we were alone again between the hedges of a narrow lane leading into more fields. They formed a wide, level plateau, with woods at the far end, but open and unencumbered, so that one could see some distance round to where the colliery chimneys stood up at various points above their slag hills to remind one, when a little older, of the campanili rising above their red-roofed, clustering villages on islands in the Venetian lagoons. They were none of them very near, there was no noise of machinery, and no perceptible smokiness in the air; but if they had the appearance of looming and floating like islands, the collieries had also this

nautical particularity which only a battleship or vessel
of war can possess, that they were inhabited exclusively
by men, and that this male population were without
exception below the water-line and never showed
themselves where they could be seen. The mists, too,
gave an aqueous, sea-like illusion, of a sea of such
lagoon-like shallowness that low bushes, on the very
hedges, would rise above its surface. But no such
comparison was possible in my mind, those days, and
so the plain with the colliery chimneys standing out
of it remained what they really looked—bulky shapes
looming out of an icy marsh.

Everything round one was sad and depressing. The
grass, with a very pale and white wetness, seemed to
consist of many hundreds of thousands of pocket-knife
blades. These, like the schoolboy's pocket-knife which
will never shut up properly from ill-usage, looked bent
back and trampled upon, as though they would neither
stand up nor lie back properly. One could see a number of ancient dandelions ready to be blown upon,
grown a little taller than the grass, and waiting there
like so many clocks by which to tell the autumn hour.
Just down at the end of the field where every detail
began to get blurred a whole colony of crows, disturbed
by our voices, flapped off heavily into the air and blew
along gradually like a handful of burnt paper thrown
up and caught away by the wind. Everything in this
atmosphere, in fact the whole of this misty glass-like
bell of space, was waiting for something to happen,
for some noise to crack the stillness. But it never
came, and sometimes this sense of waiting, and this
end-of-the-world feeling, peculiar to the district,
would last many days, and nothing would happen.

As a result of these peculiar circumstances, while the
grass would be damp enough to wet your feet badly,

the air would be so cold as to make you want your gloves and an overcoat, and yet, at the same time, you would be perspiring before you had walked very far, and want to stop for breath. Meanwhile, the solitude was not unpeopled for ever, and presently a few voices arrived very far away. At this moment one or two other phenomena presented themselves—the sun, for instance, came into view with a very condensed shrillness, and two birds twittered in a melancholy way upon a damp hedgerow. The sun, also, was very sparrowy in voice, and both sun and birds seemed satisfied for the moment, as though with a tropical-enough background for their acting. Where the path just ahead led through a small wood, the mist tangled in the top branches of the trees looked like bonfire smoke, and the air became sharp and spiked with this invasion. I must add here that in Derbyshire, a country where there is much limestone, partly from this, perhaps, and certainly as a result of the colliery smoke, the trees, when they lose their spring freshness, have a peculiar fatted, black thickness I have seen nowhere else, for it is, as I have said before, a dark misty land. So it was a deep, shadowy wood, and the road through it was like a tunnel, at the far end of which you again came into smoke, which might this time be the stream from your passage through the darkness.

The blackberries began here. Their low, briary bushes grew in great number just at the end of the wood, and on either side of a low, black, loosely built stone wall, of a sort peculiar to very hilly districts, which bordered the road and seemed to prevent the slope from running up and lifting the path on its back. Those voices we had heard far away became real now, and there was a small horde of children entangled among the thorns. They were of a very flaxen, long-headed, Danish type, and their hands and faces were of an indescribable blackness which accentuated the pallor of their skin. None of them had those ripe-apple faces you should see in England, and in spite of this extreme of blackness and whiteness, when a little way from you they faded away altogether into the background of green-black fields, green-black trees, and black stone walls. Their clothes, even, were a sort of protective colouring which associated itself with, and sank into the background, and, indeed, at a small distance from you, there was no sign of them except their high, bird-like words. They might be in the next field, or quite near behind the stone-hedge, but they could not be seen and must be taken for granted like the dandelions which you knew to be growing down there, though the very wan colour of those lionish manes made it difficult to see them, save near at hand.

They were calling out to one another, every small group being under the apparent guidance of a little girl or boy an inch or two taller or a few months older than the others. The thorns and briars were making a stout resistance, and it was pathetic to see one of these chieftains lifting up a child, hardly smaller than itself, to help it in the battle, for they had that primitive, childish strength which soon leaves us, so that there are few grown men who can carry a second man of his own size and weight. Their speech was slurred and clipped to a degree that made it hard to understand, and their noise, like the sparrows twittering on a low spray of leaves, seemed out of all proportion to the mark they made against the landscape. The three of us, my brother, sister, and myself, were luckily tall enough to get at berries which were out of their reach, for by this time they had left nothing but red, unripe

ones near to hand. While the taller children still
continued picking the berries, those of them who were
too small—hardly big enough to walk, in fact—tot-
tered uneasily round to where we could be watched in
a stupefied silence. But, by now, we had picked all
we wanted and were able to remove them in a basket
before they could recover from their astonishment.

A moment or two later they had disappeared from
view, though their voices could still be heard out of
the shrill, sharp briars; however, the wood had soon
built up its dark screen again and they were out of the
world altogether, underneath the earth, perhaps, like
mushrooms before the summer nights' warm rain.

It was the same path until we reached the public
road once more, for we had decided to go home by the
some way until we climbed the hill and reached the
gate of another drive through the park, which had the
merit of taking us past a certain walled orchard known
as the paddock because racehorses had been kept there
about a hundred years ago. You could just see, as you
came along, the hard green apples, not yet ripe, showing above the yellow, crumbling wall, and tempting
one to turn the corner and come inside. The wide
double door had an open padlock, and we were soon
walking towards the fruit trees along the ivied wall,
for the real orchard did not begin till we had got past
some flower-beds. Then the path came round an angle
and we were underneath the almost leafless boughs,
for each small leaf had a cluster of at least four or
five green apples hanging from it. But it was the completion of the blackberries we were after, and for this
purpose we wanted red currants, and not unripe apples
or pears. There were some broad rhubarb plants
growing by the wall, and we had come to pick a few
of the biggest leaves to carry the currants safe home.

They were growing all along the wall here, under the protection of nets strung over them from the ivy leaves on the top of the stone coping. The birds could not get at them with their sharp bills through the meshes, so difficult was it to stand on the thin threads or hover about them among the knotted scales. However, it was easier, though hard enough, then, for us to stand quite still—we had, at any rate, firm ground beneath our feet—and push our hands into the red clusters, which were very brittle and would break easily over our fingers. Sometimes one would miss the whole little bunch, and carry away back through the net just one small currant to eat immediately so that it was not wasted; and it had an acrid, bitter taste with the hard, black seed in the middle, though the fruit itself was cold and sharp as a raindrop. The taste of it was, indeed, precisely that of the rain when it falls upon a leaf and rolls itself into some little hollow of the webbed tracery where it can keep its form, and if you could eat it there, you would have, like the caterpillar, the whole flavour and the actual being of the tree principle, both the sharp light of the boughs which is like the green alternation you see from looking at the sun through closed eyelids, and also the wild, goatish limbs of the tree. Thus it is that the real food of summer in this country should be the raspberry, the red currant, or the blackberry, and we had set out, as I have told, to find, at any rate, two of these delights.

Having collected as many red currants as three big rhubarb leaves would hold, we started home, carrying the blackberry basket by turns because it was heavy and bulky; and, sure enough, as though to justify our tasting of the red fruit against the wall, it began to rain and we had to hurry home through the wet grass

23

to change our clothes. We came through the back-door, down a long passage, and ran upstairs.

I have given this detail of the shower that began just before we reached home, because, when I was rest-ing, as I always had to, for an hour after lunch, the sun had already come out after the rain and the hem of his fine coat of fire was among the topmost branches of some trees not very far from my window, though the long shadow of the house covered the ground for nearly a hundred yards before me. My room faced due north down a hollow valley, out of the park, to a line of hills a mile or two away which rose up into a series of moors that divided, and hid us, from the smoky stacks of Sheffield. This side of the house had a gloomy, Sunday-like outlook, as do most houses which face that particular cardinal-point of the compass. It had a long, stretched-out front that consisted of two great wings starting on either side from a recess into which the centre, or as it were heart of the house, ad-vanced in the form of a pentagon of three stories to which the porch and front door were attached. My bedroom was in one of these long wings, and looking from the window you could see nothing of the building except its long straight front and the three stories of windows all hidden by dark and smoky leaves of ivy. Mine was but one of this line of portholes giving on to the grey seas of winter sky, though now it was shining with a Sunday-like blue flatness of little depth, which made one think of grievances only half understood by the person to whom one recounts them. No amount of explanation and no subtlety of detail would be con-vincing, for the listener was obtuse and the unfolding of these sorrows was like telling a story of complicated nervous disorder to a blunt country doctor. This much of its want of depth I could understand even in those days, though, perhaps, I thought of it more in the terms of a terrible toothache, with its endless horrors, taken to a local dentist for relief. There was but little encouragement to be got out of those sad colours, and one's thoughts floated easily to the other side of the house where the sunlight came from, and where many flowers brightened the grass below the windows.

There seemed to be an endless time in which to meditate on any subject one chose, for one hour spent in this way is like the possession of a little platform from which the whole plain of life can be seen. The rivers are flowing near at hand and you can make a hazard at their course into the invisible distance, while there is not a mountain of which you cannot see all the sides, and not a tree through whose leaves you cannot see the shepherd dozing at the tree-foot, or the beasts of the field finding their shade there from the heat. Such an ineffable and incurable sadness lay over everything, in spite of the bright sunlight; this tender, thin light, indeed, seemed almost to sharpen and intensify the universal pathos which was visible even in the inanimate leaves, middle-aged, now, and heavy with autumn. The whole of that green world, and the fields of grass, as well, seemed to be but feeble trials, vain attempts at something unattainable, the object and nature of which they could neither reach nor explain. All living things, like the creatures of the field, were dumb; unless you reckon their clumsy calls, uncouth as the sharp winds among the leaves, whose bitter sighs you could not sum up into any reasoned theorem of their sorrows. You might listen to this for an eternity, as to the incessant drum-beat of the rain, in first one and then another quarter of the wind; but all these sounds only amounted to so many phenomena, so many temporary phases that showed an experiment

25

was in progress, though this mere sign of a movement or direction was all that could be deduced, and there was no possibility of knowing towards what object or purpose they were striving.

I felt myself a part of the same movement. I was growing very rapidly, and at the same time accumulating and arranging a great store of almost entirely useless knowledge. This inutility I felt severely, and was therefore under a natural apprehension of what was going to happen when I reached to a permanent stature and status of life. I dreaded the future, and did not enjoy the present.

It was a long time—not in fact until I had grown tall enough to fit my coffin—before I could arrive at any solution or explanation of my surroundings, or make any conjecture as to the future. The flowers and trees one comes gradually to understand as being slower and more pathetic creatures than the horse or cow—they cannot complain, and they cannot defend themselves—but they must, in common with everything else, have some sense of confidence, or else their stupidity is blessed. I was too young then to realise that we came here by our own endeavours, and have to look after ourselves, being in a condition of absolute liberty, except in so far as we may punish ourselves by too much greed or curiosity—and always barring the possibility of accidents, such as those that may befall any motor-omnibus, or even a football.

This being so, the only philosophy is to enjoy the speed, without caring for the distance traversed, and one should, therefore, take pleasure in growing, although one does not know what it is for, or where it will end. Too many children, unfortunately, do this naturally, and, on growing up, have exhausted their power for happiness, while they have learned nothing, and cannot console themselves with any acquired clichés or recipes of life. In the second part of this book I hope to distort the present, so as to make it full of anecdote and mythology like the past, for it is the lack of these two arsenals of motive that ruined poetry, architecture, and painting in the last century, and are being but slowly and painfully regained now at the present day. Till they are restored we can expect only the individual artist, and not a school, so that production must be sporadic and cannot be steadily relied upon.

In the meantime I must keep this part of the narrative low and sad, for I want it to contrast with the rest so as to produce some ground for optimism. Also, it was in itself, as I have said, a period of depressed spirits, because, although one suspected the possibilities of happiness, there seemed to be but little proof that such a condition had ever, or ever could, exist. There was nothing but the bare bones of life, and one little knew how to clothe this skeleton with flesh.

Clever people—and by this qualitative I mean, not prize-winning, scholastic minds, but persons invested with some amount of personality, living in an atmosphere distilled by their own words and actions—I had never yet come across; though one could tell, even from books, that such had existed. It seemed so easy to grow up and miss such people altogether, as one might live, for instance, all one's life without seeing a New Zealand Maori in the flesh; there might be meetings at which these immortals were present, but so might there be exhibitions, of an Empire, or what not designation, with a whole native village, shown and inhabited by the dark heroes; but then one could boast only of having seen them exposed in public, and was as far away as ever from really knowing them. The

27

nearer one could get, in fact, in this mute manner, the further removed did one seem from them in real fact, for it was as though one had flown near enough to the sun to realise its monstrous enormity, and had then returned to earth again appalled by its distance from us.

If only one could grow up safely, all might yet be well; but it was such a dreary, long waste before the eyes. In the meanwhile one must collect evidences, proofs of what one sought to establish as a safe and assured reality. There were luckily a few pictures in the house to rebut a despairing mood and supply some ground for optimism. A large family group painted by Copley about 1780 carried a kind of personal authority with it, as though one's great-great-grandfather had been able to speak out of the picture and tell one everything was all right and that one could go on hoping. It was painted with that convincing reality that Zoffany managed to give to his interiors, and being on a larger scale and less fussy in detail than is usual with the latter painter, this picture carried a deeper degree of conviction with it, though it perhaps lacked by this very reason the play-scene appearance that Zoffany's predilection gave to every picture he painted.

There were, besides, various other family portraits of more or less merit, with a few Italian pictures bought and brought home by my father. None of these latter was able to satisfy any really deep feeling; but this deficiency was filled and made good by what I can only consider as the fabulous beauty residing in five great panels of Brussels tapestry bought by an ancestor from the sale of the Philippe Egalité collection in London. I have already in a former book attempted some slight description of their subject and treatment, so that it is not necessary here to embark upon an inventory of their content. I have only space, therefore, to state briefly and categorically, that I have never yet been able to discover who designed them, and that I still consider them some of the most beautiful products of human genius. What else was there?

I had once been by motor to Southwell Minster, a huge old abbey about thirty miles away from our home. It looked cold and unspeakably gloomy, while the elaborate and tritely-minute carving of the stone capitals in the Chapter-house was most unconvincing. It was a poor code of art that employed the same material as ornament for the elaborately coloured and gilt pages of a missal, and the white stone capitals which were meant to be seen from twenty or thirty feet below. In any case stone sparrows seemed to be an anachronism, as did the selection of the most tinny and ivy-like leaves as detail for the foliage in which these birds were playing about and singing. The yellow-varnished, grained wood benches set out below, as if in admiration, made a fit accompaniment to these carvings; for the yellow wood suggested the thinnest kind of spring sunlight, a typical Sunday spring morning, in fact, with a sense that the Wesleyans were not far away with their harmonium, while the stone leaves and birds confirmed everything, and the twitter and bustle of their lives sounded genuine in this thinly-filtered sunlight. It made one hate the Gothic age, with all its false notes, like the unfunny humour of their fools, and it was many years before I began to realise my mistake, though I doubt if it was a mistake, for I still think the fourteenth century could be bad when it tried to be simple.

Nearer at hand there were human works of much truer beauty, for Bolsover Castle and Hardwicke were both within a dozen miles of us, due south across the

valley. Bolsover stands up on a dramatic cliff above
the gulf below, and its battlements can just be seen
above the enormous elms that grow at the foot of its
walls. The castle is cold and sad, but with a much
more deserted chilliness than the Gothic church I have
just described; for you can see at once that the people
who built the house were far above the provincialism
that produced the church with its quiet country themes
and country content. These palace-dwellers had travelled beyond their native land, and their ambition
wanted, therefore, more interesting echoes than the
harmonium or the village choir. They had fenced
themselves in here with a huge girdle of walls and
gates, so that the summer evenings seemed to live
longer while the lute echoes lasted. Hardwicke, built
by the same family, was a yet safer retreat, for it lies
in a huge park the very trees and rocks of which seem
to suggest, in their fantastic forms, the antlers and the
distant belling of the herds of deer. When you arrive
up actually at the house, it seems very far removed
from the world, both of this day and of the Elizabethans, as though it had always been remote and silent.
The windows, indeed, at the back of the house, where
there is the long gallery always to be found in the
great Elizabethan houses, give on to a wide, misty
waste of grass which stretches away as far as the eyes
can see; so that any noise you hear in the silence of
the evening, or the early morning, must come out of
these heights and hollows. But it is a language of
sound as dead as a dead speech, so that none can understand, or need, indeed, bother as to its meaning; it is
like the Latin words, half-effaced, below a statue, which
none but a scholar can decipher, and none but he
would wish to understand.

This was all; the whole extent of evidence to be

collected from one's surroundings; and, for the rest, one was back again at the starting-point, with nothing more tangible than a presumption or deduction.

It was time to come downstairs again, once more; and, as I did so, the feel of the door-handle and the sound of my feet on the little wooden space before the carpet began brought me back dramatically into yesterday, where I found it still fresh and sweet-smelling, not very far away and not very different. There was nothing that separated us, except putting my hand on the door-handle and stepping once on the wooden boards, and then doing all this again a second time. Round these two procedures, all the other events of to-day and yesterday lay, stretched like bodies, a few of them still alive and waiting for my death-blow; or it was like some one stirring in the room next door, whose every move you can hear through the thin walls. But this latter, who imitated everything I did, like my shadow thrown before me, was really the sound, which I had thus personified into life, of exactly the same things happening to me to-morrow; for I knew that there was this continual shadow forestalling me, till I should come out of my room one day and feel nothing there in front of me. That would be the day, most awful of all days, before I was to go back to school, so there was some comfort, in this particular instance, in the forest-like multitude of my shades.

The next thing I remember, in fact, was that particular to-morrow come nearer, and already, shadow-like, attached to my feet, whence I was dangling it before me on another country walk. This time we had varied our path and started in an opposite direction from the house, down a steep drive, out of the path on to the station road. I was too young, then, to remember anything from those days except mere scraps of

31

conversation, or intricate family stories of no possible interest to any one outside our immediate household. But, in spite of this, I can well imagine how we talked, and how we must have passed, so quickly as not to have noticed it, by the little rows of old Jacobean stone houses, and even over the bridges that span the two separate main lines of railway, running so close together in this part of the country as to offer an almost insuperable bribe to a child to stay there and watch the double flow of trains. These two obstacles passed, the road now began to climb up a very steep hill, curving about and stopping its ascent for a moment, here and there, as though to stay and get its breath; while you could see over the low hedges into the valley beneath, and on the opposite slope there was our home hidden away and invisible among the steep woods.

Everything of interest in the country round lay somewhere among the heights we were climbing, for this hill was one of the bastions of the steep plateau on which stood Bolsover Castle, Hardwicke, and all the other private colonies of a one-time, and usually for only one generation, civilised mankind. It is these colonies, these small family nuclei of culture, and the University towns of Oxford and Cambridge, that form the only evidence, since the decay of the Gothic age, for the presumption that any civilised communities existed on these shores. Such things were the result of private enterprise, not much encouraged by Church or State—since some one, who should have known better, was beheaded at Whitehall. Unfortunately, even the nearest of these outposts was too far away to be reached by foot; but it gave one a certain feeling of comfort to think that any people who had known

painters or musicians had ever lived, however long
ago, so near to us.

Eventually, when about half-way up this hill, we
had come to a red-brick bridge over a canal, and just
on getting to this, one climbed a stile, and ran down
a steep bank to the canal brink, which had a cinder-
bed stamped down into the semblance of a rough path
along the waterside. This was a favourite walk of
ours for several reasons. In the first place, it is always
romantic going along so near to the water, because of
the reflections and this other peculiar glassy world so
near to you. Then, again, the banks were always covered with a profusion of lovely wild-flowers, such as
you see on the sides of a railway-cutting, and this was
for an obvious reason, because the Great Central Railway did in fact run along, only some six feet from one,
the other side of a paling of huge timber stakes. It
was a delightful walk along this high, wooden fence,
especially towards evening when the sun was rather
low down and cast a number of long cubical shadows,
like the black notes of a piano, between each pair of
palings. When this happened, one had to walk through
a huge band of xylophones, sounding out, one after another, as one came to them; and, if it was a lucky
evening, an express train might come dashing past
through this continual music with a loud and most
ferocious roar of its own, while the brave plumes of
steam lost their pride after a time and drifted down in
a little drenching mist on to the wild-flowers which
prospered from this plenty.

It gave one, at once, a wonderful sense of the artificial and man-made beauty that is possible of achievement, for all the substance of which the charm of this
particular walk was made owed its arrangement, or

even its very origin, to human hands. To start with, here one was, on the banks of an artificial and scarcely flowing river, conducted with an absolute disregard to the apparent convenience both of the water and the landscape, half-way up a steep hillside. The canal stretched for many miles in either direction, coming from, and going to, unknown distances, and all along you could journey at the same level, except where the waters were drawn down in artificial cascades, on to a lower terrace. Apart from these lulls, when your boat would either float up as though there were wings beneath her, or sink down as though her wings were closed and she was settling with a swan-like difficulty and heaviness upon the waters, progress would be so steady and continual as to be almost a passing out of life altogether; for with food on board, like the provisions left in ancient tombs for the last journey of the dead, there would be no reason for ever leaving the boat, and this voyage might continue, in a network of circles, for as long as there was patience to sustain it.

Images, then, rode easily upon the water, with a life as substantial as that possessed by the reflections, which stretched into such an illusion of space, and vanished so readily at the touch of an oar or hand. This oar—and the magical hour might well transmute it into the white swan's webbed foot, a ghostly and more subtle instrument—could shiver those echoes at a touch, breaking down the roofs of the blue caves of air, or destroying, as by the iron weight of rain, trees, or the banked fields shown there. In one moment the mirror has closed its cavern-mouth and will not answer to any of the colours that are glittering from the leaves and hills; and it will not ring with a clear echo until it is left at peace again and can build up its glassy caverns undisturbed by even so much as an alien breath, for the slightest wind will ruffle and mar the reflections.

Sunset had about begun when we turned back, having covered in our walk this minute and almost negligible extent of the canal's length: and so we walked over the same ground once more, with the sun, this time, declining from about the height of the eyes down one's body, a process that reminded me a little of a system of torture I had read about, where the victim was blinded by a red-hot iron plate held in front of his eyes; and this was an analogy somewhere near to truth, because the sun, however feeble in his wane, was still red and violent enough for his glare to conjure up a whole treeful of those rayed and marred parhelions, whose coloured fires I could see burning as they dropped away from the branches and glittered violently against the hills, or even in the heart of the waters as far as one could see into their shadowy depths. At the slightest curve of the hedges, or at a bend of the towpath, this confusion became worse, for on the appearance of another landscape, the parhelions would settle themselves anew or still more of them would come into sight just above a low range of hills, or even hiding among, and blurring, their fenced folds.

Far away down the fields, and the sound must have flown somehow over the summer woods between us, came the sound of a miners' band practising in the village—a warning in itself, that to-day was Saturday, for this music had already a foretaste of the brassy Sabbath brightness whose dead level of polished coldness is the achievement of each week's striving; is, in fact, as near to a happier state as it is safe for the miners to aim for in this life. The instruments would be silent for a few moments, and would then break out

again, all at once, in some new interpretation of the
ideal, which state was not so much hinted at, as actually
achieved, by the clearest and most regular breathed
among the players, while some of them were obviously
flurried and at a disadvantage in the heart of all this
blare. It was curious to think of that concourse dressed
in their black clothes, and standing facing inwards
round a circle, for they were there in the same manner,
and much to the same purpose, as the knots of insects
you can see standing close to each other and engaged,
most patently, in some method of mental communication: but they added, at any rate, something out of the
usual to our walk home that evening, and their com-
ments were still audible as we came up through the
wood; they seemed, indeed, to drift down on to us
off the leaves whenever a puff of wind moved the
branches, and the last of their noises was dismembered,
as it were, by the door-frame under which we came
back into the house.

II

A Military Ghost

THE world of things one's eyes could see I have
now tried to describe, but a new and a greater
depth to life came this same season with the first
appearance in my memory of characters, the formalised
families and septs with whom this summer landscape
was peopled. By many among these I had been surrounded for as long as I could remember, since, in
their widest interpretation, they were as numerous as
the myriad black shades in whose midst a white man
might be living, while many years of his life were
consumed in the hot sun before he could tell one native
from another, or piece together a whole family and
its relations from such indistinguishable differences to
the eye as the black basalt of limb and feature can offer.
But, like marble under the sculptor's hand, first one
and then another shape was born into permanence out
of its matrix, and, about this time, my horizon became
crowded with more and more of these statues. Among
the earliest of them, and one that will remain a permanency in my memory, rose Colonel Fantock.

This military ghost had been appointed my tutor the
previous summer, and further acquaintance with him
that winter, at the seaside town where he lived, and
where my family spent a part of each year, had sharpened my anticipation of seeing him this season. He
had arrived, for there were various household matters
that he had to manage in addition to my education, a
day or two before we came up for the summer holi-

37

days, so that we could see him waiting on the doorstep
when the house first came into view, and I was able to
spend sunset among the flower-beds in his company.
Meeting him again was more than an ordinary re-
newal of friendship, because the full plenitude and
capacity of one particular human being was emerging
for me out of those early mists through which the
eye can only vaguely discover an object ahead, and is
not powerful enough to conjecture its height or bulk.
But now the early morning was over and dead, and,
confining my metaphors from the whole span of a life
down to the actual moment, or, as it were, the living
particle of time, I may say that the hour of sunset had
already begun to assert an indefinable depression and
sadness over me, and that the mere increase of sensibility that was evident to me in my deeper appreciation of Colonel Fantock, held in it something of sadness, as though I had already guessed that stronger
sight meant a greater uncertainty, and a deeper depression of the spirit. I can remember, in this connection, how unhappy I was on my tenth birthday,
being loath to lose what I already possessed, and nervous of what I might acquire.

Colonel Fantock had a familiar air among the flower-
beds, for he was an enthusiastic amateur gardener, as
energetic as the years would allow when his yellow
brick house cast a shadow, as it were a carpet for his
feet to tread, and he could walk out on it in safety to
those high rose bushes in his little garden; while here,
at our home, his enthusiasm was rendered keener by
the thought that he might be himself responsible in
part for these thickets of flowers, since he had the
previous summer pruned and worked a lot in the more
accessible beds. He walked, therefore, with a justi-
fiable pride, and we may imagine that his haughty

silence has given us a few moments in which to watch
him and take note of his appearance. We may admire
his white moustachios, curled gravely downward at
their ends, and his bald head, emblem, in itself, of
authority; while we have time, even after this, to
notice that his clothes are a little worn, a little too
tidily frayed, and that he has yellow boots of an almost primrose hue, which the butler will tell you that
Colonel Fantock must have worn for at least ten years
for that particular tone of colour to be perfected. But
he has begun talking now, and so one must stop the
scrutiny and listen.

That particular evening conversation was typical of
many; indeed of the whole range of days, so that when,
since that time, I have tried to summon up the peculiar
atmosphere, the very scent, as it were, of that summer,
my sunset talk with Colonel Fantock in the garden
seems like the consummation, the most important and
very last event of the day, before the less substantial
and falsely gilded affairs of the evening. For everything glittered, then, with real authentic gold—the
leaves, the lawns, the very windows of the house; and
the hour had not yet come when human beings prolong
the day with a false sunlight in their shuttered rooms.
It was such a solemn hour, in fact, that one stopped
running and began to walk slowly about as though
this steadier progression could make the dwindling
moments more lasting. But it was in vain, for, quicker
than one would have thought it possible, all this beauty
was dead and gone: the boughs had become dark and
woolly—formless as a silly sheep; the lawns were wet
and marshy; and the windows, that were just now
shining with sunset gold, had lost their echo as quickly
as a dying drum-beat. More than this, Colonel Fantock complained of the cold and went indoors to fetch

39

his hat—a resolution which, by common consent, ended
the day so far as appearances were concerned, and we
followed him inside mutely, and found ourselves in a
darkened house.

As the night grew deeper, he would light first one
pair of candles and then another, after the fashion of
ancient travellers who would take a pair of pistols in
their holsters and perhaps another pair strapped round
the waist, for every evening, as it advanced into the
dinner hour, was like a desperate adventure to Colonel
Fantock, and when he finally came down the stairs
it was as though he had been seized from his horse,
his pistols had been taken from him, and the order
given that he should be taken straight into his captor's
lair, to receive judgment. When I came to find him
in his room, he had already surrendered half his defences to the darkness, for one pair of candles stood
smouldering—just at that moment when the wick has
gone black again, but the smoke still rises in a high,
twisted spiral—upon the mantelpiece. I had come in
time to see even this escape tremble and die away, for
the two threads of smoke vanished as though lifted
from above, and he was standing at his dressing-table
in the thinly-gathered glare of his last pair of lights.
He was tying his tie, a pathetic piece of "finish"; indeed, a humble and amiable surrender, like the soft,
downy whiteness of the rabbit's stomach, which it offers
so meekly, turning on its back to the strong teeth of
the dog who has run it down. It was not so much
that Colonel Fantock, like the rabbit, was hoping for
a quicker death, as that by this conventional knot that
he tied every evening he was lashing himself to the
last mast he had left from his shipwreck, for, with the
proudly poor, their evening suit is the last convention
with which they will part. The tie again must have

been, speaking generally, in its origin, a protection
against cold, but this had long ago been frittered away
into decoration, and now, if you were dressing for
dinner, you must tie your tie, even if you had no vest
beneath your shirt. He was used to it, anyway, and did
not probably bother himself much about its excuse or
meaning, for he folded it over rapidly and neatly into
a nicely ordinary specimen, and by the time I looked
again it was sitting there sufficiently and adequately,
a little large, perhaps, and a trifle square-cornered,
but as good a specimen of its class as are, for instance,
in their own category of conventionally arranged linen,
the napkins which you are likely to find in a station
hotel, with their accompaniment of plush-backed chairs
and brushed, velvety carpet. He had only now to
brush his hair, a convention this, and one easily accomplished, and then to put on his coat—that pressed
flower of conventionality which he had lifted out so
carefully from its sheets of tissue paper in a drawer so
that it could lie for a few moments on his bed, and
this he did every day with the kind of mechanical
heartlessness you would expect of the priests whom a
wealthy eccentric might enjoin by his will to open his
coffin for a few seconds after each memorial mass had
been said, in order to ensure that he was really and
truly dead with every vestige of life gone. He did
this, just as the priests would do it, heartlessly but
dutifully, knowing that they drew so much money
for it and should be thankful for this added income;
though, in his own case, this evening suit that he tended
so carefully was the symbol of life, and if he were
forced to give it up, then all the pretension on his part
that made living endurable on such straitened means
would break down, and he would be as dead as anything, save the actual touch of death, could make him.

It only wanted one more brush after this, then a last look into the glass, and he was ready for dinner, and could blow out the two last candles on his dressing-table, and fumble his way through the twilight room between the various chairs towards the door.

As I think of the days in this manner they become filled out, blown, indeed, into the very fulness of their pride, for I have already loaded each of them with the weight of four heavy processes, daily repeated: the morning walk, the rest after lunch, the last hour of daylight in the garden, and my evening visit to discover if Colonel Fantock was ready for dinner. Thinking thus, round and upon these four cardinal points of each day, all manner of other smaller details return, and soon, by shifting the memory from one day easily recalled, through various things difficult to fix down to any particular day, towards the next that lived with a life of its own, independent of the rest, one comes to think of the whole summer as consisting of an immense day in which every repetition of the same event has become fused into one final, comprehensive performance, and the entire vast progress moves on slowly and inevitably towards its logical close, the moment at which I blew out my own candle and soon became lost in the black cavern in which I found myself.

But that final moment has not arrived, and I must not shut those pages until the ink upon them is heavy enough to keep them closed on their own motion: in the same way, I should not bring out my ghosts in their full trappings till the conventional and correct hour for them has arrived, though I cannot, so remote was my life then, avoid their interposition, and it is hardly my fault if a few of these shadows cross my stage, or throw a shade in front of me when I am trying to find my path again through the changed fields. It is

like a half-remembered tune when I think of Colonel
Fantock, for I have only a very few perfect mental
presentments of him; I see him for the most part, that
is to say, either with an immaculate finish of memory
on a piece of ground or a corner of a room that I cannot place, or else, hazily, like a yellowed photograph,
somewhere that I recall the whole world of boughs
and can hardly catch sight of him in the green air below them, or in some angle of a room where the tides
of light, broken by the leaves, have flowed unevenly
through the window, and this hot, calm river is the
thing I remember, for I can scarcely see Colonel Fantock through its troubled surface. I know that he is
there, however, for I have a third proof of his presence
in remembering his words, or, at any rate, the sort of
thing he would have been likely to say as we came
home through the trees, or lingered talking for a moment near the door.

Memory is sometimes served even quicker than by
the sunlit leaves or that yellow train of fire as it
catches and starts to run through door or window,
from some secret notation of eye or mind gathered up
and stored in the sense of smell, and kept secret and
forgotten there till you come upon a like centre with
which your memory can communicate, till you have
discovered, as it were, a reply to the messages your
mind has been sending ceaselessly through all space,
and which have never been received or given answer
to till now. A scent, with this sudden and dramatic
response, will transport you to the last place of contact,
and if a bank of flowers or the hot beds of sunlight
lining a long wall can be recalled, the figures peopling
these abrupt landscapes live again in your mind with
an equal force of vitality. So quick is this journey
through space and time that it is no real departure

from your actual place of being, and for a few moments you may live in these double centres of consciousness blown upon by the uncertain breezes that seem doubtful which side to take, for they waver from one quarter of the heavens to another. But as you draw in a deeper breath the sunlight, through this glass of memory, burns with a clearer and still deeper certainty, and soon you are living with full lungs in the centre of this warm world.

It is in this manner that I can follow Colonel Fantock back to the seaside, through a space of many miles and a span of years, but however clear my destination may be, the actual journey, though it lasts only for a fraction of a second, is like being carried along blindfolded, though the speed and direction are unerring. I am attempting, so I may explain my meaning and the purpose of my voyage, to follow this ghost back to the home that he started from. When, by means of the agency that I have described, I am able to set up this swift communication, I can lay his spectre until it no longer haunts me, because I can see him with such clearness that I understand his meaning and he need no longer trouble me to interpret him; and this is how the journey begins; this is my place of departure.

I have only to bend down, at any time or place, to pick a stem of wallflower, and its smell, as I draw in breath, carries me straight away till, in the space of a flash of light, I am with him again, just above, and in the full yellow furnace-heat of, the massy bed of these same flowers that is like the pylon, the electric tower, that receives my message and gives me my answer. It is one of those huge, thickly-filled beds which are only found in Corporation gardens, and so brimming with its own fulness that it makes one think of a spoon-

ful of jam, or of the thick cream that one eats with
summer fruit; while that massy splendour I have com-
mented upon shows a survival of the taste of sixty
years ago, when they loved to encase precious stones
as though in a solidified aura of the sun's rather brassy
gold, which they were, even then, not content to leave
alone but felt constrained to enhance its loudness of
tone by as much pinching and twisting of the metal as
their skill could contrive. Indeed, those were the days
in which straightforward loudness of music reached to
its culmination, and there has never been so brazen
an interpretation, or an anticipation so material in its
suggestion of the ideal. No one, before Wagner, had
employed such a blast with which to announce his
heroes; and the young winds—the zephyrs—of Mozart had grown in the space of two human generations
into an almost Renaissance manliness of beard and
whisker, all of which ornaments were but outward indication of the vigour within. Music, less serious in
purpose, was just as emphatic in its form, and there
can never have been so plangent a protestation of the
emotions as in the full martial waltz of that day, blown
forth and sounded out in Paris or Vienna. The battlefield was a world of gas-light; the chandeliers were so
many tropic trees that flourished exceedingly in this
hot, conservatory air, while they hung down reversed
from Nature with their fiery blossoms burning out
above the crystal branches, as though you only saw
them reflected in water; and this, indeed, might seem
to be the truth when the night grew tired and all the
mirrors took on a faint greenish tinge, like the earliest
dawn-echoes on the water. It was these strains of metal
that were still ringing in the strange place to which
this martial ghost had led me, though the echoes had
an ebbing strength and must by now have died away

45

before the newer vulgarity of crooked rhythms and intermingled currents; but they seemed that day to be possessed of an undiminished force.

The hot summer air was faintly quivering a few inches above the ground, and over this deep bed of flowers it had become merged into and drenched by the yellow blossom, so that it could clearly be seen coiling into little spiral waves, or tingling like a held vibrato in music; indeed, your hand put down into this loud interval between earth and air felt chafed against and rubbed by the moving heat. This flower-bed grew right up to the edge of the asphalt path, that winding molten river through the grass, and it had an abrupt edge, a kind of sudden cessation of colour, for the green sea of grass started off sheer from its four sides and flowed without a pause up to another island in this archipelago, in this case a sister-like alternation, of the same affinities, for it was a bed of the dark, vinous wallflower which has a deeper and cooler scent and suggests a world with a near horizon of red garden walls. Along the asphalt path, by each of these islands, stood a black and brown seat which was hot to touch and the brown woodwork of which was blistered and swollen by the sun, and Colonel Fantock chose one of these because of its nearness to the flowers, and sat down taking its central division as a rest for his arm. I sat down, too, for a few moments, because our walk had been hot and tiring, but the Colonel was so warm that he could not talk for a while and so we held a monotonous silence.

Somehow it made one feel cool to look along, past the side of the flower-bed, down the wide, level grass, and so, after a time, I got up from our seat and started to walk across, noticing, at that moment, in what a curious manner the grass seemed to run straight into

the sky as if the limit of vision was only a very few
feet in front. I seemed to have become possessed of
the insect's faculty of walking up a wall as though it
is a flat, level floor, for no sooner had I gone a few
feet further than I could suddenly see something the
other side of it, the horizon somehow took a vast leap
away from me, and I suddenly realised that the sea
lay there below me, tumbling in an idle way as though
to keep itself awake in the drowsy heat. I had now
only to get my shoulders above the wall to have more
and more of its surface unrolled before my eyes, and
in another moment I was standing on the edge, the
very brink of this wall, and there was a huge surging
bay, a kind of immense amphitheatre, in which I occupied the highest seat, while the sea was playing to us
with a listless and very tired enthusiasm.

I had hardly time to look once up and down this
wide sweep when there came a brave burst of music
from below, and one realised that, down at the bottom
there, a great crowd of people were walking to and
fro listening to the band. This was, indeed, the only
sound that rose up to me from the huge, hollow shore,
except when, during its softer strains, the sea had the
more telling tone and its waxing, waning chords could
be heard above the band that was now reiterating, and
softly arguing out some question that must be settled
before all the instruments could unite again and sound
forth the charge, when they would drop their differences and thrill the air with a vast crescendo. It was
a comic opera they were playing down below, and the
cornet and the flute, taking place on this occasion for
the tenor and the soprano, sounded out in long, rather
wearying phrases, but, before long, the hero and heroine got lost in the noisy crowd, and the loud, vulgar
measures of a chorus came along, reaching me up here

just about a beat later than their birth below. So it was, that when this banal music ended in a magnificent, scroll-like flourish, the last reverberations were as if thrown back by the sea, and one was still involved, delightfully, in this heavy foliage, though, really, it was already lifted away from one, dying with the waves.

Colonel Fantock had evidently appreciated the music; perhaps he remembered it, new and glistening, many years before, for now it was finished he stood up and came towards me, staying on the brink a moment and looking rather longingly, I thought, at the crowd below, as though he envied them being able to walk up and down while the band, like a living animal, performed to them. He had made up his mind to go and join them, and he proposed that we should walk down the gardens, bribing me with a promise that I could climb about on the rocks. So we turned our backs on the Esplanade, with its long line of stuccoed houses, and took the asphalt path which went down like a railway cutting between high, green banks and came out presently into a small valley, once, no doubt, a river-bed, though it had long ago been bridged over and cemented down. Under a municipal order this valley had been converted into a kind of distended rockery, and in an effort to authenticate this falsehood, a little rustic bridge of untrimmed logs was built across and embarked upon at either end by a nervous, wavering path which wound about and hesitated before it would trust itself on the shaking, perhaps snapping, timbers; but we came steadily down the broad asphalt of the valley-bed and walked under the bridge, which looked like the frail, wind-blown work of some insect, reaching immediately after this what must have once been the river-delta, though now

48

it was kept back and blockaded by a high cement sea-wall.

This was a continuous line of fortification that ran the whole way round the town, joining on to the fore-shore and the harbour, though the actual part of it that we had reached was the most distant defence, the very end of the line of ramparts, and beyond this the cliffs disappeared out of sight, armed with their own rough bulwarks and battlements, which fortifications they had to defend by themselves, without the help of man. At this spot it was a wall some thirty feet high and, in proportion to its scale, one had to walk some distance to find the steps leading down to the sands, and even then, so uneven and precipitous were the stairs, that, in order to make them safe, a heavy iron railing had to be embedded in the cement; while the fearful strength of the winter sea was proved by the rusting of the iron supports, for they had even stained the hard cement with this sign of their agony, and the discolouring grew more and more marked as one climbed down towards the beach where the waves had easier access to the railing, when they came running in from low tide under a strong wind.

In another moment we were treading on yielding sand, for the sea was very far out down at the bottom of the bay, though, just near the cliff, the shore was littered with pellet-like pieces of clay and with small pebbles; indeed, fine sand only began some distance out, and one noticed this particularly because if one wanted to throw a stone into the water there were never any to be found near the edge of the sea. This was, however, but a small deficiency compared with the other manifold pleasures of the sands, and so one lost no time in heading straight out towards the rocks. On our way there, we passed a whole armament of

49

footprints; first of all the tracks of galloping horses, with sometimes the smaller marks of a dog running by the side, and then, when we had come nearer to the sea, almost to its very edge indeed, there were the curious angular prints made by the feet of the sea-birds, and so fresh and receptive was the sand that if you stooped to pick up a piece of seaweed, the leaf-like strands left a mark where you had lifted them from the shore. The sea had been over here very recently, for there were a few shells half embedded in the sand that were still full of water, and they gleamed and shone as if perfectly new, with the kind of freshness possessed by the flowers, and even the very earth, in some Pacific island never before reached by man.

We might almost have stepped out of a boat on to the sands, for the rocks rose a little above them and ran straight out into the water, just as an island might do, for it would only have one or two beaches on which one could land, and, for the rest, would come out of the sea with a broken and ragged sharpness that made it difficult to approach. But it showed here, low, and fairly level above the sand, and so we got easily on to its surface, and even Colonel Fantock, except for an occasional slipperiness, could see no dangers before him. When we had scrambled out as far as the rocks went, one had to turn round, of course, to come back, and then one saw the town sweeping right round the bay with as many windows looking on to the sea as possible; with, first of all, the long stuccoed lines of houses, then the great bridge that joined the new town to the old across a deep ravine, and beyond that the old town, much smaller in scale and creeping low down to the sea so as to be near the harbour, while right above this was the towering castle hill with the ruins on it coming out above a gaunt green hillside that looked like green baize. These ruins had been built in the time of King Stephen, so I had been told, but he seemed, like all his generation, too far away to have ever existed, and his castle lay up there, high on the skyline, looking as small as a child's fort, while one quite expected the King's armoured ghost to come, glittering, through the portcullis, where he would seem tall as the walls he had built to protect him. It was no use, though, waiting for this to happen, and so one looked down, away from the Castle, towards the near cliffs, or on to the sand.

Colonel Fantock knew every foot of this level plain, for it had been his daily walk, in morning or afternoon, according to the tides, ever since his arrival in the town forty or fifty years ago; moreover, the place was the terminus of a northern railway system, and this species of finality was possessed by the very town itself, making him feel, for instance, that this daily walk was part of the insignia of his life, just as much as the last, midnight whisky-and-soda, for in a provincial town, stranded away like this on the cliffs, life to become endurable has to have all its details magnified into an almost insupportable importance, for the mere fact of being a terminus means that not very much arrives and still less ever goes away, many of the inhabitants, like Colonel Fantock, coming for a week-end and staying for the remainder of their lives. Etiquette of an endless intricacy is invented, through the webs and meshes of which the inhabitants can pursue each other to their hearts' content, all their lives. This is a trait of the human animal all over the world where such conditions exist, however much locality or circumstance may influence the form it takes. The Spaniards in their walled towns, their desert termini, may cultivate the inscrutable, the unapproachable, guarding their closed homes with a huge shield of heraldic achievement, but they live the same lives, nevertheless, and are pursuing but a variety of the same ideal. Here, against the scene I have chosen, these campaigns are waged at drawing-room tea-parties and at charity organisations: but the same victories may be won, and at the same price.

My companion was a competent historian of this warfare, being, indeed, a veteran of unsurpassed record, with so inexhaustible a store of anecdote that conversation could never weary and grow tired. There can hardly have been a person in the town whom he did not know, and he would discuss their political opinions and their poverty or prosperity, naming, if not their friends, at least their enemies. It was a peculiar sensation to go walking with him over the sands, for this bleak plain was like a great canvas on which he sketched out anything that one asked him about, and in an hour's walk he could complete several figures with every detail and accessory, though the tide would soon roll back and rub away his thin scratchings.

We were soon, therefore, above the sands in our conversation, back in the terraced, sea-viewing streets, where there was hardly a house that he had not been into as friend or canvasser, for Colonel Fantock had pronounced political ambitions, was a popular speaker, and had even edited for a time, the span between a bankruptcy and a suicide, the local Conservative newspaper. He could speak on these matters, then, with the authority of some one whose counsel or advice was often sought, while for my more youthful pleasure and information he would assume a military importance, and, on days of particular favour, would describe for me once again—it could never be too often—the uniforms of the Garde Impériale, and especially the Cent Garde of Napoleon III.

I used to enjoy asking him about the Gentlemen's Club, a structure of alarming, almost military, red, which stood just opposite the Grand Hotel near a cab shelter, and close to a railed-in plot of grass which was ornamented with a Russian cannon, trophy of the Crimean War, and a huge, rusty anchor dredged up by a trawler, and reputed to have once belonged to the frigate of the American privateer, Paul Jones. There were two great bow-windows, one above the other, in which the gentlemen, as ever a difficult term to live up to, could be seen, seated, with their backs turned so as to throw the hard daylight direct on to their newspapers, or favouring one, were it a fine day, with their red faces pressed close towards us and only kept away by a great film of glass. Those of them in whose veins the fires of youth burned brighter would cluster at the upper window round the elaborate mechanism of a telescope, like steersmen at the wheel, for it would point in any direction they wanted, but was as obdurate in its predilection for one particular arc of space as are the yachts, that continually tack in the wind, but are resolved to enjoy the sun and air in the bay, and turn therefore to every point of the compass except the line leading home to the harbour. They were looking to the right of that relic of Paul Jones, over the back of the Russian gun, and the passers-by on the promenade just opposite seemed blurred and unwieldy, while the cliff that they, and the Club itself, stood on broke sharp down in a dramatic and breath-catching fall on to the sands that reappeared again soon, joining on, in fact, to the cliff's edge, and stretching at this hour of low tide far out to sea. It was the bathing-machines and their slender occupants that the gentlemen were noticing so closely, and then there was a turn of the wheel, and they were facing, like that Russian cannon, right down the Esplanade crowded with the chairs of people listening to the music wafted from below. "A whiff of grape-shot" and, after a few jocular recognitions and a peep at the figures hurrying over the great wooden bridge across the valley, they would sweep the telescope across to the Grand Hotel at close range just opposite, hoping for some domestic revelations of humorous character. It would be a pleasant afternoon whiled away in this fashion, with tea or whisky so near at hand, and brought so quickly to the call. How quickly seven o'clock came round once more, and then they would all start off home for their dinners, not to meet again till next day, for the Club only provided drinks and the lightest of meals, and their inviolable homes claimed them for these solemn family dinners!

There were topics, other than the Gentlemen's Club, of an almost equal resilience—resilient in the sense that one never tired of the theme or its variations, so skilfully and so eagerly did Colonel Fantock return to the charge. Amateur theatricals, for example, because this excuse served to assemble under one roof everybody in the town with an individuality or an arrogance of self-assertion. Over such gatherings the Colonel presided, partly because his friends took the opportunity of making a collection for him and calling it, by way of palliation, a salary; and partly because of his store of native insolence, which selected him for the command and suited him to its maintenance. On these gatherings he possessed a whole repertory of anecdote, which he added to at each repetition, so that he could supply you with a full outline of character based simply on his observation of the particular person under this set of

conditions. The organisation of public balls in aid of
some charity or other was another darling topic of his
heart. He could expatiate, at great expense of detail,
on the choice of the supper, or the selection of the
band; while if it was a hospital ball, he could narrate
the endless intrigues of the rival doctors and their
bands of patients, for, being a seaside town, there was
a needless profusion of medical men.

In this way, while walking with him, you were surrounded, almost as if you were their prisoner and they
were escorting you into safe custody, by a whole army
of the ghosts he could evoke. There was Doctor Vale,
while we are on this subject, always stepping out of his
car while it was still in motion, and with his stethoscope
nicely coiled, like living entrails, in his silk hat (he was
the last local doctor to wear this emblem of respecta-
bility, and he held it always in his hand when leaving
his motor, as though there was not a moment to be
lost). He was very plump, wore black clothes that
made him look like a very important crow—their
mayor, as it might be—and had a red-haired chauffeur
who read *Tit-Bits* during the waits. Never very far
away, and circulating more quickly in his newer motor,
was Doctor Peploe, who had once been Vale's partner,
but had long ago quarrelled with him and set up on his
own. He was small and weak-looking, with the intent
busyness of a young fly, and an unfinished face that
wanted pince-nez to complete it. I used to play with
his two children, but they joined the Air Force during
the war and were burnt to ashes before their respective
aeroplanes crashed to earth. Their mother, a romantic
invalid, became fortified and almost visibly improved
by the shock, while the doctor, in the agonies of his
doubt as to where they could be, learned the Morse
code during those sleepless nights and always kept the

code-book near his bed in case they should rap out some words to him. But it was in vain—all in vain! Either they no longer cared for him, or they had gone so far away that the perspective of human life was lost to them, and they had no word to send and no method of sending it. Doctor Vale had children, too, a son and a daughter; the former, an imbecile, the latter, deaf from birth; and it is needless to record that these two were the model children held up to our esteem and extolled to our own childhood.

There were many more of them: Doctor Weedon, rumoured to have poisoned his wife; Doctor Thomas, with two daughters who played violins; and Doctor Thorpe, whose wife was deaf and always went to the South of France in the winter. Each of these doctors had his own tribe of patients, his own nurses, and his own nursing-home, for they wielded the same sort of power in this seaside town that the priests possess in some provincial capital of Italy or Spain. Clergymen were innumerable, also, but Colonel Fantock was no Christian enthusiast, so that I heard less of the churches and their vicars than I did of any other class of this small community.

Most numerous of all, and connected with the widest repertory, were those ladies of independent means who lived out in the new part of the town, and met together nearly every day in order to play Bridge. They lived in strong force almost within earshot of each other, and so intimate was the interweaving of their lives, so plangent the way that they bared their breasts to each other's arrows, that you might say these Amazons faced the fire like soldiers on parade, never flinching and never dismissed, using this latter term in its military meaning, for nothing save the very severest financial loss could force a withdrawal from the field. It would be impossible, in these few pages, to start a detailed account of their warfare; you might as soon expect the historian to give the full history of each day of the week, for the subjects, as well as the duration, were diurnal. We can leave them, then, under this heavy, eternal fire; and, anyway, we can see their houses clearly from the sands, whence we can look upon their lives as something peculiar and mortal, being both a part of life and a symbol of its immortality, so that if one was a drowning sailor from some ship wrecked in the huge, hollow bay, the thought of these people living such a little way away, a few feet above one on the cliffs, would be the thread of life that one would cling to with the last press of strength, just as the lives of Mrs. Wardle, Miss Fosse, or Mrs. Hebden comfort me when I am being given gas at the dentist's, for they interest me and seem by their very excess of absurdity to constitute some sign of a continuity after death.

There was now a moaning, metallic sound as a far-away tram, so little that you could hardly see it, came grinding round a steep corner of the foreshore hill, and simultaneously, as though started by the noise, a pair of lifts began travelling up and down the cliff, seeming to slide on long, grasshopper legs. They were taking away the tired, who had heard enough of the band and had finished their tea, and replacing them with fresh reserves drawn from the thronging crowds on the Esplanade above. There would have been few among them known to us, in any case, because this was a summer crowd come for a holiday from big towns in the smoky, industrial centre of the country; while the true, all-the-year-round, inhabitants stirred but little out of doors in this crush, and only resumed their parochial energies once more about the end of September, when the town returned to its normal size, and you were no longer disturbed, walking through the shopping district, by the chattering mobs on their way from the station to the sea-front.

Once the winter campaign had begun it was waged without intermission till Easter, and no quarter was allowed; there was a truce during the summer, and Colonel Fantock used to avail himself of the holiday, sometimes spending it in Derbyshire with us as I have described, for the young children who were his pupils were given six weeks' rest, though, even then, they must not be suffered to forget the examinations that lay before them, through—or rather over which—as though they were hedges and his pupils young untrained horses, it was Colonel Fantock's duty to urge them. The furniture of the room in which he taught became, every year, scarcer and more simple, as though philosophy had taken a stern and austere hold upon his conscience, so that, by the time we are speaking of, he would be sitting near an old oak dresser, which he would always tell you he had secured lately, as a great bargain, for five pounds; though it was obviously the amount and not the cheapness of the bargain that impressed him; by several plain chairs; a still plainer writing-table; a few prints by Cruikshank; four or five small framed silhouettes; many books, but all of them in cheap shilling editions; and, on the mantelpiece, a skeleton clock under a glass shade, a clock that, though intended to look so, seemed reduced to the barest necessities of existence and continuance, for there was no flesh to cover its bones. It was in very fact the cell of a philosopher, for but few thinkers can stand their rooms full of objects that distract the attention; but this ideal setting had imposed itself, and philosophy was no more the agent than it was the object of his simplicity.

In spite of all these drawbacks I imagine him to have been happy, for he had imprisoned his ambitions within such confined limits that the direst poverty could hardly have reduced them further: some pipe tobacco and two or three whiskies-and-sodas daily being his ordinary and unvarying demand, while he had two other needs that came in rotation with the seasons—a little coal in winter and a few hours of sun in summer; the price of the one, and the niggardliness of the other, formed, indeed, his two grumbles against life, and if only these could have been assured to him he would not have minded his bare table or cold bed. He had twelve children, by two marriages, but they all, save his youngest daughter, lived miles away in the south of England, or in the Colonies, and all of them were married and had large families of their own, for which reason they would have found it most difficult to help him, had they even been asked. But here pride came in and intervened, so that they were not informed of what their own hard lives rendered them disinclined to make enquiry. He was left, therefore, to the mercy of his friends, and it was one of the misfortunes of time that made his old age just coincide with the departure to London or to the South of England of so many families he knew, for this sea-side town had become fashionable about the time of the Franco-Prussian War, and as soon as a younger generation, most of whom had been Colonel Fantock's pupils, grew up and began to take up careers or marry, their first resolution was always to leave their old homes for a less rigorous climate. These facts gave a theatrical reality to Colonel Fantock's senile complaints, for his golden youth had vanished by now as certainly as it had been, once, more golden than his grey drab present.

Could there be anything more human in mortals

59

than the enthusiasm with which old gentlemen, of Colonel Fantock's years, welcomed the Great War! Colonel Fantock must have commanded, in spirit, those legions that fought, on behalf of all vested interests, against Napoleon, that last and most worthy champion of the aristocratic principle. Once more, a century later, they welcomed the agent of their own destruction, but in a hundred years they had not understood, and Colonel Fantock would tell me about the Duke of Wellington's funeral as though it had been a national tribute to the victor over anarchy. Napoleon, appearing before the actual industrial revolution had begun, seemed to offer in a parodoxical way an amendment and yet a hope of permanency for the thousand-year-old European system of which he was the culmination; but the kernel of this paradox lay too deep within its hard walls, and the very system he had set out to perpetuate on a modernised and strengthened basis brought him down. Even then, the ruins were considerable and required one more explosion to bring them to the ground; but the survivors, while they lost everything of good they had ever had, kept anything obnoxious they could save out of the new system Napoleon had invented, and retained conscription, the one thing most calculated to make them hated by their own subjects, just as compulsory cricket at the schools has both made the game hated and professionalised, and, therefore, spoilt those most disposed to be good at it. This second blast has now come and gone, and, until the smoke has cleared away, it is difficult to see how much is left standing.

It is surprising, even thus early, to see how many sheltered lives there still are, how many complete existences removed as far from any contact with poverty as a drawing-room carpet should be from the winter

rain. This thought gives a luxury to eating one's breakfast at ten o'clock, and makes the mere demand, at the hotel desk, that one should be called at such or such an hour in the morning, an act of audacity; which seems bolder still when we think of the huddled forms sleeping on the window-sills under the colonnade.* There are of a certainty many small pleasures for the superman! The Norman barons may seem a long way back, now, but they were there, once, like the wolf at the head of every dog's pedigree.

Leaving public wars of politics, and coming to private wars of the intellect, I believe men of exceptional ability to be able always to get their work done, in the teeth of the most appalling obstacles and in spite of every species of opposition, so that, however impaired their lives may be by enmity and poverty, there is at least some trace left after them, some more permanent footmark than the crowd with their heavy feet can leave. There are the men who are important in their generation, who form indeed the only evidence and leave the only relics of their age! in fact, they do the work of their own contemporaries, so that one poet can typify and give voice to many thousands of mute and immaculate nonentities. These are, then, the true workers; but a certain interest attaches also to their patrons, and this importance, which lies in what they do with their leisure, can only be found among those who have a little time on their hands and can afford weak nerves or insomnia: for the others, in their huge majority, go to bed too tired every night and open each day too busily; the former, by an early rapacity exercised many generations ago, found themselves on a firm foundation in the shifting sands, where each grain could only see its near neighbour in the flat plain, and

* The Ritz Hotel, London.

knew no name attaching to itself save, perhaps, those of its two immediate generators; living in the very heart of them were the "strong men," for thus did power begin, living in cages that they had built for themselves and within which they intended to remain. The "strong men" of our generation are with us still, and they are no coarser and no more brutal than their colleagues of a thousand years ago, only they are working in a conventionalised brutality that seems more awful to us because it is bloodless. Slave-owners could not "give notice" to their slaves, but if you are a job tailor at work in a heart-rending slum, you can be thrown on to the cold winds at any moment, and may then bless liberty: unless your eyes are too weak, you may read in this sweet leisure, for that is the surest and quickest way to find out how unhappy you are. Ghosts of an important exterior, like Colonel Fantock, did not bother much about these lesser comedies of life, they were too safely tucked away from sight down the slums: the streets he lived in were straight and well-trimmed, with lawns at appropriate intervals, and so may we typify his aspirations, the Duke of Cambridge at the end of every vista transmuting each lawn to a parade-ground. Yes! with Colonel Fantock it was decidedly a life of outside appearance, of the exterior, and a great part of the game consisted in hiding behind your own façade.

This secret in his life I had learned long ago, and in order to find my way into his conscience, into his soul, if we prefer calling it by another name, I found that many of those dark cells required to have their windows flung open that they might be flooded with light, and so I would travel down his memory, that long corridor, going into one room after another that led off it, following this continuous thread of connection in all its ramifications. In this way he was a true teacher, not overloading my own mind, but allowing me to travel about in his experience, where I could find an answer to every question I wanted to ask. He could tell me anything between 1840 and the summer before last, that stage from which I was prepared myself to keep, as it were, a full journal of memory; and he would start off with the earliest historical fact, as against those of a personal or family nature, that had made itself known to him as something worth remembering, and this was his story: that he used to see some withered, wizened objects stuck, like coco-nuts, on the masts that adorned the Temple Arch, and these were, so he told me, and I have never had the courage to find out if he was wrong, the heads of "traitors" executed after the 1745 rebellion. Close on this, as I have said, followed the Duke of Wellington's funeral; he had seen him, in fact, lying in state with that great hooked nose, and here he joined on with my grandmother who remembered him well, as her great-uncle, and could describe his yellow nankeen trousers and pale blue coat with silver buttons. It was a pity that I could not ask that old lady, sitting remote in her arm-chair, how much she remembered of her own grandmother, for that distant paragon had been the daughter of Admiral Boscawen, and then we should have got, at one bound, into the middle of the eighteenth century. But she was too huddled, too crouched in mind over her own descendants, as though anxious, when she fell, that she might fall among them, so as to be carried on a little further in that half-light, memory.

It was symbolic of the way in which she was dwelling on the future, and not the past, that her eyes were always wandering across the room towards a leather travelling-clock on the piano, for she used to wait the

whole day for her son to come in and see her, and the
afternoon grew longer and longer the later it got, for
after perhaps six o'clock of a summer evening it was
hopeless that he should come. In fact he came very
seldom, and these delays seemed to prolong her old
age; for instead of a drawing-in of the strings of life
and a compact and comfortable decline, her last few
years were a staccato, and agitated dropping of the
faculties, because the one person she really cared for
had grown out of her possession, and nothing she could
do, no little signs or pledges, could win him back again.
Her arm-chair was drawn up by a window, and during
these waits she used to look out, the house she always
hired for the summer being just by the Gentlemen's
Club, and watch the people crossing the bridge to the
Spa and the new part of the town, beyond. This may
have comforted her a little, for the sight of those hundreds of people doing mechanically what she had so
often done herself, walking just the same side of the
bridge, looking at the same tree below them on the left,
catching the first sight of the Castle Hill over the second lamp-post, and listening to the gear being moved
on board the fishing fleet in the bay, seemed to bring
her down to the level of ordinary people, and minimise
her unhappiness by the very multitude of its similarity.
Thus, for the individual, death in a big war, or being
drowned at sea in company with many others, seems
both more futile and more easy from its commonplace,
than to die in a little frontier fight, or to perish all by
yourself out of a small boat; then, for the moment,
life and death became more comprehensible to her; for
all those she saw walking out there must have had
parents, and a great many of them, like herself, must
have descendants; but soon the memory of her own
importance dragged her down again into the abyss,

64

and she was far away as ever from other peoples' sorrows, railed off from them, indeed, by the glass panes of the window, that harder and more unyielding iris to her eye. It was time for tea, now, and that slow gentle warmth was a truce with the enemy ahead of her.

Just at the end of this line of houses, Cliff Bridge Terrace it was called, a private bridge led over the sunken road below into her son's garden, though this path, in the fashion of those days, took a long time reaching his house, for it wound about, serpent-like, through groves of laurel and lauristina, past clumps of that sad plant, the American lilac, till it eventually struggled free of the bushes and came out by a grass knoll where there was a pergola of roses. This was where they used to have tea in the summer, for there was a good view of the sea; and the house was only a few yards behind, near enough in fact to cover you with its shadow. It had been built on a peculiar fan-shaped plan so as to get its three separate projections all facing the sea, and from a rule of "ancient lights," economy, or a mere caprice, the whole building was of only two stories, so that most of the servants had to sleep in another house near-by, at the end of the garden. The stone was of a beautiful orange-lichen colour, and this, indeed, gave the only note of permanence, for my uncle's family seemed only to encamp in the house for July, August, and September, and this had been their custom ever since my great-grandfather built the house, ninety years ago.

A long brick wall, white-washed in a nautical manner, kept the public road away and wound along past another house to our own home, which had also been built by the same local architect in a similar style, reminiscent, ever so faintly, of the work of Sir John Soane. All three houses had long, deep gardens, so

65

that the tall trees growing in the wildernesses of their lowest reaches held up their higher branches on a level with our Bœotian façade, and in the spring, through your bedroom window, you could watch the crows building their nests. Appearing at intervals through the leaves there was a steep road, used by those who did not wish to pay a toll each time they crossed one or other suspension bridge to the new town beyond. You could see, every morning, Shentall the greengrocer's van, or Doctor Peploe swirling down in his car on the way to an operation, though perhaps he would call in here first on his daily visit to my mother. Half an hour would while away easily waiting for such clock-like happenings as these, and then all the time, above this road, there stood those astonishing white-brick villas opposite. A dentist and his brother, another dentist, lived in the lowest of these, and then came the red-brick, towered and turreted, house of Dr. Vale, the home of those two young geniuses I have mentioned: in the garden there stood one of the conical, thatch-roofed summer-houses of untrimmed logs, built in the fifties and sixties, but suggesting that woad and the ancient Britons were not so far away from us as convention would have it; and against this rather simian background, the precocious son and daughter might be seen playing in a break from their lessons. After this, white brick came once more, of a terrible porcelain consistency making one think, on a wet day, of the sensitive dentine which those skilled hands two doors away could never relieve. Next, another white house, lived in by a stout lady of formidable appetite, whom we used to watch in her dining-room through an opera-glass; after that, for a change, a house of yellow brick, and finally on the brink of the cliff, at the head of the Spa bridge, and at the corner of the Esplanade, in a

66

strategic position, therefore, the Esplanade Boarding
Establishment, an immense white stuccoed affair like a
block of flats, with a precipitous garden in which you
might sometimes see the maids walking in their white
aprons.

This view from my window had a mournful sameness, and it was apparent to one, even as a child, that
there was in all that "civilised" prospect no sign that
any kind of beauty was believed in, or even attempted,
and that no one, within sight or sound, cared for anything except a "view." This panorama had therefore
a terrible, tame monotone of interior comfort, as it
might be expressed in gas-chandelier or horse-hair sofa,
utterly at variance with the hard facts of nature,
molten, metallic heat, or fierce, Northern wintriness.
How different this summer day, for example, from
those horrible drizzles of February and March! It
would come down, thick and heavy as a woollen
blanket, not so much flung out of heaven, as lying on
one, like the real authentic blankets of sleep. The
houses opposite glistened coldly, as though their whiteness was but a mildew on respectable, ordinary brick,
and the bare branches between us looked soft and un-
breakable as deep-sea plants. Or, another day, it was
the snow, even and unremitting, as regular in its
rhythm as the waves that broke on the lighthouse in
the harbour below; and it covered the ground and lay
an inch or two deep on the window-sills and branches.
The white houses you could hardly see, though now
and again for an instant their high-pitched roofs
loomed out, now loaded with a level, matt surface of
snow; while even the pinnacle-like obelisks on the ridge
had a sheath of snow covering their points. One
might have stayed at the window for ever, for now I
had become slightly mesmerised, as will happen if you

67

have been reading a long time and then go to the window for a rest, for the more open spaces rest your eyes, and you find yourself looking involuntarily into this freedom, while your eyes point you in this direction and will keep your mind fixed there. It was in this fashion that I had changed the seasons, and gone in imagination from a summer day into the noiseless deeps of winter, and I should have stayed at the window perhaps even longer, had not the church clock of St. Martin's chimed out four o'clock, prefacing that quadruple sameness with a tune which divided itself into quarters, and was only played in its entirety at each hour.

I was growing older, and had gone through another gate even as the clock struck. Slight as its measures were, and trivial though they might be in importance, such a scene as this remained a permanency in memory, for it was one of those moments of telescopic vision when one can see oneself many years older in the act of remembering every detail of this long-dead day, saying to oneself here by the window, Shall I remember this when I am twice as old as now? and answering that same question at once, as in a second's journey, ten years ahead of time.

It will all come back again at once, with the glass— that water-film—between me and the strange world outside. It is the same hot summer blown to fire once more, and so friendly in its soft, warm touch that every one not bedridden has come out of doors. It only wants a little trouble, a little shifting of levels to find any one you set out to seek: for there are the road down to the sands, the streets of shops, and the gardens on the cliff. It is not a Sunday: the churches are empty, therefore; and the sun has so melted the cold limbs of the invalids that the doctors are taking their leisure away from the bedside. The bands are playing and their honeyed sweetness is sure to attract any one who is ill or unhappy; while the sands are so fresh and golden that the bolder spirits venture right out on to the rocks for the cool, salt breeze; and I find myself out there once more with Colonel Fantock, starting for home over the weedy boulders.

In those intervals when one can look up from picking out a path among the rocks we may take a last view, before this vision fades away, of the town where I was born, and to which I shall probably never return. Nobody that I remembered had then died, and this remote contingency, seemingly but an alternative to life, lay too far ahead to be considered in its effect. They were all there, and it seemed as though they would always be so. I did not know, then, that the beauty of jet bonnet, or white moustachio, was but transitory, only a phase in something that was continually changing and growing older, with an adaptability, even, that had a little spark of the chameleon about it, for if white moustache and beard are indicative of the snows of winter, one may say that the black lights of jet show the sombre sparkle of the hearse in their gay facets. In fact these two flaunting figures, male and female emblems of their race, were standing near enough to catch the reflection, be, themselves, part of the shadow, as they showed against the snow, or stood at those mournful windows framed in jet-black panelling.

Nothing, certainly, could have seemed further away on the day I am describing: death was as far off from us as sleep from waking, or night from day.

The huge mass of the Grand Hotel, with its peculiar French floridity of detail, for it had been built like the hotels in Northumberland Avenue, in the sixties, when

François Premier and Henri Deux, or Quatre, were
well studied and admired epochs, stood up like an
enormous natural bluff or headland above the town.
In fact its size almost rivalled the bulk of the Castle
Hill, and it looked like a great lion lying with its paws
stretched out towards the sands below. The Spa buildings, nearer at hand, were built, on a smaller scale, in
the same bastard style, and from the rocks one could
see very clearly the crowded promenade, the thronged
terrace where people were having tea, and that strange
tower, built for no reason or purpose, up which there
climbed every day, on its thin metal spiral stair, our
only local alpinist, a young man suspected, not without
just cause, of being perilously near the border-line of
insanity—in fact he has now, long ago, crossed into the
tropics, where one may hope that he is happier. Above
the Spa, gardens ran right up to the cliff above, with
many winding paths through the different groves of
trees and shrubs. On certain grassy knolls, left bare
for this purpose, there were hundreds of coloured
lamps inlaid into the grass, in preparation for to-night's
firework display, and they were arranged like beds of
very metallic flowers, or like the stars, and rayed suns,
that distinguished personages wear across their breasts.

Now and again the elastic contact of the wind,
stretched out to seemingly its furthest extent, would
reach to us at the same moment that it hovered over
the band playing by that battlemented wall of the Spa
promenade, and part of one of those incessant comedy
overtures would arrive out on the rocks, a little inap-
propriate, as though one ate strawberries and cream in
a sea-pool, or was sitting out here under the boughs, in
order to be rested by their green surge and swell in the
wind. We were alone upon these pinnacles, for those
people who were energetic enough to take much exer-

cise had moved on from here, and were already far ahead and would soon disappear from view round a corner of the cliffs, into Cornelian Bay, the next inlet in the coast. Colonel Fantock, for bright sunlight always calls up Utopias of the fancy, was telling me about his chicken-farm, a project which had for years seemed unrealisable, but was now coming slowly within his grasp. There were only a few more pounds needed, some forty or fifty, and then he would be able to retire from all this wearisome teaching into the country village he had chosen, a few miles away, and near enough to come in to the town for luncheon two or three times a month. There was a little orchard behind the house, where he could keep his hen-coops under the apple trees, with an arbour where he could sit in the sun, and just a few little beds of flowers for him to tend. A red cinder-path ran along the stone wall, and made a walk for him when he wanted to smoke his pipe, for there was always an objective at the far end, where the wall sank down a little before turning a corner and travelling round to complete the square, and at that particular point you could pause for a moment and take a look up and down the road to see who was abroad in the village street. This would keep him busy six or seven months of the year, and in the winter he had a good sitting-room, that looked out quietly into the same wall-bound enclosure; big enough for his writing-table and bookcases, and making at the same time a good dining-room for the three of them. In fact his wife and daughter themselves preferred the idea of this room to the rather frigid and forbidding parlour with its dull and heavy lace curtains that hid the street, and they thought that the former would make their general living-room, especially as they would both be busy most of the day in the house or after the chickens; while the Colonel, it was understood, must have time every day for reading or writing. He would like to move in there early in the autumn, October for preference, for then there would be time to prepare, not only for the winter, but also for their first spring in the country. They could make things comfortable before it became too cold.

We had come, by now, to the edge of a kind of inland sea, which spread out over quite a considerable area among the rocks, and to which I always made a point of coming whenever I walked on the shore because of the extraordinary beauty of the sea-plants to be seen growing out of its shallow depths. There were long palm-like fronds that floated, serpent-wise, upon its surface, for, until the wind was so completely silent that you could see the long tree-stems on which these fronds were supported, they seemed, in very fact, to be moving, slow and serpent-wise, across a glass world. Sometimes one of the little ripples that the wind made would tower up into a miniature wave, and it was astonishing how this appeared to be charged and concentrated with the violent blue of the deep sea out beyond the rocks. Indeed the continual force of the wind, so strong that it was like a great host of people running past you and all of them heading for the same direction, together with its salt, stinging smell, had the power of transporting one altogether, till the fronds of sea-weed became real palms, gliding and shaking themselves in the grasp of one of those blue tropical winds. At the same time, the sea glittered all over its huge mass for as far as one could see, and the sands showed themselves, for once, as a likely ingredient in the making of glass, for they were shining with a crackling, transparent fire.

The fishing boats in the bay were caught up and

transfused in the sunlight, so that while any polished
or metallic surface was thrown back violently on a
golden line that flashed into your eyes, the universal
and fathomless blue of the air had penetrated into
every corner and crevice that it could reach.   In this
way the hulls and even the complicated web of rigging
became ingredients of, and not objects in, the atmosphere.   The hull seemed a blue body converted into
the substance in which it lay, much as insects turn to
amber within that sweet and cloying matrix; and the
rigging seemed to climb through tubes of blue air; the
ropes, in fact, were so many glass rods sparkling with
blue, electric fires, and as the boats moved slowly
through the ethereal brightness they had the force and
the majestic movement of stars, for one can well
imagine them tacking with the same freedom across
their blue plain, with sails like a snow mountain to cool
them, and firm rudders that beat down steadily the
ripe-haired fields of foam, leaving a temporary destruction in their wake.   This pool in the rocks, by
which we were standing, had exactly the same blue intensity as the sea, for that colour came out of the sky
with equal violence, however small the surface on
which it fell.   When an edge of water was lifted a
little by the wind it would splash upon the rocks and
leave, for a moment, some little trace of its colour till
this was quickly devoured and taken up again by the
hot sky.

In just the same way, the salt began to die out of the
sea air, and the band far back at the cliff's foot never
seemed to reach us now upon the wind, so that some of
the machinery of memory must be failing, some contact must have been severed and disconnected.   Sure
enough, in a moment or two the whole scene had faded
and vanished into thin air, taken up again as had been

73

the fate of the edges of water on the rocks, and in very fact the only thing common to both these worlds was the hot sky, under whose influence I had been dozing through part of the summer afternoon. I arrived back out of this unconsciousness to find myself once more in Derbyshire, and sailing with Colonel Fantock on the lake at my home, a frequent delight of ours on the hot afternoons, when lunch was over and one had rested for a little.

There was a tall, steep hill down from the house to the lake, with long grass that was always a little damp even on the hottest day. Very soon you came to a point at which your feet were on a level with the tree-tops, for there were some clumps of trees, mainly chestnuts, upon the hillside. They were now in full leaf, and so thick and intense was the foliage that, once you came down among the leaves, the very shadow over which you trod to get under the boughs was scented and seemed part of the motionless and patient animal to which it was attached. The whole tree was as if close-furred, so full and thick that every leaf was an important, live part of the whole; and yet, being too cloying and fragrant for an animal, this chestnut tree was more like a hot, brimming honeycomb. There were, as I have said, several of these combs to be tasted on the way downhill, and then, just where the slope ran into the ground level, came a hot, iron fence with almost molten tar to coat its rustiness. Once this had clanged-to, a few more yards over the high grass brought one to the wooden landing-stage, near the padlocked door of the boat-house. Colonel Fantock fumbled in an aged way with the key, and at last he had turned it and we could push the door wide open and begin to pull out the boat. This was always difficult, because the boat-house was much bigger than

74

the punt it contained, and so the boat was always to be found down at the far end, where nothing except a walking-stick at the end of a long arm could reach it. The method was to push it as hard as possible against the far end, whence it would rebound and come out to us on the landing-stage. These boards were rather worn and old and used to creak ominously under Colonel Fantock's weight, while, for there was a certain amount of wind, we were trying to hoist a big white sail on to the punt. The waves broke one after another, for we were only some three inches above them, and the Colonel walked a little nervously upon the platform, as though about to address a public meeting. Indeed, as he drew away each time before a new wave, he seemed to be shying at the hundreds of clapped hands sounding out together, for the waves as they were shattered on the side of the boat, on these boards, and on the wooden walls of the boat-house, had exactly that rumbling detonation. It was an authentic fear that caused him to behave like this, for he was afraid to get his boots wet and spoil that primrose colour to the perfection of which, as I have already described, he had devoted so many years; or, to bring down the matter to an altogether lower level, he had no other boots to change into should these be spoiled.

Once the sail was hoisted and tied safely into position, we could take the painter out of the ground and start off for the centre of the lake. There were some great shoals of weed to be crossed on the way, but there was enough wind just to carry one through these, though the rudder after one of these passages had to be violently shaken to free it of the weed that had collected there. The pace was, therefore, alternatively quite fast and rather slow and drooping, so that there was some reason for the drowsiness that overcame one

75

after a half-hour under the afternoon sun. When I became conscious again, I found Colonel Fantock sitting rather stiffly upright, in a position that suggested that he was too old to lie flat down without experiencing some difficulty in getting up again; he was propped up by a number of cushions and was smoking his pipe in a contemplative mood. After a few moments' silence, he produced a heavy gold watch from his pocket, and said it was time to start home for tea, and we must, moreover, be punctual this particular day because of the visitors who had come over.

We had only to turn the boat's head round to find the wind ready to take us down the whole length of the lake to the boat-house. The sail filled out in a moment and the whole boat leaned over at a delightful angle against the wind, while the swell caused by the rudder welled up angrily almost to the height of the gunwales, and there was a bubbling, prismatic sense of speed as we flashed past foot after foot of blue water. About half-way down we lowered the sail, and were carried on by our own speed to a point where one could arrive by a magnificent sweep of the rudder right alongside the landing-stage. We had, then, only to lift out the cushions, and push the boat back home into its house. It seemed a weary way up the hill carrying those light but awkward weights, but when one stood still for a moment to get breath, there were views of the whole stretch of water below, with the banks of sighing, green reeds, the dark, turbaned bulrushes, and the wooded island, dark and inaccessible now, in the middle. Colonel Fantock was puffing and blowing, always a little behind, but steady and sure in his pace, so that he was the first to reach the top, and make that familiar clang of the little iron gate that led into the bottom of the garden.

76

III

The Polish Musicians

THERE was the sound of heavy footsteps first on wood and then on stone as Henry, my father's Yorkshire servant, passed on his way to the ballroom, where the family were having tea, and soon his enormous form came out from the kitchen-passage into the hall and I saw that he was carrying them a second supply of hot water, an indication that we were rather later than I had imagined. He had just time to make a face at me indicative of his opinion of Colonel Fantock's military prowess and was then gone beyond recall, as swiftly and noisily as a train upon the last lengths of its journey. I followed those echoing footsteps across the hall through a lobby, and into the huge and deserted drawing-room through which one had to pass. There were seven great windows coming right down to the floor, and two more of them at the end of the room; while, as though to stress the importance that the builder of this drawing-room attached to his creations being sufficiently lighted, there hung down from the middle of the Adams ceiling a great ormolu chandelier which spoke to one at once of George IV and the Brighton Pavilion, while the glass shades of those numerous oil lamps contained, as do so many unconscious details in decoration, a true confirmation of their date, for they had exactly the silhouette of the dress of fashionable women of that period. A tall Georgian mantelpiece lay in front as one walked down the room, and on each side of it there were two mahogany doors of great height, tallying with two equal doors on the wall opposite that flow of windows; the walls themselves being occupied by huge panels of tapestry, one of them very dark and faded, and the other curiously light and "cleaned" in colour—probably because it was over the fireplace and had profited to this extent by winter fires. One had come through a door, now, and turned the corner into an ante-room, beyond which the ballroom could be seen stretched out to great length between the opened double-folds of another tall mahogany door.

This room was even longer and higher than that through which one had passed, and the far-off ceiling had a stucco design of a rare and cloud-like lightness, which made the heavy structure really appear to float above one's head. There were three more panels of tapestry upon the walls, one of them opposite the door through which one had entered; and indeed these were the five that I have mentioned at the beginning of this book as having exerted an extraordinary fascination upon us children. At this second mention of them I am unable to resist a few remarks about them.

They portrayed five triumphs, of such abstract qualities as justice and commerce; but it was a world of Indian suavity and opulence, and Indian in the poetic not the geographic sense, for it was the East before artists had learned the difference between India, China, and the El Dorados of America, and so it contained subtle exaggerations on what the designer considered as the mean level of this trebly-distilled land of beauty. There were elephants and black slaves, bell-hung pagodas and clipped hornbeams; in the background were clouds tacking like fleets of sailing ships, and, lower down, terraces with pots of orange-trees upon their balustrades, and continual fountain jets that gave a cool note to the hot summer portrayed in every

78

other symbol. Some great folios lie open upon the stone steps, as though the lady in her plumed headdress who sits above them had lately been read to by one of the slaves who is waiting upon her. She has had them put to ground, for a horn far away in the distance must be the prelude to some new procession that will come out of the distance, slowly climbing one terrace after another till they come almost to her side; though they pass her and fade away again as easily, for it is one of the laws of this paradise that only the scaffolding, the bare bones, the actual fact of being alive, are unchanging and permanent: leaves, clouds, and water showing as much change as they are capable of, so that there is hardly any monotony except the heart-beat, and all externals are mobile and differing in their phases. It is necessary, then, for these laws that such tragic intervals as a procession can fill must die like music, and it has never yet been expected of music that it should have greater permanency than the span of its own bars; for even with the gramophone or pianola you have to play the piece over again, and it cannot stand except on those very jointed and mechanical legs.

Tea was by the fireplace at a round table, which was hidden like a baby in long white clothes. The evenings were getting earlier, and so the tall windows which a projecting angle of the house hid from the fires of sunset gave little except a waterlike and limpid light, which explains why the tea-table had been dragged across from the windows and put by the fire. Another of those tall eighteenth-century mantelpieces allowed the flames to leap up from the grate higher than the silver kettle on the table and the pulsing and flickering light reddened every face and made the near ends of the sofa and the tablecloth difficult to touch because of their heat, while after half an hour, or so, these flames would build up a baking, red furnace, unchanging and insatiable till near midnight.

In a few days we should be going back to school again, my parents would start for abroad, and the house would be shut up once more, deserted save for the occasional voyages of a very aged housekeeper till the following August: so that this was one of the last days the room would be used. It gave a poignancy and a kind of special pathos to the occasion. All sorts of things would leave one or be taken away from one, including, I always feared, Colonel Fantock—one of my few friends. This was in fact the beginning of ennui—of depression. One hated—old men call this decadence—going back to school, though surely that regret is a tribute to one's happiness at home, and one longed—as depression was inevitable—that since one had to be unhappy it might at any rate be away from a football, and of a tapestry-like peace and regret. When as young as that, one regrets mainly the future —a proof, surely, that time is a dimension, because by doing this one can place oneself at either side of it to prove that it is limited and finite.

I suppose this particular depression had its origin in fondness for one's home, and in the feeling that something awful would happen and one would have to leave it. Its incongruous size and unwieldy extent must be partly responsible. I suppose the same sense that enables artists—Rossetti, for instance—to invent a kind of woman some time before she appears and is apparent to the public, enables every one to be a little of a prophet in minor matters; and so it was probably this same area of sensibility that registered the opinion that in future houses of such size would only be inhabited as hospitals or hotels. There was something of the extinct monster about it, a miniature of that melancholy interest that attaches itself to such old skeletons as Caserta or the Escurial. One was very fond of it, and rather frightened of it. The two great eighteenth-century rooms that I have described were terrifying to be alone in, or even to walk through by oneself, while being asked after dinner by a relation to fetch something she had left in the dining-room was an excursion fraught with horror. Naturally the walls were red—they always are in English dining-rooms— but the solitary candle left burning without its shade made those dark walls palpitate with shadows. High up among them hung several portraits of wigged ancestors, all of them painted in such fashion that their eyes followed you and their heads seemed to be turned in your direction whichever part of the room you stood in. Then again, there were four formal mahogany doors, any one of which might open suddenly, and with a more terrifying possibility in the case of those two of them that had cupboards concealed behind them, and led nowhere. Perhaps now, at this twilight hour, it was even more frightening than after dinner, because there was at any rate, then, the certainty of a few oil-lamps in the passages, and these would not yet have been taken round by the man who cleaned them in the stillery-room. It was getting darker and darker.

It was so dark that you could hardly make out the faces of the people sitting at tea. We were going to have some music afterwards, for my sister played the piano well, and our guests that day included a family of Poles, father, mother, and son, the father having been, as a young man, a player of some merit. They had driven over in a high dog-cart from their son's rooms in Bolsover, where he was engaged in some industrial concern, and they were extremely fond of music, which is more than can be said for any one else

81

that we had met up to that time. Talking, and listening to the music, were, therefore, like getting outside one's own skin, and not being imprisoned in some one else's, but free to wander at will and fancy. Also the fact that they were Poles made them romantic, and the old gentleman was himself fully alive to this, and could tell one harrowing stories of the last Polish Rebellion—in 1863-4, I think—which he could vividly remember as a child. Snow plains, sledges, and Cossacks were words that occurred as often in his talk as you may hear technical terms in the gibber at a golf club, and he had in addition a kind of noisy general humour which is supposed to be the inalienable prerogative of persons who dwell in artistic circles. He would, of a sudden, sing with loud gestures, or could at a moment's notice improvise knife and fork, or shovel and tongs, into musical instruments. Such are the tricks of exiles making the best of their banishment; for you never find natives who thus enjoy themselves in their own country: but only Poles in Paris, or Spaniards in London. Life was a perpetual picnic, and he had grown used to any discomforts that it might entail.

Colonel Fantock was nowhere to be seen: he hated music and despised musicians. Probably he was smoking a pipe in the arm-chair in his bedroom. It was irritating to think that he, or any one else in the house who disliked music, could if they pleased sit in the room, get nothing out of it, and spoil other people's pleasure—one liked him the more, therefore, for staying away; but it was maddening that people had even the power of listening who were too stupid to make use of it. In the same way the thought of its railway-station grates on one's memory of Venice, and a great hero's reputation suffers when one imagines him in the grip of a cold, or having to take doses. These, again, are the faults of young criticism, because, in reality, Venice being able to survive its railway, and a hero overcoming his colds, or his weak constitution, are the tests of supremacy; and one learns to despise anything that has had no obstacles to contend against. Very soon, for the same reason, one must try to live without the past, for it becomes, after a time, weakening by weight of association; producing the same effect that Socialists ascribe to a settled income. Circumstances were luckily so favourable on this particular evening that the servants had even taken the tea-table away before the music began, avoiding that apparently inevitable interruption.

Everything was congenial, therefore, and I suppose that the very atmosphere of the room—the sense that everything shortly was to "close down"—helped and intensified the interpretation that one put forward for the music. The Romantics of eighty or a hundred years ago showed, unconsciously, exactly the same characteristics as the reactionary politicians of their own generation whom they most disliked; and none of the ministers of Charles X, or of the Ferdinands of Austria, Naples, and Spain, can have felt more acutely the transitory and passing life in that which they were seeking to recapture and re-establish. So old and tottering were those principles, after the hard knocks of the Revolution and Napoleon, so soon would they inevitably die, that the hope of continuity was transferred from those old breasts, avoiding the middle-aged who might be supposed to be inoculated with the poisonous ideas of their own young days and became installed in a youthfulness that was almost too tender and young. Thus the Comte de Chambord, as a forlorn political principle, perhaps even those two young Queens, Vic-

toria of England and Isabella of Spain, tally curiously
and with some significance with that hero-worship
which the circumstances of their early deaths caused to
centre round Shelley, Keats, and Byron. Merit was
distrusted in persons of over thirty years of age, and
it would be difficult to find a hero or heroine much
over this age in any book, poem, or picture of that
period. We feel this extreme youthfulness wherever
the poetry of Keats, or Shelley, crystallises, so rarely,
into a human character; and surely the same thing is
true with the music of that period, and most evidently
so in those few instances where we get the same characteristics perfectly expressed in prose, in Gautier's
Mdlle. de Maupin, for example, itself the work of a
young man of nineteen, and a book of astonishing
genius.

It is because of these circumstances that the music of
Chopin has such an immediate and overwhelming effect
when one is young and first hears it; later on this
supremacy is sure to be questioned and reacted against,
but in the end there is something endurable that nothing can destroy, and so long as he is neither nocturnal,
nor Italian, he remains as nearly effective as when first
heard. There is no hoary authority about his tone, and
he does not seek to justify wisdom with white hairs;
nor are his ideals of excellence and authority bearded,
as they are with Wagner. It is this hirsute cleanliness,
immaturity almost, that makes one associate his music
with people who have not yet reached middle-age, and
have, by dying, taken steps to ensure that they should
never do so. It is romantic, therefore, like the tomb
of a young lady, or a young knight; but it has autumn
as well as spring for its completion, and we must picture this alternate hero or heroine, young but resigned,
or wounded and nearly dying.

There is a limitation of personality, a somewhat re-
stricted list of actors: those suitable, however, spring
easily into the imagination, and without hesitation, for
they are appropriate to nothing else. The background
is never very intricate, and every detail glows with an
even light; nor is a scene far removed, often, from the
house. In Schumann you may be miles from a human
dwelling; but with Chopin, if you see a landscape it is
through an open window, and only that on a warm
evening. The ceiling must always be high, and the
window, like those in the room I have been describing,
cut down low to the ground. Heavy curtains, chosen
because of the velvet shadows that they throw, and
which hold the sunlight as steadily as a cut topaz or a
pane of yellow glass, while thousands of little dust-
motes dance in the crowded sunbeams that are dropped
like celestial gangways joining infinite space to such
humble objects as chair or carpet, are pressed back in
squeezed and violent folds behind the opened frames
of the French windows. The shadows are filled with
such unequivocal shades as that of Madame Hanska,
a material embodiment of romance, and the long
sledge-journey to meet her would seem to stretch out
infinitely from some intangible point that will make
itself manifest as soon as ever the window is shut, and
winter may be said by this act of symbolism to have
irrevocably begun. She is in her Russian castle, sitting
on a low divan, drinking tea, and with true barbarian
impassivity has remained in one room out of the many
dozens available to her for two or three weeks together.
She will be as impassive, as uninterested, on the day
Balzac arrives; and he will feel the half-satisfaction of
an archæologist who digs a splendid statue out of the
desert, but cannot tell its subject, or more than hazard
its date. Some of the serfs, the idea of whose abject

obedience had been one of the motives that induced
Balzac to this journey, are sweeping the snow into two
lines of ramparts, so that there shall be some kind of
path across the courtyard; and the sound of their
brooms suggests dead leaves that are being brushed and
rolled off a damp path into little heaps. Both reality
and supposition are dead; they both are useless and
serve only to cumber the ground. Another window
that looks over the countryside shows many hundreds
of bare larch trees, and armies, just as numerous, of
fir trees and evergreens, the former appearing to be
prisoners of the latter who show better equipment;
both hosts are perfectly motionless, being kept stiffly
in position by the loads of snow upon their branches.
Every tree, whether with leaves or without, is as
prickly and jagged as one of those cylindrical rollers
that pass with the artful jaggedness of their raised
points over and over again in a steady pattern through
the vibrating comb of a musical box; and indeed that
is very much their purpose and effect when the hoarse,
rasping wind comes sweeping over the plain. The
snow falls off the branches like a sustained tattoo of
drums, heavy and hollow on the ground thick with
snow; and the notes rise shriller and more sustained
from the denuded boughs.

Such might be an idealised interpretation, narrowing
it down to tree, roof, and room; but these same
simulacra seemed to fit themselves, to become locked
into the set of surroundings in which we were ourselves
living, so that the transfusion of idea from one to the
other could be accomplished without difficulty. Those
green-black fields, for instance, that I mentioned early
in the pages of this book formed an admirable alternative to the Russian plains, and the coal-miners might
well stand for serfs whom we may suppose, by dispos-

ing arbitrarily of some twenty years of history, to have been but lately liberated from their serfdom, so recently, in fact, that they still retain the listlessness and apparent lack of interest in life by which you can distinguish those whose livelihood is barely guaranteed and who are not allowed to profit by any extra show of energy from those who prosper according to their degree of hard work. A sempiternal wintriness, only rendered more acute by the few summer weeks of sunshine, ranged its bitter, rasping weapons at our side.

I have said that one set of circumstances seemed to lock themselves into the other, and the same term can be used over the similar and deadening effect of winter. In this sense, though, it is not so much a lock as a seal of silence. Everything suffers in a complete and immobile vacuum of sound, which is undisturbed and unbroken except by wind and by rain, or by the human noises of road and railway. So dead is this long sleep, so devoid of any movement that is not a shaking or a rattling given violently by some foreign hand, that it is a matter of surprise that the flowers and trees should ever presume upon such lack of evidence to raise their heads again for the sun. That they should do so is evidence of a pathetic confidence, of a patient optimism, almost Christian in its implicitness and in its insistence on the survival of the best. Such was the prospect of winter that lay ahead, and it was as insistent and unavoidable as one's return to school, only to be postponed by a few days' lukewarm sunshine as sad and enervate as the cold in the head, or the sore throat, that might by its rightly-timed appearance put off the months of agony for a day or two.

Soon everything would be very different, and who could tell whether for better or worse? I was nicely hedged round, still, and protected from the delights as well as the dangers of life outside, though I was soon to learn not to take either of these two poles of life too seriously. Meanwhile with the aid of music I was able to unlock one cabinet after another of memories. I was playing in a window with my brother at building houses with wooden bricks; and putting them down to look out of the window at the fishing boats in the bay, stared too closely towards the sun and was rewarded by a whole heap of his shining counterfeits which jangled together like a handful of coins, and then turned blue or red, and moved swiftly down the rows of houses on the cliff opposite, or up Oliver's Mount, the square hill behind the town. Or, a second later, was walking with him along the sands which were stretched out, uncovered, like a vast sketch-board. Most of my memories seemed to be connected with this seaside town, for we spent at least three times as long there as we did in Derbyshire. In particular, one had the memory of long afternoons, which had at the time seemed interminable, and now in all their accumulated hours had only a second's life. Perhaps, when one was old, the whole of forty years would only take some five minutes to live through again; and even that span of moments be interspersed with many intervals of trying to remember. If the kind of music we were listening to brought the great plains of Russia or Poland into one's mind, it was equally certain that one's present life was as difficult to escape from as those twin lands of passports and police supervision.

Such was the outlook, the obvious trend of affairs; but there were in the meanwhile consolations, narcotics that prolonged days of enjoyment and shortened weeks of suffering. At that time, from being surrounded by padded softness and a kind of bevelled bluntness of attitude, one was inclined naturally to-

wards a sharpness of expression: one had no inclination
to read anything that only made one sink yet deeper
into what one was seeking to escape from. Robert
Burns, therefore, or the milder moods of Wordsworth,
held little attraction, and one felt the need for a violent hand to break the glass and let one out. That
arm, as is fitting to a race that has produced so many
swordsmen and bomb-throwers, was Italian—and it
belonged to the poet F. T. Marinetti. He then
possessed the combined attributes of the actor, the
pianist, and the orator; all of which he had mingled
and changed into another complete entity which he
made use of as his means of expression—his vehicle—
giving to this process and its results the same mental
attitude as that of a traveller who when his train is delayed charters an aeroplane, and has no time to hesi-
tate as to his choice of transport. Complete absence
of rhyme, by giving him entire freedom, allowed him
to move without, so to speak, a speed limit, and without having to deviate for metrical reasons from the
direction in which he was travelling. Speed being his
object, he could give one the sensation of this speed,
and his poetry presented a quicker and more easy
escape than any other. He gave one many other effects
of speed; the sudden way in which a prospect became
clear, as in a flash—and the constant changes of scene
as one was carried along. Also in his glorification of
mechanics he had little room for sentimentality, and
this gave a strengthening and an enlargement to his
range; just as a powerful motor, which will take you
out further from home than a weak one, gives you a
more extended experience. It was refreshing, too, to
be told unequivocally and in so many words the oft-
concealed truth that poetry is, in great part, the art of
metaphor. The reliance of this Italian upon metaphor

is indeed most encouraging counsel for any young poet, since it teaches expansion of the imagination as against the rural contraction into which it is so easy to fall in this country. The new perspective to poetry is in itself a slight intoxicant to the fancy, and it substitutes for the osiers, the pollard elms, and the church bells, something with a greater depth and more variety of sound and colour. I believe, also, that "free-verse," when it is not mangled and cut into arbitrary lengths by any American poet, is a much more sure method of learning the true music of poetry—the use of rhyme—than the customary method of beginning one's first attempts at poetry with this adornment. The will to write is necessarily stronger than the ability, and rhyme, which holds certainly not more than half the potential beauties of poetry, has often baulked the creation of the other half of possibility. Luckily this very difficulty acts as a deterrent; for poetry, which must be a self-taught art, has need of this protection from its apparent easiness; while it is never needful to encourage real talent, because it always finds expression, however stern the obstacles in front of it. All the same, I believe content to be more important than method, and the former should most certainly be the aim of the poetical neophyte.

To revert to the poetry of Marinetti, there has seldom been an output so charged as this is with ideas, a quartz so heavy with ore; and any one of his images, if it could be taken away from its context and exploded, would give themes for a whole set of poems. Of course their effect was due to the period at which they were read, and perhaps now a solemn and austere perusal of his works would leave one dismayed at the effect that it had once produced; but it acted then like a restorative taken at a critical moment.

It is easy from this to guess one's other admirations at that age. It was effect by which one was entranced —the professional trick—the apparent complete expression of the subject; and of course there is nothing easier or quicker to this end than Hokusai's prints— they are like a three-penny ride on a mountain-railway; where in a few seconds you are surrounded by an artificial scenery, consistently volcanic, and rewarded with a dizzy and varying perspective, while you return home again with the kind of repute for mild courage which you might earn by living in the suburbs and hanging Japanese prints on your walls. The thirty-six views of Fuji, the Waterfalls, the Bridges, the Chinese Classical Poems—these, then, were my Amusement Park.

For more sentimental moments there were the German Primitives, and rarest and most treasured among them, any reproductions one could obtain of water-colours by Dürer. The bunch of violets, the rose-tree, the rabbit, the jay's feather, the cornfield, these seemed beautiful beyond any value that money could give them; while still lovelier were his drawings of castles, and little Alpine lakes, like the green pools in the mountains above Salzburg. I used to think there could be nothing more romantic than a steep hill with a citadel at the top, and a long winding climb to it through those ranks of fir trees which on a hill's slope look like hundreds of spears held steeply in the air. The time should be about six in the evening; if possible, the early autumn. There must be a river winding away in the distance, whenever you stop on the hillside for breath; and smoke rising up from the red roofs in the town below. At a corner in the path must sit Mr. Edwin Evans, bearded and pilgrim-like, resting by the wayside with an open book upon his knees.

Higher up, by the first gate, there are the "land-sknechts" with their very masculine adornment of beard and whisker, striped clothes like a wasp or a Swiss Guard, and chests puffed out with pride. Now and again a bugle is blown. There is a faint touch of sharpness in the air, like that sudden taste when you pick a green apple off a branch and bite into it, but it might now be occasioned by the first hint of frost ahead, or even by the bonfire-smoke that drifts up the hillside from the fires of heaped leaves.

Or we are back again among those noisy and dramatic prints. The water is pouring down in its chains of linked foam and a number of coolies with clothes tucked away above their knees are employing every pretext the artist can think of for getting soaked and drenched with the spray. Even the trees curve with this sudden precipice and are involved in the waters. Another waterfall has, at that point where its blue water is changed by a jagged line into foam, the staccato and angled contours of a flash of lightning as it can be made permanent by photography: the line flickers, even in the print. The Views are yet more "snapped," more momentary, as though the artist thought the closest he could get to reality was the shortest-lived fraction of time that he could seize upon. The snow-capped volcano is seen in the trough between two waves, as those two blue mountain-ranges sweep after one another down the bay. Another time the latten sail has suddenly filled with a gust of wind, and the volcano is seen through the strained meshes; a moment later it shows in a ghostly reflection between ears of corn. This veteran monomaniac became yet more feverish, more ecstatic, when confronted with small inanimate objects, a lacquer box or two, a tea-set, or a group of sea-shells, as though he must get them down on paper at all costs before they jumped away. Such are his "surimono" prints, where he has accentuated the terrible virility of his drawing with inlays of metal, and the most elaborate lozenging and diapering, the whole affair printed in the most violent and alkaline colours. It is surprising that any piece of paper can withstand such savage treatment. So illusory is his reality, so parallel to—while not being a part of —the truth, that his counterfeits have the audacity and swiftness of a tremendous poetical metaphor—a sort of explanation, by parable, of the subject. Such gymnastics, which demand a scantiness of costume on the part of the executant, cannot fail for this reason alone to strike the conventional mind as vulgar; but there is the additional element of admiration, in the case of Hokusai, that these works of such youthful muscle and vitality were only brought to this pitch of execution by him when between sixty-five and eighty years of age. He has, therefore, a kind of personal glamour superimposed upon his achievement; like the histrionics that made Marinetti an inspiring figure apart from his *vers libre*.

Something quick and emphatic with a dramatic perspective were the qualities for which I admired a thing, and there was too deep a tinge of natural melancholy in my surroundings for any admixture of this quality to be necessary to my appreciation. I am proud, therefore, for, if nothing else, this announcement may one day have value as a commercial advertisement, to make the statement that my æsthetic education was confided by myself in large measure to the gramophone. More particularly did I rely upon the early records by Paderewski, which were the prizes of much economy and endeavour, for they then cost twelve shillings and sixpence each. This mechanical friend, who was will-

ing to play for me, when and as often as I asked him,
held in his very compliance a kind of refuge and
alternative from depression. Besides, one had been
led to believe that everything new was ugly, *ipso facto;*
and that bold step on the part of a great musician to
place himself at the mercy of mechanics, or even more,
to profit by and rely upon their rigid obedience, showed
some ground for optimism about the period one lived
in. His fiery, incisive touch was made manifest the
very second one of his records was played; and he
managed with that magic which is the test of genius
to convey, even on to those flat, black discs, the kind of
angular and passionate force which one may gather
from the ordinary white pages on which one can read
Swinburne, a poet who has some parallel in his art to
the playing of this other master. I used to think that
at the time; and long afterwards I read that Burne-
Jones drew Paderewski's head because of his great resemblance to Swinburne as a young man. What there
lay to be learnt in these records one can categorise
under two heads—the absolute maximum of expression
on a given subject, and the ability to produce a sense
of personal style from the first second the hand is
shown. Often, since then, I have heard a pianist,
Busoni for example, who combined the same, or even
greater technique, with an obviously much greater
mentality; but I can never imagine anything to surpass
the older musician in that peculiar quality of fiery and
poetical personality which broke in upon one, even in a
gramophone record, with much the same force as the
effect when Swinburne is read for the first time.

It seemed to be more creditable to bring fantasy to
bear upon the ordinary events of life than to invent an
enervate paradise—which has been the aim of so many
artists. I started, thus, with the presumption that

pessimism was only tolerable, or called for, in private affairs, and it took me several years to find out the mistake. At that time I liked things to be short and violent, like a kind of melodramatic book-illustration which I can only imagine and have never come across any evidence of; after which preliminary and youthful work we may imagine the painter turning to larger and deeper subjects. I liked the actors to be close up, in the full blaze of the footlights, with only the simplest drop-scene—a mere curtain behind them, so that you could get the fullest expression of their emotions without the extraneous aids of music and scenery.

Of course the next stage of appreciation runs to the very opposite extreme. Arrived at that shore, we hate every single work which has been carried out in execution of a commission, and only believe in excellence which is not appreciated. The mere fact of a work being popular turns favour against it. One likes to walk in a land which few other feet have trod, and Robinson Crusoe could not have felt more horrified at the footprint on the sand than we would be on seeing a stranger, or still worse, an acquaintance, in front of a picture that we liked. Thus one's pleasure in looking at an early cathedral could be spoilt by the advertisements in a tradesman's window opposite; and a single cough at a concert would ruin the whole flow of music. In the same way, the delight in arriving at a town that one had always wanted to see would be entirely vitiated by the necessity of unpacking before one could leave the hotel; and any delay on the way to palace or picture-gallery would send appreciation down in a descending scale.

Having given this faint contour of things that interested a child about fifteen years old, I am now bound to admit that one's point of view with regard to all human achievement undergoes the most drastic modification soon after that age, until a condition is reached, perhaps preferable ethically to any other, in which one can never cease to wonder at human beings having ever been able to accomplish anything at all. More especially is this the case in contemplating any of those works of art that must have required qualities which one can only define as a perfect breathing apparatus and heart-action so as to keep up the same level of progress; and this is particularly true, much less with buildings than with a great cycle, say, of frescoes, such as you may see so often in Italy, wherein the most extraordinary subtlety and sense of beauty have had to be maintained for a stretch of years. Such slow miracles are in reality much more wonderful than the quick lightning-flash of an inspired drawing, or the few moments in which a poet can write off his lyric.

Meanwhile we may consider the evening to be quickly closing in, so that the room we were sitting in was dark in all its corners and only preserved a few pale streaks of light near the windows, and the red patch given off by the glow of the fire. The music was still rumbling fitfully from the piano, but it had apparently reached to the same degree of life as those hot coals which continued to give off heat without bestirring themselves, or taking thought for their future. They no longer, that is to say, sent out tongues of flame that, like the roots of trees, would twist themselves into any shape, or even bridge small chasms in the air in order to get sustenance for themselves. Those red-combed warriors had withdrawn behind their fiery walls, where, to all appearances, they might well be feasting on their accumulated spoils and afterwards be drowsy and unwilling to defend themselves. In just the same way this music that we had been listening to all the evening seemed now to be satiated and contented.

I have been trying, here, to describe another of those moments, like that with which this book opens, where we have the feeling, as though projected to us out of the future, that we shall always remember this particular arc of time. It is a similar feeling to that which we experience some time before leaving a place, when the sensation suddenly breaks upon us that we have already left, and we know that from now onwards the intervening space of time between this and the instant of our actual departure will pass like a flash and nothing will arrest its movement—and conversely, with the sentience of arriving at a place before, perhaps, one has even started on the journey.

So it was in a trance, almost, born of the steady heat of the fire and of two hours of music, that we all stood up, and after a few inefficient words of farewell, moved along the echoing floor to the door, and filed along like a caravan down the darkened vault of that great drawing-room I have described. So confident did one feel of the future of this memory that one hardly troubled to take note of what happened, and I have only some muddled recollection of helping our friends into their coats and opening the door for them to go out on to the porch. Their dog-cart was waiting for them, having been driven down by a groom from the stables. Colonel Fantock was on the doorstep, smoking a sunset pipe, and he bade rather a stiff farewell to the Poles, for he disapproved of foreigners. They climbed up into their seats, and the father, who with his great Polish moustachios looked like the portrait of Nietzsche, took the reins that were handed to him, and sweeping his hat off for the last time, drove them away towards Bolsover. Then one turned round

and saw that long front all covered under its battlements with the rook-green ivy; I call it rook-green
because it is always associated in my mind with those
fat glossy birds, who seem to be whirled heavily into
the air like scraps of burnt paper till they can balance
themselves on the wind and sail down its reaches on to
their boughs among the limes and elms they live in.
Also, ivy has the same glossiness, the identical white
light upon its darkness. There were no lamps yet in
any of the windows, and except for ourselves by the
doorstep the house might have been empty and deserted. Then as the front-door clanged-to again and
rattled slowly into silence this memory fades; and I
can only suppose that we talked for a moment or two
and then went upstairs to dress for dinner. It is my
last memory of that summer, and after this lapse of
time it is difficult to say to which year that momentary
consciousness belonged, for it is typical of all those
years that we fuse into one whole and call our childhood. What is true of the part is true of the whole,
and I can define the ingredients of all these memories
and think of their similar headings that make those
memories co-ordinate and hang together. Such may
be—looking for blackberries—walking by the shores
of the lake—the rooks in the tall limes—deserted
rooms and declined grandeur—orchards, and the netted
fruit upon their walls—or Colonel Fantock and the
Polish musicians.

IV

Miss Morgan

THIS is to be a tea-party, and I extract or distil it out of quite a hundred examples I have to choose from. Indeed, I dare say I must have been to tea there many more times than this, considering that I used to do so from the age of three until less than two years ago, but I am trying in these pages to take a whole average of what it used to be like, and so, as far as I am myself concerned, I had better be at a nebulous age—somewhere between three and twenty-three.

It is the seaside, again, at the place where I was born, many of whose characters I have mentioned before in this book, and as the signal for my leaving home we may take the clock of St. Martin's Church, which struck the quarters up and down a little irritating and optimist scale of four notes and then struck four peremptory blows, like raps upon the knuckles, on a bigger and better bell. I had been told to come early, and so I at once put down the book I had been reading—it may well have been G. A. Henty—took my hat from the hall and started off.

In a moment I was out of the drive and walking down the long, white-washed, sailor-like wall that formed one half of the Crescent. Behind this wall my uncle's family used to live in the summer, and opposite them in the two horns of the actual crescent there were some forty houses, nearly all of them containing characters worthy of epical treatment. I could, had I the space and my readers the necessary inclination, conjure up at least a dozen perfect and complete households, each one of them worthy, as I say, of three-volume treatment.

Gentle summer tappings from the discreetest and most genteel of mallets signified croquet in the Crescent Garden, and through a high iron railing which ran along by my left hand as I walked, I could see, where sight was possible through the laurel groves, several people I knew engaged at this game or sitting about on the wooden garden-seats. But I forbear mentioning their names or who they were, for fear of being drawn aside from my narrative.

It is strange to think how much money the English have spent upon unnecessary iron railings, and how they fortify even these barriers with a thick hedge wherever they can scratch together enough soil to support one. The platitude that "An Englishman's home is his castle" they support with an unwise, harem-like spirit of seclusion which puts at doubt the truth of many of their vaunts. Why, for example, hide this innocent game of croquet, and then permit the inmates of the local Rescue Home to walk to church every Sunday morning in a "crocodile" that strikes horror into the heart of the beholder? This is to make recreation alluring from its reticence, and repentance ugly and unpleasant.

Those fat croquet balls waddled through their hoops in a manner which it is difficult to think of apart from the people who propelled them on their easy careers. Such a rolling, easy gait, managing in the end just to squeeze yourself into your objective and enjoy the pleasant life beyond that one short strain: surely this was both the epitome and the whole ambition of life? Oh, of course it was all right for them, but so far as I was concerned, to-day was a typical Monday; there was that particular air of slight crossness and trouble ahead that follows close on the day of rest. With me, these apparently natural phenomena were due not to Nature but to an injudicious feast of chocolates the day before, and here I was going out to tea again to-day and heading directly for more trouble. As though to help me out and give me an air of innocence, I am bound to admit that the sky had done its best to be like a Monday, for that rather starched and staring blue was hung with some ragged laundry-work of cloud which blew about ominously in the wind.

The long, white wall ran round at a curve finishing the crescent; the garden railing sprang round in the other direction, and the road went down a little run like a tributary sweeping into its river, this latter being a main road from the town to the seashore, with a double line of trams enlivening its shopless quiet by shrill bells and the piercing groans their wheels make going round corners. Across this road and along the level plateau on the other side were the best streets of shops in the town, the Grand Hotel, the Gentlemen's Club, and a number of other curiosities of the kind. In order to get there from this main road you could walk up Albion Road or up St. Nicholas Parade.

This was the threshold of my afternoon, and to begin my tribute I must build a temporary altar here. Between the lodgings of Albion Road and the private houses of St. Nicholas Parade—in fact exactly at the corner—stood the house to which I was going. It was Number One, which means that like the prow of a ship it looked out in every direction, in front and to either side; moreover, to make this easier, on the south side, facing the sea (you couldn't see the water, though), there were bow-windows on every floor.

Now for my temporary altar, though I seem to be

not so much praying there as addressing the congregation in a few sentences about some parochial project. Who was I going to tea with?

Miss Morgan—and her name, though one never thought of her as anything but Miss Morgan, was Elizabeth, or rather, Ella.

Her house, we have noticed, was but a short distance—a couple of hundred yards, perhaps—from our own, and from our seeing her so frequently and being notoriously her best friends, one might imagine that she had come to live near us on purpose.

I suppose every one has some friend whom they always remember with white hair, whose hair must have gone white when they were quite young, and whose precise age must be, therefore, in default of any exact information, a subject of conjecture. This is easy enough for the experience of one generation, but Miss Morgan had been the friend of my grandmother; they had been friends for thirty-five years when I first remember her, and my grandmother did not know her age and would not discuss it, and knew nothing of her history and was too loyal to her to mention what there was of mystery in it to others.

She had first appeared thirty-five years ago when my father was a young boy, and then she had this same white hair and seemed neither younger nor older than she would do to-day, when I had rung the doorbell and she came downstairs to open it.

My grandmother, who was bitten with that mania for home industries characteristic of the "seventies" of the last century, had first met Miss Morgan at Cannes in the studio of a French artist who had perfected a particularly horrid new trap for the "artistic" in the shape of Cloisonné pottery. Every year there had to be some new invention of the kind—the tracing of ferns with sand upon specially-prepared cloth, a system of pen-painting, or anything of an inutility and violence of design appropriate to the new flowers that were produced every year, for hardly a season went by that was not made memorable by a calceolaria, a lobelia, or some strident, hairy, and caustic product of the East Indies adapted and still further intensified for greenhouse use.

That particular year, as I say, it was Cloisonné pottery. The inventor, as also his pupil, Miss Morgan, had worked in the factory which produced the blue china cupids and vases so beloved in the "sixties," the name of which factory—it was in the South of France somewhere near Cannes—I transcribe as nearly as it was pronounced—Valérie—though I happen to know that it was spelt entirely different from this, and have never, since I was ten and stumbled upon this information, been able to find out any more about it or how the name was really spelt.

Even as long ago as that it is apparent that Miss Morgan was something of a mystery, for when my grandmother met her in that "artist's atelier" there is no doubt that her condition of life was but little removed from starvation. She had been stranded on the Riviera through all the heat of summer, and this was but the beginning of a new season before business had started again. When, therefore, it was suggested that she should come to England and start the industry there, even her employer was delighted at the thought of these missionary labours, and the whole project was arranged almost as soon as discussed.

I gather that as the season wore on business went better, and with this increase in confidence the Frenchman became tiresome, perhaps jealous of her plates that were better than his, and so when the time came for her to leave they dissolved partnership without much regret.

So she came to this seaside town, and had been there ever since.

By this time I was underneath the bit of porch: I say "bit" of a purpose, for it jutted out and overhung, reminding me—for those were days when I had more than a passing interest in railways—of the hood an engine generously allows its driver. I rang the bell— a bell which answered with strange vigour to the slightest pull at its cord—and the door was opened.

Miss Morgan cannot have been more than four and a half feet high, and her appearance was one of the most remarkable I have ever had the good fortune to see. She had, as I have said, white hair, and this grew in a series of little tight curls upon her head, while her face was of a dazzling whiteness and she had extraordinarily good features of the particular sort that are enhanced and look their best above a stock, and this, or some form of a silk handkerchief, tied round her neck, she always wore. I can't describe her kind of dress, but it was always covered with a white smock, which associated her in one's mind with some kind of benevolent activity, not hospital work, for there were none of those dreadful anæsthetic smells about her.

We used to go up two flights of stairs, passing on the way the first-floor sitting-room, which was put to other uses. At about this point memories of what the house looked like begin to take their place in my mind.

The staircase walls had a lot of her plates hung upon them, and these were decorated chiefly with paintings of birds; for instance, there was a china plaque on the landing painted with two ravens, or perhaps it was one raven and a hooded grey crow with it, and these bore a strange likeness to Gladstone and Disraeli. Both birds were on one flowering branch of a tree and were in a kind of Japanese-Riviera convention, which even in the days that I first remember must have been forty years old. Then there were plates of the regular Cloisonné order decorated with strapwork and fretwork, often in white or yellow upon a mulberry ground, very heavy in design and rather like an open jam tart, with the jam showing between strips of pastry.

At the top one left hat or coat upon one of two chairs on either side of a small table, and went to the righthand side into the drawing-room. What loveliness lay round one, and how terrible to think it has been dispersed under the hammer of the auctioneer less than two years before the time I write this!

The whole of this room owed its decoration to Miss Morgan. On first taking the house many years before, she had procured a pair of steps and frescoed the top part of the walls all round the room with blue ribbons tied in bows and with a kind of running fire of roses between these blue, silken supports. Below this, and covering the whole of the lower part of the wall, there was embroidery by her—again roses, on a cream or vellum-coloured ground. The curtains were made of material she had embroidered; the furniture, chairs, and cupboards were painted by her in a clever imitation of inlay that made you run your fingers along where the edges of the inlay should have been, to see whether it was true or not. The tablecloths and chair-covers she had made, and, of course, there were some plates and vases by her hand upon mantelpiece and shelves.

The bow-window had elaborate window-boxes arranged with a whole shelf of *hors d'œuvre* to attract sparrows, finches, tits, or what other small birds there were about, and on a table just near to the window were three or four miniature greenhouses filled with dwarf cactuses, some of which even flowered occasionally under her encouragement.

I hope it is now manifest how many activities she had, how many interests to divide time and give her life point. These were not nearly all of them; but the others must be developed later when occasion arises.

Just at this moment it was tea-time. Tea mixed with green Pekoe out of a beautiful tortoiseshell box, plates of two or three different kinds of bread, and a jam made by her out of vegetable marrow and tasting better than the most delicious marmalade. Also two plates of chocolate biscuits, and some tea-cakes, which had formed themselves under her instigation into a sandwich for a layer of Demerara sugar, cooked into a kind of liquid toffee and yet preserving its marvellous crunch under the teeth, a sound like some one walking on the sand of a desert island, romantically conjured up for one by the very name—Demerara. Even the tea was not what one was used to; since she mixed, as I have said, a teaspoonful of orange or green Pekoe with it, and this gave it a romantic zest so that one felt on one's travels when drinking it.

But these preparations—I had only just sat down—were interrupted by a strangely familiar voice, followed in a second by another ghostly evocation of well-known tones, both these disturbances coming from a corner of the room behind the door. A cage stood on a table there, and in this lived a "Minah" bird—a large, black, glossy creature from the Indies, and by far the most accomplished talker and mimic that I have ever met among its bird rivals. It knew all our voices, and hearing me talking had at once reproduced first my father and then my mother. I do not want this bird to assume the proportionate character of the raven in *Barnaby Rudge,* and so I say no more about it here, except that all through tea we may imagine its voice breaking in from time to time and always at an appropriate context or an awkward silence, while it made little plucking, quill-like noises moving from perch to perch.

I suppose that at the time I am talking of she knew practically every one that I had ever heard of or seen. She used to come and spend the summer with us in Derbyshire, and therefore all possible topics of conversation were common to us both, and it was hard for one of us to get out of contact with the other.

I have said that her house was like the prow of a ship, and certainly from this vantage-point we enjoyed a mental as well as a physical panorama of what lay round and below us. Miss Morgan and Colonel Fantock, between them, knew all there was to be known of fact, or fiction, concerning any one whose name you might mention. But even gossip on so portentous a scale as was here possible one must not allow to obscure other issues.

Very soon we shall all be left to ourselves—our generation, I mean. Therefore if a contact with even the past of twenty years ago is interesting, how much more so something of such antiquity as this turned out to be in the end, for until she died two years ago none of us knew her age.

She always told us that she had been born during the Crimean War, producing in evidence of this a story about her having been left in charge of an uncle while her father went to the war, and of how she was so inextricably confused with her uncle's daughter of just the same age as herself that identification became impossible, and her father being killed before long she had, perforce, to be brought up as an alternative and pendant to the other child, there being nothing better

than a presumption to give her the authority in thinking she was who she gave herself out to be and not her
own cousin, instead, or as well.

But even in the days I am speaking of, this date for
her birth was most obviously an exaggeration in her
favour, and later it became apparent that so long ago
as the year she said she was born, she was grown up
and living in Paris, in the earliest days of Napoleon
III. She had, in fact, lopped off one whole generation
from her age in an attempt to be young for us, since
I really do not believe that vanity had much share in
this diminishment of her years.

Her mind was of a childish stature. She derived an
equal amount of pleasure from fine pieces of china,
from a picture by Watteau or Boucher, and from a
tin-enamelled biscuit-box. This want of discrimination
was most obviously, therefore, to her material advantage, for she could be as happy on a shilling as on a
hundred pounds.

The amount of childishness and natural youth in her
composition was balanced by all the elements in her
that took one right away from the present with its
trams and cheap sweet-shops into a kind of Dickensian
antiquity. It is sad to think that what seemed, then,
the immortal and live-long present has changed into
something far off and intangible with as much of
legend clinging to its rags and clouts as was to be
found in Miss Morgan's mythology of her own youth.

Of this, with all its details, she was not sparing to us.
The frondage of her improbable and fantastic family
tree shone like a green aura about her little figure as
she moved, duster in hand, from treasure to treasure
round the room. She would pull out a plate of green
apples, or take from the same cupboard a chocolate
cake out of a tin box, both of these being supplements,

and quite unnecessary they were, to the many plates of cakes and biscuits upon the table. Then, perhaps, she would move to the window and be greeted by a loud chirping from the tits and chaffinches that were feeding there. A coco-nut, or two, was threaded from a nail in the woodwork and dangled in the wind, clashing against the green, summer paint with regular and rhythmical beat, so that sitting there in the sun and falling into an afternoon stupor the clash of those wooden pates broke in upon one's thoughts like a vague but undeniable Eastern music. The coco-nuts were swaying against their own tufted leaves, and just as these threaded skulls that Miss Morgan had bought from a barrow were climbed into and devoured by the tits and chaffinches, so were these on their native trees lifted by some agency of sun or wind, lifted, and swung lazily but firmly against the flat and nest-like top of the palm from which they depended. To this kind of summons by drum some savages were climbing the straight stems by means of a piece of bark-cord, the ends of which they held in either hand, while they leaned out their bodies as far as possible from the stem, pressing out with both feet, and at the same time lifting the cord a rung or two higher up the tree, while they moved their feet along in an alternate motion to the noose they held. Bending out their bodies like a bow from the stem, so as to keep themselves where they had climbed to, they would reach out and pick the fruit and then go a little higher, breaking through the outer leaves and so find themselves upon the flat, nest-like summit where they would sit like so many stylites, hammering in the rind with a shell-knife and drinking the milk they had taken so much trouble to procure. There would be two or three palms, each with its occupant, riding, in this peculiar fashion, down the sunset

wind and falling from those gourds of milk and from
the cradle-like movement of their perches into the
identical stupor to that in which I found myself sitting
in an armchair in the hot cage of sun which Miss Morgan's bow-window turned to during the late afternoon.

I began again to listen to what she was saying,
though even now there would be a little flutter of
wings against the sun, or a faint bashing of a coco-nut
upon wood as the weight of some small bird made it
move against the window-frame. The sun went con-
veniently behind a cloud, as on a Monday morning
you can see a housewife hidden at her work behind an
apron or some other piece of linen hanging from the
strings in her backyard, and this very change in the
day's fire, this sudden and momentary falling-in of its
coals, keyed down and stilled my thoughts so that I
was back once more in her direct focus, almost, I might
say, within what I described as the green aura of her
improbable and fantastic mythology.

She was talking about the "big house" she had lived
in as a child. It stood on what is now the Embankment, next, so she said, to Waterloo Bridge, but this
was before Northumberland Avenue, or any of the
great hotels, were built, when there was a steep shore
to that sluggish yellow stream wherever the houses did
not stand right at the water's edge. I remember her
telling me that she had been frightened as a child by
what was known as the Waterloo Bridge murder. A
carpet-bag, with a design of sunflowers upon it, was
found on one of the projecting piers, and on being
taken up by a scavenger or one of the bridge workmen
it was found to contain a great many small morsels of
human flesh which from the black hair adhering to
them the police stated to have been the remains of a
male. The bones, if I remember rightly, they did not

find and they must have been disposed of by some other method.

Now this story was one of the first indications I was ever given of her age, because not long after she had told me about it, during the summer term at Eton when I should have been playing cricket and was, according to my custom (the game was compulsory, and yet I only played cricket three times in two years), reading in the School Library, I began, having completely exhausted the Art section, to read a compilation called the Annual Register where crimes were written up in a language that the journalism of to-day would emulate had it the good taste to appreciate those finer shades of horror. Reading backwards through the years from the Northumberland Street mystery, that frightful and mysterious death-grapple for no apparent reason between Major   , I got as far as Palmer of Rugeley, and somewhere just about that point, I should say it was 1854 or 1855, I fell directly upon the Waterloo Bridge murder and realised that Miss Morgan, supposed, according to her story, only to have been born in one of those two years, had been telling me this story of which she had a pretty full memory about something that had frightened what must from her knowledge of its details have been an adult mind of sixty years ago.

As I think of her story and compare it in my mind with what I read upon that non-cricket afternoon, more of the scene comes back to me. It was almost the first of what I should call the "modern dress" murders, crimes, that is to say, that were committed by and upon persons who led lives and wore clothes not so different from those one can remember oneself, and which from these very reasons have an intense and waxwork horror about all their details. It was, as I say, about the first of them, and this period goes down as far as Crippen.

At the inquest upon these scraps of flesh some circumstances about the mystery were pieced together that were what really gave the affair its notoriety, for after all the ordinary finding of a dead body in the Thames is a fairly common and not particularly awful incident in the history of London crime. The toll-keepers at the ends of the bridge gave evidence that a woman passed their barriers carrying this identical bag and in a hurry, so they surmised, to catch the midnight train from Waterloo. They noticed the pattern of sunflowers on the bag she carried, and they observed that she had a thin moustache and faint indications of a beard which lent colour to their suspicion that this woman was a man. No more was ever discovered about either the perpetrator or the victim of the crime, but this was one of the earliest ghosts to haunt with this peculiar tinge of horror that area of London where, even now, if you walk about Lambeth, the spectre of Neil Cream is incessantly abroad in the mean slums.

After these horrors of the river-slime it is pleasant once more to be back in the peaceful sleep of that tea-party. Miss Morgan, for I am taking an average in these pages of the many, many times I went to tea with her, was now going through her usual cupboards of legend. I suppose the thought of the Embankment that had destroyed her old home and led in a dreadful cast-iron curve like the deck of an iron-clad along the foggy river took her mind away, past the sight of St. Paul's dome, towards the docks and the wharves of the merchants. In fact it was an extension of her home into her "uncle's" business premises, though the actual nature of his work, or even his true position as uncle, were other mysteries as unsolved in their different way as the Waterloo Bridge problem we have just discussed.

He was, so we were led to believe, the owner of various merchant-ships trading with India and China, and one of the best among these vessels he had converted into a yacht for his own personal use. For a year, or so, he would use it and then it would go back for a time to its normal work, starting off, after refitting, from London Wall or Deptford and coming back at an uncertain time, for it might be expected any day in three months, according to the disposition of the winds, being held apparently to the will and pleasure of those capricious tyrants. Very long voyages were then the rule, for we know that whalers were more often than not three or four years away from port and would return without any warning with every inch of surface covered by the barrels of sperm-oil that they had carried in an uneven, rolling gait from the Pacific or Antarctic seas. Indian merchantmen were less than this length of time away, but it was probably eighteen months or more before they reached London again; and, according to Miss Morgan, the first intimation her uncle used to have of his ship's return was the arrival of "old Davey," a kind of personal servant of his among the sailors when the boat was in use as a yacht. This whiskered and pig-tailed old tar would drive up in a cab, generally towards the middle of the morning, the ship having been cleared of the customs by the night before, and its leather seats would be absolutely covered with the parcels brought back from China and the Indies either to her "uncle's" orders or in the form of presents for himself and his family from the captain. There would be Chinese toys, paper flowers, sets of carved chessmen, lacquered tins of tea, pieces of silk, paintings on rice-paper, Indian idols, hammered bronze ornaments, printed cottons, joss-sticks, perfumes, and every conceivable bazaar product of the East.

Who were the family? Besides "uncle," pronounced in her delightful fashion, for long residence among the poor had made her assume some of their accent, "oncle," there were her brothers, two or three of them, and they had all gone into the Navy and were dead years ago, and "m'cousin," who constitutes the key to the whole of this strange life, since any reader will know who Miss Morgan was if they can recognise her brother, for brother he really was and not cousin. His Christian name was Wyndham, and he had been studying medicine for some little time when the American Civil War broke out and he went across to the United States in answer to a call for doctors. There, during the long evenings in the winter, he became an amateur actor and found this to be his real profession, so that when the war was over and he came back to England he gave up his former work and went on to the stage, having by this time, for a space of more than forty years had gone by since he took up the profession, become one of the leading actors of the time and the owner of several London theatres. He was not only Miss Morgan's family hero, but also her support in life, for her income was a small allowance from him. He was, therefore, a frequent figure in her legends and assumed a more genuine stature than that we can accord to her brothers or to "oncle." As for mother, were it not for the truism that every one must have a mother, one might have felt inclined to deny any possibility of this position towards Miss Morgan on the part of any other woman, so little was she referred to during the course of these conversations; but I gathered that she died very soon after Miss Mor-

gan's birth, of typhoid I think, and that she had been
English on her father's side and Belgian on her
mother's, her father having settled in Bruges after
the Napoleonic Wars to live there for the rest of his
life. A miniature of a woman with a little child that
hung by her fireplace Miss Morgan used to refer to
indifferently and according to her mood as portraying
either herself and her mother or the Duchess of Kent
and the future Queen Victoria, varying this alternative
according to her caprice for realism or grandeur. Now,
this very shifting of personalities in total disregard
of what was obvious and plainly to be seen brings me
to a phase of her character that cannot be too strongly
stressed in relation to the portrait that I am trying to
draw of her.

I suppose it came of living alone and having to rely
upon her own company for amusement, and I leave
these few words in a paragraph of their own, so that
they can stand for the whole tragedy of her situation.

She never left the town she lived in except to stay
with us in the summer, or to come to London for a
few days about Christmas, when she was always able
to get seats for us, through her "cousin's" influence,
at the Drury Lane pantomime, and after a day or two's
shopping she would go back once more through the icy
silence of the midland fields that must have seemed,
each time this happened, to be forming itself into as
complete a copy as possible of her first journey to
the north from Cannes. She was going back from
London perhaps so recently as the middle years of
the War, and yet her thoughts and the very scenes
that moved before her eyes must have taken her back,
infallibly, to the familiar environment of long ago.
In just the same way that you can move the furniture
in an old, accustomed bedroom, having resolved at

length upon some changes in its arrangement, and still push against those household ghosts standing sentry at their ancient posts where the eye and hand are unwilling to forget their old slaves, so did Miss Morgan still surround herself with all the paraphernalia of art, comfort, or fashion to which she had been accustomed.

The halt at Peterborough station meant, as it did to me, till these wayward luxuries were abandoned in some flight of national economy, small packets of Rowntree's chocolate biscuits, the very name and origin of this delight being a sign of the northward journey. Behind, and very far behind now, lay the palm trees and the promenades, the gay parasols, the flounced skirts, the whole convention of the Riviera. Her journey led from one hollow shore to another, and having arrived at this more northern destination the changes in the seasons or in the fashions announced themselves like a slow rotation of Time's finger upon the clock. It amounted to moving one's bedroom from one side of the house to the other with the increasing sun, and not much detail of the actual transition remained in the memory. Like two sets of window-boxes we may consider the gardens, on, respectively, the Mediterranean shores of the one place, and the English cliffs of the other; but this window-box towards which she was travelling was a long way still from bearing flower and what had seemed like the young summer of France turned itself into the solid grey ice-block of our island as the journey proceeded. The ridged and stark fields with but a few crows upon them occurring against that drab plain like scraps of burnt paper from, perhaps, a tramp's fire, and who, when they took wing at the train's approach, flapped clumsily into the air as such charred rags might do with the rushing wind of that straight arrow the train made in its attack upon time and space, this deadness, and such a very little dark life, what comfort was there to be got from looking out on this through the frosted window?

The stations of Grantham, or Newark, or Selby, with the line of black "four-wheelers" outside the iron yet impermanent building, the very blackness and discomfort of this "get-away" from so hasty an arrival, the shabby streets and mean shops seen near by just before or after the moment's stay under that sea-green arch of the roof, all this made towns but little less depressing than country. There was at any rate this much about her destination, that it was a terminus, there was not that hollow, that transparent gloom which clung about places through which the railway passed straight like an arrow wound, and a wound through which the arrow was being continually re-shot, and to this terminus there must be attached, therefore, some degree of the comfort that any permanence must attain to, unless it is a hospital or prison of the senses. York station had a twisted and grooved turn to its shape that was made memorable by the way in which the glass panes of the roof curved into the main spiral girders and followed the rails and the platform beneath them, so that the whole affair was like a huge sea-shell open at both ends. And from this point onwards the whole of her mental scene would be coloured with anticipation of her home and its little beauties and conveniences, though even this pleasant focus was projected back a little into the past and away from what was, owing to the War, an universally terrible present.

Her maid, Annie, would meet her at the station, and this robust and highly coloured farm-product brought up in communion with geese and sheep had become in my eyes from familiarity as natural and inanimate a part of Miss Morgan's house as the china she had painted, the tea-cakes, or the chairs and tables. Such was her home-coming, though even in the warmth of that welcome I doubt whether Miss Morgan would eat more than a rosy-cheeked apple for her supper, after which, as I so often saw her when walking past, she would sit in her drawing-room with the blinds up and the acetylene burning, while she read the *Daily Mail* through a pair of steel spectacles.

At tea the next day, for we may all have travelled back together from London, she would, from some stimulus that had been given her by her trip, manœuvre the conversation back on to her uncle's yacht once more; and there were but few places in Europe, Madrid not excepted, at which that problem-ship had not cast anchor. She had even combined the aristocratic independence and arbitrariness of direction that are implicit in the possession of a yacht with the profession she had practised in the South of France in a story where she alleged she had taught china-painting from the vessel in the Sultan's harem at Constantinople; but this town was the limit of her travels, and having escaped the importunate Abd-el-Aziz, she resolved to persuade her uncle never to go so far afield again. There were a Frenchwoman and more than one Italian in his harem, and Miss Morgan might have had her share of the Sultan's unbelievable luxury of living.

In fact it comes to this, Miss Morgan managed to live in a kind of double mist of romance which consisted first of the mystery of her origin and history, and second of the aura of improbable legend that she distilled around her—for example, she had been Gounod's favourite pupil at the piano. Now, of this there was no true denying, for there was no proof to

the contrary, since every one else living then and able
to answer questions was long ago dead. She had been
with Gounod to some of Rossini's Sunday-evening
parties, and this was so delightful to me that I dared
not ask any questions for fear of demolishing it.

She existed in a light that continually shifted as it
played round her, and I hope the reader will now understand why I have not been able to attempt what
might have aimed at being a Holbein-like outline-
drawing of her character. Instead of this I have
adopted towards her the process of some of the pictures by Picasso or Braque, where there are two or
three profiles thrown towards you, and in this quivering white light of theatre or café—here with Miss
Morgan, let us think of it as sunlight or acetylene—
we can see the body moving and breathing and hear the
guitars of the comedians, or, in our case, the dithy-
rambic platitudes of Miss Morgan.

Her whole life, like her stories, I had grown to
look upon as being likely to go on for ever, since there
was not even the slightest perceptible change in anything. Winters came and passed by without leaving
any mark upon her and life was apparently one long
groove, though, as I think of it now, I can see that
this smoothness was a steady slide down the snow-slope
with some inevitable stop at the bottom. It had been
smooth running for some thirty or forty years and
there seemed little reason that it should ever end;
life was now at its quickest and most comfortable,
gaining in speed before the blow fell.

As if to show her to the most memorable advantage
I can see the whole of that bow-window quite alive
with sunbeams, and their stairs and ladders, broken
against by lifted or lowered boughs of leaves, made the
whole room seem to be part of a process of weaving.

This began at the same time every afternoon, rather early and before tea in the summer days I was there, when the sun having crossed the roof of the house lifted his looms in steeply through the windows while he came down hand above hand through the branches at a more reasonable angle to his work. All the time this happened Miss Morgan was elaborating upon her own pet themes, taking very often the same story every day for her pattern but varying it with such endless and audacious detail that, like the buildings decried in guide-books, the whole affair became lost in a maze of endless ornament that wearied the eye to follow. The tragedy of living alone was most obviously responsible for this prolixity, for such were the channels in which her mind and imagination ran when the household work was finished and the *Daily Mail* completely read. Indeed her *Daily Mail* and her vacuum cleaner were her nearest contact to modernity, who, in everything else, lived in some indefinable antiquity of her own which was most certainly not later in date than the reign of Louis Philippe.

She knew, I need hardly say, all those local inhabitants whose faults and intrigues I used to discuss with Colonel Fantock, while to this store she was able to add some few characters unknown to him and about whom she possessed a whole repertory of anecdotes. I can only wish there was space here to go house by house through the Crescent, and even when this was done I could expatiate at equal length on some thirty or forty other households about the town.

I shall never forget one day not so very long ago— as I say, she has only been dead some two years—taking, as was my invariable custom, some book for her to look at, for she liked turning over the pages and glancing at the pictures; and on this occasion it was a book I had just brought back with me from Paris on the artist, Constantin Guys.

It was most interesting to watch its effect upon her. The visual part of history deeply concerned, necessarily, with the sartorial particularities of the time, must begin as a rule with the rich, and at this period the extremes of fashion began with the Empress Eugénie. Guys is probably the best draughtsman who ever went sufficiently near the Emperor and Empress to draw a fleeting glimpse of them as they rolled past in a carriage surrounded by postilions, outriders, and the Cent Gardes. The nervous and embarrassed shade of this artist stands, therefore, quite near to that old-fangled figurehead, Monarchy, though disguised in this instance under the new and journalistic invention of Empire.

But there are other sides to his work than this. When Guys was dealing with the subjects in which he was most obviously interested, in the sense that he must have drawn them for his own personal delight and cannot have anticipated their ready sale to the illustrated papers from which he derived his livelihood, he comes out as the equivalent and peer to Baudelaire. Just as that genius, the first Frenchman to write true poetry since the days of the Valois Kings, hovered most ethereally, most authentically "left the ground," for I purposely apply this aeronautical simile as the test between what is and what is not poetry, when, moth-like, he was attracted to the lighted altars of the dark god of prostitution, just so is Guy's finest work a comment upon and an epitome of the "demi-mondaines" of his time. Such are the best drawings out of the series that he personally offered in his old age to the Director of the Carnavalet Museum, where a few of them, but too few of them at a time, are to be found

hung in a dark and unlikely corner of the Salle Na-
poléon III. They must, therefore, have represented
what he himself considered to be his most final and
characteristic work.

It is impossible to imagine an easier and yet deeper
insight into the whole history of two decades, for these
single figures drawn so easily on to the paper mean
everything that constituted those twenty years of
French history, not only that of the Emperor and his
Court but of the whole two million inhabitants of that
bourgeois paradise. They have something dark and
satanic about their glamour, as though it was an epoch
of perpetual gas-light with no alternation to the milder
and more accommodating sun. It is always night, in
fact, and more generally that late hour when the
theatres have emptied and people are moving slowly
home, for there was at that time no quicker passage
through the city than that of a trotting horse.

I have qualified gas-light as being opposed to the
mild and gentle sun-rays, and this is positively so, for
that white incandescent glare showed everything with
a flat evenness and no depth, so that nothing was hidden
and every face wore its authentic animal emotion without subterfuge or concealment. Greedy people must
have looked greedier then than they did before by
candle-light or oil-lamp, or than they do now when
electricity can be turned about, shaded and concentrated, or filtered slowly at will. Every other emotion was heightened accordingly; hooked noses and
deep lines indicative of Oriental cunning became un-
mercifully magnified in their scale, while hair that had
always been suspiciously fair burned now like a rough
untidy halo above a rouged face.

The beauties out of this world of pleasure were of a
type far removed from the criterions of modern at-

tractiveness. They were tall and thin and pale-skinned with a remnant of that Spanish atmosphere about them which had descended to them in the social scale from the fact of the Empress being a Spaniard, and from the Romanticism of thirty years before that had made Victor Hugo and Theophile Gautier settle upon Spain as the land of their ideal. Their masculine friends were of a type strange and unprecedented; persons of doubtful origin became ennobled; there were Barons from Egypt and from Armenia, while Pashas from Egypt and Turkey were accorded a warm welcome and a foretaste of that Utopia which is now dangled before slender purses by the Riviera news in the Continental *Daily Mail*. When a male is speaking to these women in a drawing he is so hidden by his top-hat and so muffled by whisker and moustache as to appear just a male animal and hardly a human being, which is again like the world of Baudelaire, for males hardly ever break into his slow, lethargic world, though, should they do so, his satirical ennui and bitterness at life would disguise them in the identical top-hat and with the same whisker and moustache as they are shown by Constantin Guys.

Except for such small records as these there is nothing left of those millions of lives; for there is no trained observer who could now write down for those days the exact appearance and animation of a street, or of a party, in the manner in which it has been done for the later seventies and eighties by Mr. George Moore. They are dead and gone completely, with no more lasting life than the tones of a human voice that lift like smoke and are dead as soon as they have broken upon door or ceiling.

Miss Morgan took the book in her hand and put on the steel spectacles that lay before her on the table.

The Minah-bird talked, at least as intelligently as the chatter of most of the people at a party, and Annie's heavy, substantial tread could be heard on the stairs as she came up with the tea. Meanwhile, in order to be out of the way of that bustling shape, I moved into the bow-window and sat down on a low chair in the middle of that cage of sunlight.

I was just in front of the two small glass-houses of cactuses that I have mentioned before. My brother had bought them years ago at a bazaar and Miss Morgan had promised to look after them when he went back to school. They had by now increased from one glass-house into two; for every year she took shoots from them and reared this tiny progeny with the most extraordinary care, watering them continually, covering them in winter, even in the moderate warmth of her drawing-room, with little squares of sacking, and feeding them with spoonfuls of tea and little morsels of bread and milk.

These were her tropics; and they were to a thin purse what lacquered cabinets stand for to the collector of rich furniture, or vases of famille rose, or noir, to the amateur of china. But far from being lifeless and dead in her hand, these increased, as I say, as though they were works of art gifted with powers of fertility. In these few years they had more than doubled in number, and time and patience together could put no limit to their increase. Those little, sloped glass roofs sheltered a whole world of poetry.

One or two of the plants had little pink flowers of a waxy or creamy surface growing at the very end of their ivory spikes that shot out from the deepest and thickest green of their centres. They seemed like a kind of vegetable unicorn with little howdahs carried on the end of their horns. Others of these plants, far from that ostentation, concealed their blossoms as close as possible to their leaves, so that these had to be lifted before they could be seen. Of course in all, there were only some five or six of the plants in flower, and the rest of them seemed muted and decorous by comparison. It is a different universe altogether from that of the rose or the elm tree. About these two factors of garden or landscape, as such are to be seen almost anywhere in Europe, one is never far in mind from the Cathedral and the Town-hall. The two glass-houses held, on the contrary, a whole miniature Mexico of invention and imagination.

In their direction "old Davey" acted as a kind of King's Messenger, traversing such distances in what was, considering the extent of his journey, the remarkably short space of eighteen months or so. Even then, he only reached the very frontier of those regions, and you could imagine almost anything you liked for the interior.

For my part I liked to think of new races of men built not so much upon the lines of the Apollo Belvedere as following the lopped curves of a prickly pear or aloe. A knock with a "machete," or obsidian axe, even if it took off a limb, inflicted a wound that was easily repaired, and this constant mending and bridging into the impossible carried every factor of beauty right out of the ordinary canons of possibility. The golden sands of poetry really became shores upon which anything or everything might happen, and if you wanted an almond tree growing out of a small cloud, or the mast of a ship breaking into a vine, you could have them there, then and now. Human loves became intensified in their sorrows and pleasures by this admixture of flower-blood, so that the ordinary standards of human beauty were far exceeded when skins

could take on the hues of flower-petals, voices be like
birds' songs, and limbs have every imaginable grace
of branches and wind working together towards this
sole end. As for the painter's hand, no one would ever
wish to look for ever at the same scene, and so we may
imagine frescoes falling into dust but a few hours after
their gleaming freshness had come into being, as if
you could explode some lovely cloud soon after it has
borne in towards you from the horizon and long before
it has become a shade-throwing bulk: and sudden drawings like the theatre petrified into the rock of poetry,
with all its glamour taken alive out of the very trumpet's mouth before the heroes we would like to see
against the endless boards. In fact I liked those paintings not to be on board or framed canvas, and little
enough upon walls, unless, as I say, these crumbled
into powder before they grew old and had many days'
shadow upon them through the glass-less windows, but
to lie on great or small screens hiding things that are
easily broken in upon. The Japanese screens of deer
under green pine-trees in a plain of snow I take as the
very threshold of this world, as far behind what is
possible of perfection as outlying pine trees should be
from banquet-hall or music-colonnade.

There are hunting-parties through jungles greener
and far more full of flowers than any Persian drawing, against red or blue hills and great heaped snow-
ranges capped with fire, with here and there, away
from any regular sierra, a volcano that rises out of the
plain like the Tower of Babel and lifts its charred and
scorched glacis, that no army can scale, thousands of
feet into the air. The green or yellow hair of corn
waves ripely upon more gentle hillsides, and at the
distance of the husbandman's journey to his work there
are Indian cities floating in shallow lakes, their battle-

ments and turrets so gilded by the setting or rising
sun that they seem roofs of authentic gold above the
plumed and ruffled water-shallows. A causeway like
a giant umbilical cord joins this tiny universe to the
earth that gave it birth.

I should demand, also, a great many convents and
monasteries, and if the former must be venal I expect
the latter kind of asceticism to produce an art distinct
and separate, as should be the case with this neutralised
manhood. It must be fortified into extremes by this
abnegation and the utmost elaboration of ornament
must contrast with a Cistercian bareness, so that you
have huge cliff-like buildings that are pools or wells of
filtered sunlight, and then sudden rays and haloes given
out by artifice alone. Apart from the rhythmical and
timed workers in the cornfields and the orchards, the
convents must produce gleaming cascades and brilliant
parterres of needlework or spinning, but with needle
and spinning-wheel working in the richest of materials,
so that entire theatrical wardrobes are made ready in
a week of summer.

Poetry becomes transcendentalised into wilder and
more accurate music, and it may be imagined how these
two arts flourish together, inspired one by the other
and still further fired by the actors and the fresco-
painters that I have demanded. Dress must be, at its
simplest and most unimaginative, on those cockscomb
lines preferred by the Elizabethans, and breaking out
of that starched stiffness it can reach to a degree of
significance that even the periwig or the quilts of the
samurai never attained to as an expression of dandyism
or family-feeling. What a poet has called the "long
lacquered afternoons" burn up out of all this glamour
into a most extraordinary nerve-consciousness and fertility of invention and metaphor. Under such influence

127

there is no apparent limit to the remitting or recording of sensations; in the distance and from any direction, as though you were on the roof of the château of Chambord that was specially built and ornamented for the ladies to wait there and listen for news of the chase in the great and antlered park that lay for miles round, comes the sound of the hunting-horn, and the huntsmen in their green dresses, darker than the wet leaves or grass, move across vistas in the distance, and their sound is swallowed up by the briars of a wilderness between these alleys until it sounds again in some clearing in the trees. Men are walking past laden with great screens just finished and gleaming in their newness, and out of the opened end of the theatre poetry sounds out through giant megaphones above full orchestras that are interpreting and exploding the metaphors while they stress the rhythm. The evening and the night are ahead and one is not feeling tired; besides, and this is a condition of the Paradise, we are all to remain the same age, just as old as we are now, and no older.

But here came the crisis, the very gate of that antlered park, and it advanced with a loud rap upon Miss Morgan's door and a stumbling and stair-blown voice that announced Colonel Fantock, who came slowly into the room and sat down with a significant weariness that was not a bit out of place. For I was young and had walked myself in those greenhouses into a Paradise of my own choosing, where everything was young and moved under the most favourable conditions of sun or gold in case you are ethical or mercenary in understanding. Now all the dying things round me in that old house broke into life; I realised Miss Morgan's voice, I sat beside Colonel Fantock, and the Minah-bird imitated my father and mother far better than I could do myself.

Miss Morgan was off on one of her favourite topics, and it struck me (need I say why?) with a doubled pathos—the French châteaux. These, by a confusion of date, she always attributed to the reign of "Angry Cat," giving by these words to the debonair and vulgar Henri Quatre a kind of fantastic alertness and sharpness of whisker that was not out of keeping with the dandyism and self-assertion of those buildings.

But I could not follow her to-day with the enthusiasm that I generally contrived to put into my conversation with her when she was upon one of her pet themes, for I liked encouraging her over these own hurdles of her fancy and usually contrived to run by her side in encouragement. Instead, I felt bound to interrupt and draw her back again on to this new subject I had started for her reminiscences. For some moments I was unable to do so, for she showed a vigorous keenness upon "Angry Cat" that made one think she was anxious to go on talking about this architectural culmination and lose sight in its absurdities, which she thought beauties, of what I wanted to know from her. And so I had to let her talk herself out.

Colonel Fantock leaned forward and helped himself to a tea-cake, then he relapsed again into the back of his arm-chair and seemed agreed, like I was, to suffer her dissertation in silence. I had now got these two pivots of my recollections safely in front of me in the same room, one of them silent, and the other talking but not listening.

I thought of all the years Miss Morgan had spent in this house, the summers like I have tried to indicate and the winters that she treated in the spirit in which one would have taken an invitation to the Russian

Court before the Revolution, for she only had little
walks to the near shops or round the Crescent to our
own home, and these excursions through snow or rain
she took as though her sledge was near at hand and
she had left it just for an experiment of walking. I
feel bound in honour to record her one weakness, a
very occasional affair occurring but two or three times
a year. When moved by this mood she sent across,
wet or fine, to an old lady who owned the boarding-
establishment across the road, and this old lady (these
were the only terms of their acquaintance, the only
time they met) contrived inevitably that her mood
should coincide in time and sort with that of Miss
Morgan. Together, and in high gala state of both
dress and spirits, they would drive round the whole
town, not neglecting to notice any one they knew who
was abroad in the streets, and paying as much attention
to their enemies as to their friends. This mysterious
and high-spirited friendship continued for a couple of
hours, while these two boon-companions talked and
laughed together and changed this for a mood of grim
vengeance at the sight of an enemy, as though chastise-
ment was possible and on the eve of infliction. When
their circuit was over and the carriage came down the
other half of the road towards Miss Morgan's front-
door, the two friends had reached the point of wanting
for more sympathy, both in their victories and their
troubles, and so they would get down from the carriage and, after paying the complacent cabman, go in
to Miss Morgan's house, where they remained until
the acetylene was lit, and even prolonged their feasting
until after midnight, when no one was about in the
streets and that short journey across the road to the
boarding-establishment could be embarked upon as a
vagary that entailed no ridicule from passers-by.

To-day, I am bound to admit, it was an entirely different Miss Morgan from the one who undertook those gaudy excursions in the carriage, and all the sweetness and gentleness in her character come back to me. Later on that very summer when she came to stay with us in the country she arrived with a camera and installed in her enthusiasm a dark-room in some cupboard in the house. She took a number of photographs of the house and the garden as though to get an outsider's opinion on these scenes to which through the years she had become so accustomed, and at the same time directed the taking of some flashlight groups of the whole party staying in the house. In these she remained still and looked towards the camera in so marked a manner and with such a degree of concentration that even now, if I see one of these groups, it seems to me that she was anxious to leave her likeness behind. In fact the whole of that summer was a stocktaking, an inventory, of what she had in hand as regards her own life, and apart from what you read of or see as a spectator.

In any case that pathetic struggle with what must have been a failing memory took place later than the main scene of this chapter, and in its irrelevance, therefore, we leave it at that, having merely recorded what was a contingent curiosity on her part. Everything was slipping, slipping away in front of her, and against this steady descent into the abyss she wanted to turn back and have a last look at the scene she was leaving. So for that matter did I, but with a very different purpose, for I knew that a great deal still lay in front of me, whereas, with Miss Morgan, there was nothing in front, and, had she realised it, but little reason or point in trying to remember when but a few months meant the complete break in everything. To look out from a prison-van upon green trees for the last time for many years to come, there would be point in such a sentiment as that, for memory lasts and probably even flourishes in that lean environment, but why try to remember on the very brink of nothing? Such an endeavour is like the condemned man's breakfast that one reads out of in the paper with porridge, an apple, or some other item out of an ordinary day chosen in order to fortify that bitter dawn.

I had reached that moment, so rare in a lifetime, of seeing the whole of life as it existed for her and for me in its exact shape and tone. It was, for one's own personality, therefore, a moment like those that one loves in history when the exact focus is applied that we long for in our want of information and we find it in such things as the talks of Ben Jonson and Drummond of Hawthornden, or Madame D'Urfey's *Travels in Spain*. We find the same thing where we get two people living at the same time who never met, to begin with the simplest instance it is to be wished that J. M. W. Turner and Hokusai had made each other's acquaintance, shown each other some of their drawings, and perhaps even made each other's portraits. We can wish, too, that Ingres had made a few pencil drawings of Napoleon instead of merely an official and rather poster-like portrait; we may imagine meetings between Titian and great Oriental painters, Sesshiu for example, and whole hosts of other introductions of this nature. Here in my own humble life I found myself in my attitude towards Miss Morgan drinking in all the peculiar style and glamour of her life and surroundings much as though by some magical invention I was able with all my apparatus of memory and comparison to go back for a little space to some strongly marked age interesting to my fancy, the Longhi period in Venice,

which Guys worke
all over this brigh
fog from the ligh

Perhaps the th
wiser not to ment
and attentively at
ment. As for Co
look at them, whe
or because he kne
and they bored h
would he say, eithe
went steadily thro
air with which pa
want their childre:
getting very often
than they do then
harm in my seeing
stand what they po

They left her ir
her to say good-by
more fondness th:
leaning out toward
away that it was al
meet. But I coul
and that I unders
only moment in al
ages and our mind
no more a child :
woman, but the w
vided into two ha:

I did not go bac
I knew that had I c
repeated. Indeed,
again, for I left th
ing I was leaving it

for instance. In fact I was part of Miss Morgan's life and yet quite outside it, and knew well that I should go on long after it was over and finished, for it was unique and a thing to itself that would never happen again, so I must take every opportunity of remembering it in order that somewhere at any rate there should be a record of its strange and personal nature.

I had been thinking but a few moments before of what I may justly term my own Paradise and I came back out of it to my own present and future and to what we may regard as the very dregs, the very last particles of sand, in Miss Morgan's hour-glass. For Colonel Fantock there was not much more, either, and in fact the whole of this phase of my life was nearly over, and as regards my friendship with these two old people it was as though, having measured how much time there was to come for them both and seeing its inevitable span of days, I had looked aside and away from them, for, in fact, after this summer I saw but little of either of them again. He, indeed, at his mature age moved down to the west coast of England and I never saw him again, while Miss Morgan I saw but once or twice and then left the town, not quite realising I was leaving it for good, and that she was left there and I should never see her again.

Well! I must deal my death-blow, I thought, and so as soon as tea was over, by talking of books I manœuvred the conversation back on to Constantin Guys once more, and brought the book over from the table where it had been moved to make room for the tea and placed it in Miss Morgan's hands. Then, since she was unwilling to talk of it, I opened it, turned over the illustrations and pinned her down to some attention to my questions. Colonel Fantock I made sit beside her

133

or five years more, indeed she only died two years ago from the month I am writing this, and it was only then we discovered her true age and that she was eighty-five years old when she died. Of her history or origin we know nothing; and the whole contents of her house were put up to auction and sold by the indifferent actor-relative who inherited her property.

Colonel Fantock, I had better add, since I am on the question of death, died two months ago and was eighty-six. I never saw him again, either, so that the afternoon I have described was really my farewell to them both; and most obviously, on the part of Miss Morgan at any rate, her farewell to me. They were not friendly to each other, for each suspected the other of being a liar, and so it was a rare conjunction of circumstances that brought them both together.

Here, the whole of this series of summers, so far as I am concerned, come to an end. Every year, necessarily, they recede further and further from me, though I do not regret the speed they travel because my memory of them is so complete. That final tea-party, with my perhaps rather cruel attitude towards their respective ages, gave me exactly the information I required to pose them really accurately in memory.

Their silence when looking at that book is an additional help, for then in that little lull in time I can see all the most salient things I connected with each of them playing round their bodies like a kind of spiritualist aura of their quality and achievement. However, all these things merge down to that one view of them sitting quiet in the bow-window full of light with boughs dancing in a delicate water-measure, little birds knocking the hollowed coconuts' wooden pates against the window-frame and the Minah-bird talking and

136

talking, trying, no doubt, to help its friend by distracting all time-sense with its chatter.

It is, at any rate, an external summer in which I leave them; for it is summer outside the window, if, so far as their minds and bodies are concerned, it is cold winter within. For me, like it was for them, it is all compressed into one day, into a short day so full of happenings that all things seemed to go on at once and not in a sequence one after the other. I have finished with them in a hot afternoon not yet turned into evening; and I suppose they will go on sitting there without speaking till the whole of creation turns grey with age and even the Minah-bird, talking and talking to distract Time, stops his chatter and drops his red beak on to the black and funeral plumes of his chest.

Part II: All Summer in a Night

I

The Moth and the Flame

A METICULOUS interior scene projected itself outside the window as though it was travelling along beside the train. In its depths I could see myself on the oozing and damp velvet of the settee with my five fellow-passengers counterfeited on the left-hand side instead of the right, so that while it was true that they now surrounded me, I was none the less able to keep a watch on them which they could not inflict on me, for they were too far away to catch any distinct reflection of the carriage. This sister-world I could breathe upon and hide, but the mist of my breath was easily dissipated again with a rag of newspaper, with the back of a glove, or with the fag-end of the broken and useless window-rope. As I looked closer, a number of points of light burned steadily through the reflection, and at last those lit windows came crackling towards me through the drizzling evening and announced a thousand back-bedrooms, with a white, powdery bulb of gas to each, for all of these brick boxes were tenanted by somebody just come back from his work and every occupant could produce one of these blossoms at will upon this dark, invisible tree, whose branches had grown into nearly every house among the suburbs. It was just that particular hour when all these flowers shone out with a waxy, shining light that glowed evenly through its creamy petals, like the camellia or the magnolia; but the train ran too fast by the glistening windows for one to see anything else but these white flowers shining out from their dark leaves of shadow.

A few minutes more and we should be rumbling like a line of chariots, iron upon iron, over the river, braking our speed from the bridge-end so as to make a triumphal entry into the station. This heroic rattling came with an abrupt suddenness, and in another moment we were sheathed by the sea-green glass of the station roof, while every one lowered the window nearest to him, or lifted down his luggage and struggled into the twisted arms of a heavy overcoat.

The lights of the town were very raucous, very strident, as one drove away from the station; and of course it was drizzling with rain—not too seriously, but with the degree of wetness that one can incur from standing too near a fountain on a windy day. The passers-by looked pained and hurried, and there were one or two traffic crushes in which the motor-buses and great vans looked like barges held up at some lock of a canal. Gradually each house and every corner grew familiar, and the street-lamps and shop-lights seemed to burn in their accustomed places. The distance was interminable, like a long-held breath when one dare not take fresh air into one's lungs; but at last I came to the final turning and was back home again. Even now there was the luggage to be taken upstairs, and a number of letters to be opened.

These are moments when the pathos of personal possession takes hold of one. Familiar objects are seen again after long absence and take on their true dimension and proportion without that kind of invisibility which we accord to things by which we are for ever surrounded, in the sense that we hardly ever look at them and never try to arrive at any just estimate of their appearance. So may we imagine a prisoner who, after years in the solitude of his cell, has at last obtained a mirror and can now satisfy what has tortured him even more violently than his hesitating conjectures as to the passage of time. A mirror can fortify and determine what one has long guessed at, in the same way that absence gives one a fresh angle towards objects and establishes thereby a kind of geometrically-proved certainty as to their distance and dimension. Now at last we can see everything in its true light, what is friendly and what is inimical. Certain things by their very crudity—a bowl, or perhaps an ornament—appeal to one like the most patient of dumb animals; others— perhaps a mantelpiece, a cornice, or something for which we are not responsible in a leased room—seem aloof and almost hostile. Gradually, every day a little more, those old familiar appearances creep back again out of the strangeness, for now that we are back in our cell, imprisonment quickly regains its monotony.

It was early—not much after seven o'clock—but the journey had made me intensely hungry, so that dinner seemed welcome, however premature its hour. During the waits, while a dish was being removed to give place to another, the electric light had a strange, cat-like fascination for tired eyes, so that it was impossible not to sit with head tilted back looking at it, which induced a dazed tranquillity of mood like that we can obtain by looking intently into a fire. It was a relief to break this spell by getting up and walking to the window, whence one could look out on to this typical scene one had missed for so many months. The public-house was as bright as an aquarium with those elaborate brass rails and the steamy heat upon the windows. Occasionally the door would be flung open and out would come one of those nearly extinct specimens with bonnet and ragged feather-boa, of which the public-houses seem to be the last preserves—as it were the National Park. Undoubtedly the land of Congreve—and of Phil May! Such figures emerge, as though spilt, out of their retreats; they come out into the street on a sort of yellow flood of light, like the fly which you might spill from a tea-cup on to the table-cloth; and they crawl off, dripping and bedraggled, into the darkness. One moved away, having seen the last of them, and sat down by the table, hooking one's eyes again on to the light, which dispelled the time, almost like an orchestra playing between the courses. Dinner was soon finished in this way, and there was nothing else to do except listen to that aerial music, so near at hand, while thoughts could move in and out of that persistently beating metre, for even the staring electric light has undoubtedly its own rhythm.

So is it on a railway journey where the thump-thump-thumping over bolts and sleepers strikes out a musical notation which the speed of the train harmonises. You can sing one tune after another, and occasionally it will lock itself for three or four bars together on to the rhythm of the railway, and then disentangle and move off again on its own orbit. After a time, suddenly, and with surprising insistence, the train leads off on a motive of its own, though the fact that this is some well-known tune seems to postulate that these little sequences of notes, once invented, become universal and general property, and are no longer the exclusive pleasure of human beings. This is therefore, in such an instance, an extraneous music imposed from outside; and this is exactly the manner in which, while I looked steadily at the electric light, something broke in of a sudden upon the rhythm of the light by which I had been thinking, and altered it, eventually, for something very different. It was a barrel-organ which had anchored for a few moments in that yellow swell outside the public-house and was lending its cheap and bright gaiety to the brass rails and cloudy windows within. Now, what is expected of cheapness is that it should glitter; that it should in this case gild those brass bars, and either altogether clean the windows, or impart to them that authentic cloudiness against which every one can place, as on the softest of couches, the predilection of his own mythology. For a tune or two the organ played with one's thoughts as did the railway-train with the tunes one sang; it either, that is to say, did not interfere with them, or it tripped them up, muddled them, and made itself a nuisance, until, like the co-ordination of two clocks which begin to tick together and at last break apart, one was free again for the moment and paid no attention to the organ. But it was relentless and meant no mercy. It repeated this behaviour for once or twice more, and then made its complete and unconditional conquest.

Submission was in itself an agony, but there was no hope of resistance and no alternative to surrender. At the first—as it were—syllables of those familiar notes there was nothing else to do except close one's own thoughts and listen to the ideas coming out of this empty husk of last year. Yes! it was emphatically a husk; just as it might be a shell a long way from its shore which still kept a murmur of the perpetual surf if you held it to your ear, or the dancing skeleton of some person one had once loved. By some magical predestination the organ played this tune immediately over again, so that it was like an imperious summons which one could not contradict, and which left no doubt as to its meaning. This was not difficult to obey, at least in the immediate sense of the command, for the piece was still playing and one had only to go to the theatre.

I have described this memory left over from last year as a sort of husk, or skeleton, and this is, in its essence, true; though it is possible to fortify memory by stratagem, so that what one remembers with the eyes one can assist with the ear. We may illustrate the mixture of these two or more ingredients which go to make up memory by imagining our prisoner-friend, whom we have, this time, been allowed by a kindly indulgence to supply with chocolate, and also, so that he should enjoy this privilege by making it last longer, with an extra ration of bread; for chocolate is never so satisfying as when eaten with bread, and this method has also the advantage that the chocolate does not make you thirsty, as when eaten by itself. In fact, one thing ekes out the other, in the same way that aural helps out visual memory, so that this prisoner or one's own self, whichever it may happen to be, finds life made easier for him by this combined palliative. I ascribe these powers, then, to memory, and have noted the ingredients which go to make its potency.

The street-lamps and shop-fronts moved like chessmen into their appointed places as one passed them quickly by, and they seemed, on this occasion, like so many victories, so many prisoners gained, as they flashed past the windows to either side, moving in this manner from battle-front to base. This journey seemed quick, in comparison with that between the station and home, for the rapidity of one's thoughts eat up the slowness of the drive. Thus actual time, in its conventional measure, and apparent time, are alternatively giant and dwarf to each other, and according to whether you are the slave or the victor you enjoy yourself like the conqueror, or find time slow and heavy like the slave. At this moment I had deluded myself into a giant's stature, and time was cowering before me, so that the distance was nothing and we seemed to arrive almost before we had started.

You could hear music even on the doorstep of the theatre, but once the swing-doors were open its violent loudness was intensified to a degree almost beyond belief. It had a horizontal, panting, and sonorous pattern, where one pictures other music as progressing along the earth, or a little way above it and on a parallel curve to its surface. In fact, it moved on a different system, and from the very instant it started, this peculiar character was discernible. Indeed, if you could isolate a few bars and examine them apart from the context they would reveal their identity as certainly as the smallest fragment of Greek sculpture, or as the few square inches that we may imagine cut out from the middle of a picture by Mantegna, which latter would show its authorship just by the brushwork of nerve or muscle, in the rendering of fold and contour, even though there might not be a head or a hand left there to determine the ascription.

They had just reached that moment when the whole piece ends with a bitter and terrible shuddering of the brass, and its effect on my emotional understanding was as though a dagger had been thrown into my chest, and, even before it had stopped quivering there, the person who threw it had come close up to me and taking the dagger by its hilt had worked it up and down with the utmost violence of which he was capable, in order to drive in the point still further and enlarge and lacerate the wound. It stopped there, as though satisfied with the harm it had done, and there was a deathly silence.

All the players wore white linen coats as though

they had intended to serve drinks and were only turned musicians because this work was quicker and more intoxicating to the senses. They were grouped to one side of the stage, posed as if for a photograph, and they held their glistening instruments quite still for this purpose. In a moment the march and battery of their music would begin again.

The horizontal and striped movement of the mechanisms that their music formed in space, for indeed these sounds were as hard and brittle as though you could touch them, carried one immediately into a brightly striped and chequered shade. Indeed the leaves, for we must conceive most of the trees to be palms, clanked and rattled like an armful of swords, and threw down ribbed and spined lights through their interstices. In and out of this web of sound and light the music built its sliding and abrupt machinery. A nucleus, a small shape or pattern, lived a second's life in a complete homogony of human circumstance; complete with toothed appetite, drowsed sleep, and every intonation between love and hate. Such clinches or spreading fans of notes as these might really be had that kind of close and absurd parallel to human emotions that one may experience by watching the sea-horses in the tank at an aquarium. They have the same curvetting pride of movement as a real horse, they are altogether ludicrously and exactly like the other animal, and yet, because its very improbability makes what is natural to the one, supremely typical, though quite impossible, in the other, it is no surprise, it is in fact only what one expects, to see the sea-horse moving proudly down those open water-fields, propelled by the little whirring fins on each side of its tail, or, most incongruous of all, sitting upright and stiff in the branches of a little marine tree.

THE MOTH AND THE FLAME

These little soul-centres have, as I have said, but a second's life; before you are aware of it, one has died away, to give place to another. Some of them may sum up in that instant the bitterest degree of poignancy and the very extreme of petulance, both of these stretched and intensified to a point that might endanger their structure. They are so incisive and sharp-cut that any interpretation of them must depend on a similar dramatic speed. They resemble so many doors passed one after another lying open in a lurid light; yet, though each is so separate from the other, they blend together into a co-ordinate whole.

It is towards such a miniature but complete world as this that we may imagine a deity inclining for a moment while he reads off quickly in this manner the full history of humanity since he was last able to spare a moment to watch their activities. We must conceive of him, too, as being only interested in them because he is not responsible, so that sometimes his conjectures have been right, and at others, events have contradicted his hazards. So may we imagine ourselves at the aquarium tank; deeply interested in the sea-horses and all their antics that we have studied so closely; but incapable of begetting sea-horses, though these little creatures might owe everything to us except the fact of their being alive. In just the same manner we may station ourselves at one side of the music, able to watch its evolution, but powerless to encourage or check its development.

I have said that its mechanisms were sliding and abrupt in their formation. What I mean by this is that they have to live absolutely on their own merits, for the hard theatrical life in which they thrive has no mercy for what is too clever or too weak. They are thrown upon their own resources and have to exist on their skill or prettiness.

Ornament, in the structure of this music, has a new and peculiar vitality. It is not so much decoration, as it is the jointing and stressing of different parts; so that the weight of the whole piece depends, at times, on one slender, flying bridge at the far side of which the melody will take up again and continue. There are moments, then, of great daring and confidence; perhaps it may be a great fanfare on four saxophones which projects itself like a kind of scroll or bracket into the air, and which a second later will be supporting the whole weight of everything upon its flourishes. At another turn it takes on such an unexpected and imperative air that you feel you have yourself been kicked on to the stage, without warning, and told to entertain the audience till some one else is ready to take your place. It has changed again in an instant, and nothing could now be more mild and alluring than its tone, though this kind of chasm of sentiment into which it has descended ends in a sheer wall of rock up to whose summit you are whirled with a fabulous ease and swiftness. But in all these alternations this music is mercenary; you pay for it, and it gives you no more than it has promised.

It contained this infinite number of gradations, ranging from a kitten-sound to a lion-roar; and every separate instrument could be heard, as the voices of democracy should be audible in a republic—that is to say, every instrument had an equal responsibility and all of them were treated as individual beings. The advantages of this lay in both directions, combining an extraordinary individual subtlety with a possible maximum of sound out of all proportion to that obtainable on an ordinary orchestra. The players showed as much degree and diversity of hue as did the results of their playing; for they seemed to be drawn, as to their places of origin, from such divergent directions as the Baltic and the Caribbean Seas, while China and the Congo had also sent their quota, and the whole was co-ordinated and permeated with a Semitic strain, in weak or strong dilution. Their haunting and mordant vulgarity hung about them like a strange smell, so insistent as to make one unable to forget their presence.

Such was the male side of this music, but, as so frequently happens, an ugly male produces a beautiful female; and we must conceive of all this American music as a sexual ornament or introduction to their females. The music was an elaborate framing, a doorway through which the other sex were meant to advance, and every ornament and stress we may translate into terms of seduction.

At this point the whole world of poetry breaks into life and we know that it is linked indissolubly with music, however mordant and vulgar its strains may be, for poetry is a kind of primæval and more obvious music, and the latter, as a more recent and exploited hypothesis of pleasures, carries this older art along with it. Poetry, then, which we may take as the personal translation and exposition of music, followed close behind, and, as I have said, now broke into life.

One had to tumble about in this rough sea of sound till one's feet felt the ground, but now that it was at last a certainty it was easy to get one's head above the waves and look round. If poetry has always to be made of certain things, like architecture which has to be built out of the numberless variations of pillar, wall, and arch, so most certainly was poetry present here in all its familiar ingredients. They were shown, though, in new and strange combination like the phenomena that are visible when a new poet arises; it is like a new shuffling of the old pack of cards.

What I mean by this sudden appearance of poetry is that one felt that airy substance breathing and quivering near to one as though it were a kind of living animal. All through one's life up to this moment it had been faded and lifeless with the degree of immortality that a flower possesses pressed between the pages of a book. It was precisely in this manner that one had had to recapture and distil it, and when one was thoroughly drenched through and sated with reading it would rise up from this incantation like a ghost produced by some necromancer's rite.

Having once appeared by a definite birth, it was never very far away and would come up again as quickly and insistently as the tune one has heard once and remembers at dead of night.

Now it was violently pushed and thrust against one, and from being a quiescent, if evocable phantom, it was transformed into a very live and terrible force. In fact it had the violent and precipitate rush of falling in love for the first time.

While one's own life passed into this fresh phase, all those old and dead mental adventures which one experiences in reading burned up into a bright flame with this contagious fire. One could understand, thanks to this new flow of vitality, the process by which that sensation of a breaking of time was formed. Now I suppose that every attempt at creating a work of art is connected, generally, subconsciously, with this same endeavour. Being remembered means being paused over, so any works that a man leaves after his death have the effect of so many brakes or drags on time. Unfortunately these will not work unless they are applied, and so long intervals may elapse during which they are ineffective. It is this fact which gives a particular pathos and poignancy to very old poetry or music, because architecture or works of painting and sculpture have an unavoidable bulk, a kind of secondary existence behind and beyond their artistic content, which is formed simply by the space they take up, and the fact that everything which shows craftsmanship has a certain marketable value, which is likely to help towards its conservation. It is far otherwise with music or poetry. Poetry, indeed, has that further restriction, the bar of language, so that it appeals in any case to a vastly diminished audience. It has a distension, an exaggeration of effect, which is out of all proportion to the space it takes up, and its material value is nothing. In fact poetry is so ethereal in texture as to be like an omelette made without eggs.

This is true, absolutely and entirely, of the finest lyrical poetry, which will begin of a sudden and within the space of time that it takes to sing to oneself, say, a tune by Mozart, will create, out of nothing, a complete entity, a kind of universe of emotion and experience. Then it stops, leaving nothing more to be said; and the whole phenomenon is completely inexplicable, most of all, perhaps, to the creator, or intermediary of it.

Now, although I have stated, an obvious truism, that the material of fine poetry is always the same, and that it depends for a new organisation simply upon fresh dispositions, ending in fact with the thesis that all poetry can be judged by the same standard, I propose, nevertheless, to confine my researches to that which is my personal taste, and makes for me, therefore, a somewhat eased task.

The mechanisms formed by the music, those extraordinary little sense-groups or soul-centres as we may conceive them to be, form by their close relation to poetry any number of little flying bridges on which we can walk out, moving from one to another of these twin planes of creation. Perhaps by this method it may be possible to explain, or, if not that, to stimulate those strange experiences. Other music, of a much deeper actual significance, when played in a concert-hall exerted upon one only a fragment of this mysterious force, the obvious reason for this discrepancy being the fact that the personification of its characters, the filling of its rôles, was too hazy and indefinite; whereas, in this instance, they were here ready for one. As I have tried to suggest, a little way back, the combined force of all the senses of sight and sound, and all the revived memories that are evoked again by this tawdry theatrical music, act upon one with a strength that it is difficult to experience elsewhere, though one may imagine it existing among the more devout of a religious congregation.

The most marvellous feature of all was the manner in which only the first few bars of a tune would bring out a complete set of characters who moved with astonishing ease and freedom; and where the way in which they interpreted the music on the stage was faulty and deficient you could supply your own translation. Thus, moving with the emphasis of the music, you had the sense of control and direction and could ignore the conventional interpretation offered by the management.

We will give an instance; and may as well choose for this purpose a scene of such banality that it would seem impossible of improvement. It is a night scene, on one of those haunts made familiar to us by their being chosen so often as background for a comedian; in fact, the Thames Embankment. Rain is falling bitterly and a suspicious-looking man in check trousers and top-hat is offering his escort to a young woman. She cannot get a taxi, it appears, and above and beyond that she seems predisposed to accept his company. The whole scene lasts only two minutes; but it is fortified and given a kind of permanence by the music. That intense atmosphere of Shaftesbury Avenue and Charing Cross Road is given in a simplified, even reticent, shape; so that those strange beings have a real, authentic vitality to our eyes. A little photograph, seen in next Sunday's paper, of these two dancers, with that monocled face held intently towards all that web of fair hair that we can just remember, becomes typical, no longer a part but almost the whole of one side of life.

We may pretend to ignore this, but it is nevertheless true, and you could find no event, no record so true of this life in the work of painters. Those agreeable contortionists of a recent past, and a past which was, at that, the personal vision of a French recluse, can show us nothing so typical of our age. The scene I have described is indeed a privilege, though one which can be easily refused. What poetry lover would not have been present in that long gallery at Chambord when the King scratched a name with his diamond on the window-pane? Yet in such a scene as this we find ourselves in the very heart of all that constitutes our age. All round us, if we are in a London theatre, this decaying and nearly extinct art is showing its last glimmering lights. Quite near, perhaps at the Alhambra, there is Little Tich singing his grocer's song in a scene that shows Holborn Viaduct, and might just as well consist of a street of houses from a print by Hogarth.

When, by one of those lucky chances on which the theatre exists, music and dancing happened to come up to the same level, one experienced the sensation of seeing the history of a whole century—(most of it still to come)—contracted into the space of a moment or two. No amount of research work in museum or library could construct so vital an epitome. Every detail of physical appearance bore the same relation to the whole; though, apart from the unavoidable beauty of being young, the results of so much strain did not, perhaps, quite justify the effort and the obvious hardships undergone for the purpose. On the other hand, the nature of this concentration on the moment, the grasping of that once-given gift that we have just mentioned, could not but attain to a certain poignancy. It was remarkable, as well, that any results had been arrived at at all, considering that the whole art of acting had been neglected and hidden behind prettiness. In fact, one was left with the impression that this latter quality must possess, of itself, some dramatic value one had not suspected, and this was of course aided by the music which dramatised and completed that partial emptiness.

A part of this peculiar seduction, one could not help knowing, lay in its utter distinction. There was an almost Turk-like tyranny over the other sex in feeling their ignorance and lack of interest in those things which gave one's own life its point. They were invested, therefore, in that one direction with a kind of dumbness which attracted by its blatancy. That they must be possessed, on the other side of this, with a copious volubility of their own, towards which one was oneself dumb from ignorance and lack of experience, formed a yet deeper attraction.

The caressing steadiness of the lights, together with the impertinence of the music, had already by singling out and giving special prominence given one a kind of exaggerated acquaintance with several of the characters. But acquaintance stopped on this side of speech to them, so that one could read any meaning into their movements and every surmise remain unanswered. They had, therefore, a mythological reality, for, a little way removed from one, they led an apparently ordinary life, but were aloof and unapproachable. This was, indeed, the first occasion and apparently the unique method by which such realities could be reached, and they were possessed of a very genuine and authentic importance. From looking at contemporary pictures, and from reading the Russian or French novels of one's own day, one could obtain no contact with imagination, but only a sousing in realism, or that most contortionate of poses, an affected simplicity. It seemed, then, a surer method to approach beauty through prettiness, since it is no part of optimism to suppose that ugliness demands to be searched for.

Also there was this additional force to it, that these emotions were as ancient and traditional as any that can be roused by a religious service, and that now religion was dead there was perhaps no other way left by which they could be stimulated into life once more. It would be equivalent, of course, to telling the point of a story before narrating its progress, if one was now to disclose how, once one had climbed among them, these lights and all their radiance seemed to be in no way different from the ordinary daylight, how they lost, indeed, that particular glamour which their inaccessible nature gave to them.

The particular moment, indeed the whole lives of the participants, seemed to be circumscribed by a kind of barrier or thicket of music which formed yet another fence against intrusion. One could not imagine them living apart from these conditions, and once, on whatever pretext, out of this frame those very things which had showed to best advantage became tawdry and diminished in effect, so that they looked dull, or painted, or lethargic. Their clothes were either black and economical, or of a shrill and exaggerated proclaim, as if ever anxious to attract attention. In fact they seemed to leave something on the stage which they could not take away with them into private life, so that their personality was thin and diminished in this latter condition.

It was this divided personality, this sense that they were instruments that would play, given favourable circumstances, that lent such peculiar interest to their unprofessional existence. The sight of a provincial theatre was enough at that time to give a tinge of romance to the damp and wintry streets, and one more definite than that imparted by strolling barrel-organ or wailing concertina, the only other itinerant arts.

We come back, here and now, to the barrel-organ which can at its own caprice bring a most drastic influence to bear upon one's sentiment. This mysterious force was intensified to a superlative extent a moment or two later when those very strains through whose medium the organ had worked upon one's emotion were played once again by the band. It was a lifetime compressed into two or three minutes, and every nerve and muscle in one's body became taut and as it were tuned to this music. The spotlights were moving in a slow and deliberate dance about the stage, appearing not so much to follow the dancers as to go before them, showing them their way. Sometimes a figure would be left for an instant just outside the edges of light and would then suddenly come into that sunlight with a flower-like blowing of the limbs, as though these were curved and held there by a moment's low wind.

At such moments these brakes upon time were applied with a jarring violence that scattered all one's senses.

One particular face under those vibrating and held lights showed a point of sensitiveness which it was impossible to measure. That interval over the heads of the players, between the audience and the stage, gave a kind of hieratic and aloof importance to her, so that one could attach supreme meaning to every movement. That her actions were only an epitome of some scene of ordinary life served but to give one deeper scope for interpretation. The fact that she was possessed of extreme conventional prettiness was another platform for optimism. Had her beauty been of a conscious nature, compressed into straight lines and folds to conform with the label "artistic," or wild and disordered with a reliance upon the chance accidents of "tousle" or shadow, which fortuitous confidence is held to justify the term "intellectual," the possibilities of the art that she practised would have been relegated at once to the outside edge, that perilous verge round the endless circle of which the ghosts of such mundane consolations as Cosimo Tura, Clément Marot, or Maria Edgeworth may be said to circle between oblivion and the equally careless chasm of fame. As it was, she possessed a power of appeal that was religious in its large nature and universal diffusion, so that her art possessed numberless themes, and not only, as in other examples I have just mentioned, many variations on just one contingency.

At the other side of this glass wall, beyond that mysterious space that divided us, though it was transparent and visible in every detail, there lay a land of new experience into which it seemed impossible to break. The cruelty of the situation lay in its clearness to the eye. Poetry, as I have said, broke into life there and seemed to thrive more easily upon banality, as though it was a plant which must grow out of nothing and could not be forced. Wherever music showed a ledge or cranny, poetry could be found growing there, and it even flourished by itself out of the tides of light, as if that electric substance was a deep and rich soil for its increase. It was alive now where it had always been dead before, and one had at last discovered where it grew and flourished. It sprang up in a clear and glass-like visibility and there need be no more of those mournful and indefinite mists to conceal it. The sparkling limbs that had then gleamed fitfully as though moving behind leaves in a glade were now bare and unshadowed before one's eyes; and every feature and lineament could be followed through its changes.

In spite of this, there was another side to these discoveries that gave them a kind of mortality only to be compared with the dead, the sentimental aspect of poetry. This was not evident just at the beginning, but it soon lay behind and burned through the thin film between, so that it continually thwarted one by the signs of its presence. Although more alive before one's eyes, these scenes were as aloof from one in their own fashion as age and distance could make them. The persons who moved in them were just as inaccessible as if they could only be read about, and were no longer alive to be met and talked to. They even had a dual rarity about them, for their private lives were as secret and mysterious as their public performances. But there was something even more plangently emotional about them, and this was the knowledge that, however poignant or sympathetic they might seem to be, it was only a delusion to expect to find the same qualities about their actual lives.

Their chameleon temperament enabled them by its

properties to take on the exact strength and colouring
of every situation. No sooner, therefore, had they
come within the orbit of all these lights than they assumed at once the measured and rigid smile of the
theatre, beyond which they would never penetrate into
true emotion. After a time, these very conventions,
these set and appointed limits, began to be a fascination
to one, for it was extraordinary to watch the emotions
of the audience being led up to that impassable frontier
beyond which there was no advance.

I have tried to describe the renewed effect of these
feelings on some one who had often experienced them,
and then, having gone abroad for some months, was
induced by the sudden and insistent barrel-organ to
repeat the authentic experience once again. This time
the summons was too emphatic to be entirely ignored,
and the appearance of a certain familiar name upon the
pantomime-bill in a town in the north of England led
to a short visit there for that particular purpose. This
occasion built a kind of emotional milestone out of the
twenty years that life had lasted, a species of half-way
house between birth and death, and it cannot consequently be denied some degree of attention.

Beyond those borders one conceived that something
strange and beautiful by its freshness must exist. It
possessed therefore all the attraction of travel with this
much added to it, that one's discoveries would be alive
and not dead. The peculiar slowing down and distortion of time that took place within one whenever any
of this tawdry and glittering music was played drew
upon all one's emotion and even upon that solemn
residuum, one's historical sense. If one could keep an
eye open for Stravinsky, or for Picasso, one had surely
a little time to keep the other exercised upon something
less trying to follow. The history of any generation

is mainly, but not entirely, the lives of its greatest artists; but even these draw their strength now and again from the banality or the sentiment of their audience, and therefore any one who wishes to be a good observer must follow both alternatives with his eyes. Sometimes, the cheaper things are, the better they turn out to be; and, in any case, the noises of the fair may keep one awake, however gilded the room one lies in.

II

The Oasis in Winter

I BEGIN once more with a railway-journey, and I
suppose this is, in its small way, symbolical, for it
means being taken away from one set of circumstances
and given into the custody of another. Such separa-
tions, if you follow them down to their logical source,
start, I suppose, at the moment you are taken away
from your mother and given to a nurse. So it continues: until old age, or bad health, reverses the order
and you are no longer taken away on every such occasion, but are always coming back to something—are
beginning to return, in fact, towards the direction from
which you originally came.

Here we were at last—this winter evening—near to
the station: after this five-hour journey that had been
as level as a sledge-drive past all the mounds and
hillocks thrown up by the mines. They stood up out
of the water-logged plain, like so many icebergs ready
to tilt over into that freezing sea, and as I watched
them out of the window, I could not help thinking of
the sights one would see revealed, if one of these huge
heaps were to topple over and spread out, as on to a
great delta, all the guilty secrets that lay hid in the
two-thirds of its mass that must lie, if this were really
an iceberg, below the level of the water-line. In those
days of child-slavery that were only just finishing when
the foundation of these mounds was thrown up, this
was the favourite murder-ground, and it was here that

163

a lover would kill his mistress, two rivals would fight to the death, or the newly-born baby, the seal just as much as it was the cause of every broil, be carried in meek folds of brown paper, like a picnic dinner, difficult to arrange tidily in a parcel. Then, when she was dead and you had kissed her for the last time, protesting your innocence in a louder and more heroic whisper than that reserved for dark and echoing hollows among the hedges, you let her head drop back more heavily than you would allow it if she were alive, so that it made a nasty hollow boom, like a mallet hitting a stone, and then sat down by her side, still hoping that the warmth of your body would be a kind of hot-water bottle to keep a little life in her dry and stringy veins, that must by now be like the things one's knife slips over in cheap, thin meat; or, hardly realising you were the only survivor of the duel, hit and hit again your victim's head with every weapon that lay ready to hand, with first the handle and then the point of your club, with a heavy stone lying close by, or with anything hard out of his pocket, knocking in his head first of all, lest he could think again, his ears, lest he heard and remembered your words, each eye, in case he could open them and recognise you, and, last of all, his teeth, in case he might eat and take strength to know you, and now, of course, his heart had stopped, and you could let his heavy arms fall back each time you lifted them; and, in the third instance, you laid the parcel down with an exaggeration of its weight and the strength it took to lower on to the ground, as though it were some heavy package left over from a house-moving, and forgotten till there was just time enough to fetch it by a short-cut before the sunset was over, for every one knows how little a newborn child weighs, and no one could expect such a light core for so bulky

a parcel. The last and final phase of work was easy,
provided the light was low enough and night was beginning: you had only to scoop a deep hole in the slag
and cram the body, or the parcel, deep into it, and then
shovel the slag over it again with not even that measure of precaution in his tidiness that the ordinary
murderer has to show when he buries his victim, in
keeping the surface level and showing no trace of the
spade, or no sign of the boards and flag-stones having
been lifted and put back again, for all this work of
smoothing was done for you by a kind and co-operative
providence working on the united labours of all the
miners at work down below in the galleries. And it
happened in this way—every three hours a toiling,
panting engine pushed along three or four trucks full
of the molten slag, till the railhead was reached, and
the engine stopped with a last creak and grind of its
brakes, and then, with a lever, tilted the trucks up on
one side so that the molten slag rattled out and slid
down over the hillside like running lava, that piled the
hill up a foot or two higher each time, while it
broadened the slopes as though reinforcing the founda-
tions to bear a greater weight of mountain above them.
This was providence working for you as though you
had even laid the rails to guide his lumbering car in
the direction you wanted, for his molten lava poured
down the slope, right over the improvised grave you
had dug—in one moment eating up all but the bones,
and working over the grave so that there was not one
sign of it showing through the new layer that was now
cooling, in order to form its part of the scorched and
fire-marked hillside. And there the bones lay like a
ghost within a kind of clouded and horrible amber,
with this difference, that when, if ever, they came up
to daylight again and were exposed, unlike the insect

of whom there is nothing left, once its amber coffin is split open, here the bones lie, so that you can pick them up and ticket them, but there is nothing to tell whether it has been an accident or a murder, or one of those strange cases where a tired and foot-sore tramp lies down on the side of such a hill as this, to profit by its shelter and by the treacherous warmth, that will break like a foaming, molten wave over him while he sleeps.

It was with just such a sudden flow as that of the red-hot slag over the sleeping tramp that the glass of the carriage window became misty with my breath, as though the clear glass, through which I had been look-ing a moment before, was a fresh open sky, into which the wind had suddenly herded his clouds as he began to blow up for a storm. As soon as one rubbed away this fog, the brick-chimneys and slag-heaps came back again and stood up clear to see in the icy air. It was just that most painful moment in the long winter agony when the ground, which has been entirely water-logged and made lifeless by the floods, is now on the point of freezing, while the waters, as they begin to evaporate, or sink perhaps a little way into the earth, leave ragged, untidy edges on the higher parts of each field as they ebb away. The ice is forming quickly, and if you stood on one of the dry parts of the field, you would not hear a sound, for the whole of the world that is out-side human interference is motionless, as though wait-ing for the death-stroke to relieve it from its pain; and that these expectations of the sharp sound of steel may not sound out of place, it is curious how the cold seems to infect one with the same fear of sharp edges and the sound of blows. One felt dread at the thought of touching the metal parts which held the racks together to carry the luggage overhead, and sorry for all men whose work lay in open air in the rasping cold. I remember particularly visiting some great carrier's warehouse in the City, where there were a score of workmen who had to stand in the raw cold of the yard and hammer out, or gouge away, the screws that held the huge wooden boxes together that had arrived that morning by sea from every part of the world. They had to fumble with their fingers along the splintered edges of each box, until they found the head of the screw that was torn half out of the wood into which it had been driven, and in this process even the strongest hands become torn a little and bleeding from the sharp, spiky splinters that always run for the nails, or the quick, as though on purpose to make the pain more intense. The jagged edges of wood, the splinters, and the icy steel instruments for sawing, hewing, and gouging out, became so many personifications of the cold.

One looked away from the luggage-rack, and from the train of thoughts that it had evoked, and turned to the window once more, that showed a thin strip of platform just beginning; in fact it seemed to run out towards one, like the first jetty, as a ship comes into harbour. Everything looked as cold as ice, and each lamp had a little frosty halo hanging round it. There were no porters. Luckily, the solitary bag I had brought was light enough to be carried easily down the platform, and out under some archways into the icy air, where two or three outside-porters plied for hire with their barrows. The hotel was a couple of hundred yards away at the back of some elaborate station-sidings which were distinguished between in the jargon of arrival and departure platforms. It was a real and true Sunday night, so wind-blown and empty were these back streets, with no noise sounding through them, except the occasional banging and flapping of a noticeboard or poster against the wall on which it hung.

A porter, with the bulk of an athletic burglar, burst out from a swing-door and seized the bag from the barrow-man with a brutal violence. He then stood with one hand ready, and as soon as one had stepped into that revolving cage, gave it a push of such force that one was whirled irresistibly into the marble hall, with that giant bulk close at one's heels within the next compartment of the door. A flight of steps, lined with palms, led up to the enquiry desk, where a leering young woman, who seemed at first suspicious of one's motives, consented after some evasion to provide one with a single bedroom. This room was long, thin, and narrow, but the fact that it looked on to a court, and was therefore away from the trams, and that it possessed a good electric light over the bed, which made reading a possibility, made one choose it in preference to other noisier, if more luxurious rooms. After some moments the bag, seeming after this separation like an old and valued friend, was restored to one, and the melancholy task began of unpacking and arranging one's few personal belongings. This was equivalent to hoisting the flag over some small and desert isle, for the sight of one's possessions gave confidence and a sense of ownership over this mercenary, one-night tenement. Turning on the hot water was another comfort to the nerves, because the way in which it started at stone-cold and then came at last, through various stages of warmness, into actual and intolerable heat, seemed like some kind of help that one could summon from a long way away, when needed, and which always arrived once one had invoked its assistance.

At last all this was finished; everything was unpacked, and even the coat and hat hung from their hook upon the door. It was Sunday night, and a chill struck into one's bones, thinking of all the miles of white-tiled passage that there must be in this hotel, with every individual brick damp and cold, as every separate inhabitant of this huge town must be. However, it was early—not yet half-past nine—and so it seemed advisable to come downstairs for a little; not using the lift, but walking down the stairs in order to get some knowledge of the building. This meant a long descent, to be undertaken at stately speed, for if one were to run down quickly, making a great deal of noise, all the porters and maids would come forward to investigate the cause of the disturbance. There was flight after flight, with this muffled carpet to tread upon, and then, when one least expected it, the whole stair took a great sweep round, changed somehow on to the grand scale, and swept with a generosity of curve that embarrassed one into the hall.

A number of small tables were edged up to the walls, and a kind providence had reserved just one that was unoccupied. This made another fortress, an advanced post, projected from, and covered by, one's bedroom; and out of the shelter of this shallow fastness one could observe the beings one was to live among for two days.

There were never more than three of them at any table, and this third person had always just come to them for a moment's talk, and would soon move away to his or her own table, to sit there till a companion arrived. It seemed, therefore, as though these couples were interchangeable; as though the evenings of two or three months would exhaust all the possibilities of change and bring the original pairs back to each other again. They were drinking whisky or lemonade, and in some instances were slowly nibbling from a plate of biscuits, so that a few of them, it would appear, had had no dinner. They were about equally divided between two races; the florid North of England, and the lizard-like Hebrew of that special variety, who seem to thrive in the lounges of hotels without any definite habitat of their own. So much for the males. As for the women, it was difficult to distinguish between them, so alike were they in dress and feature; indeed, they might be wearing each other's clothes in rotation, so equally suited would each dress have been to any one of them. This common denominator in them all I take to be, also, Semitic in its origin; for they possessed, in addition to that definite lustrous quality of eye and limb by which one may know Jewish women, that look of a pretty Italian or Spanish peasant woman, which accompanies those dominating features when they have become softened into attraction.

Only a few seconds had elapsed, and already with desperate haste the waiter was rushing towards me from his pantry. They had sighted a stranger through the glass panel in that door, and sent out the chief waiter of their group, for strangers are notoriously nervous, and may therefore be browbeaten into something "big" —perhaps a half-bottle of champagne. He was appropriately hectoring in manner and ready, at a sign, to sink his arrogance into fawning. His side-whiskers had a false look, as though the hotel manager had clipped them on as a badge of this waiter's servitude, but he had made his weakness into strength in the same way that soldiers and bull-fighters, whose lives are in the abstract more servile and abject than those of any other class of men, pose as heroes of a voluntary system, however compulsory may be their profession. I quickly explained, in accordance with my diagnosis, that I had already dined on the train, and only needed a glass of Benedictine now, and at the same time, so as to continue my offensive into the enemies' country, asked what town in Italy he came from. On his replying "Ferrara," I then displayed great historical and topographical knowledge of that city, which I had, in fact, visited twice. He was now, for the time at any rate, my slave, and so I dismissed him as though disinclined for further talk.

Every table had a circular glass top, held in place by a brass rim, each table supported a combined matchbox and ash-tray; the walls were of porous, steam-heated, sham stone; the carpets too soft and too thick; the ceiling of glass, florally divided and designed; and the whole scene peopled with a forest of palms. Every table was taken, and there was not an empty arm-chair.

So far there had been absolutely no sign of the person in search of whom I had arrived; and I felt too embarrassed to ask any questions at the desk. Since it was Sunday night, with consequently no performances at the theatre, one would have expected to find her in one of the sitting-rooms of the hotel, but no one was to be seen except these people I have described, who came in every evening from outside; a few commercial travellers making up their books, and occasional bursts of business men, who would move in batches, noisily talking, from, and then back to, the private room where they had been dining. Where she could be was a mystery, for I knew there was no other hotel or restaurant in this huge town! However, the way in which new people kept constantly appearing seemed to show that the evening was just beginning, that the amusing part of it lay ahead still, and that it was therefore worth one's while to wait and see what happened. Also, it was reassuring to have a theatrical poster before one's eyes, with that familiar name upon it, on every suitable piece of wall in these rooms; and to know that the theatre belonged to, and was only some twenty yards away from, the hotel.

Very soon the reason for these arrivals and all this waiting became apparent, for a band began playing noisily in a ballroom just off the hall. This was exactly what was needed, for these various couples sitting round kept constantly getting up to dance, and therefore the hall was half-empty most of the time, and any people there were left had their attention entirely occupied by the music. No one stared, and there was a noisy peace.

All the same, what a delightful mechanism it was for thinking! There was almost continual music, on the wings of which one could be carried to a great distance; and, the more blatant it became, the more abrupt was the journey. Now, this intrigue on which I was engaged was swiftly undertaken, and of precipitous duration, by which I mean that I was complete master of my side of the situation. I had resolved upon it, and I could enlarge its scope, or telescope its length, and cut it short at once. Also, I was entirely by myself in this absolutely strange town, which gave one, at once, a kind of martial alertness, as though death and ruin lurked at every corner. This aloof and dangerous living was the same, I hoped, as that of the people surrounding me, and of whom I had come in search. It was equivalent, therefore, to arriving in Spain and at once buying a Spanish cloak and a sombrero hat; for these very recognisable and salient details should make one uniform, and like every one else in the country which is their home; and in the same way, appearing to have no home and no ties of that nature, should make one usual and unobserved in this hotel setting. This new life was as acid and biting to me as could be any visit to such a cliché of romance as that country I have just mentioned.

Nobody knew one's identity, and nobody would

care if one was ill. These two facts, alone, seemed part
of the warrior's life; and, more typical of it still, nobody would complain of one's extravagance, provided
enough money was produced at the critical moments.
One's own character lay, then, completely submerged
under this flow of people coming and going, and this
very exhaustion of personality made it easier to appreciate the characteristics of others. I had set out to
investigate a land that was, to me, new, peculiar, and
perhaps perilous. Having read during my school-days
every book that was to be found on places of mystery
like Tibet or South America, I had now discovered
something equally baffling much nearer to hand, and
which could only be solved by experience and not by
reading. I think a dusty and damaged book called *The
Life of an Actor*, by Pierce Egan, a Regency ruffian,
with its many curious and Cruikshank-like coloured
drawings, had started my interest in these equivocal
lives.

There was the young actor, of necessity pale and
thin, learning his part and speaking it aloud in some
corner of a public garden of that day. A romantic
pool, a weeping willow, and various vases and urns
seem like the stage properties that accompany much
travelling and a low wage. It is blank verse that he is
shouting, and we may imagine its sense to be sharp and
confused, distraught and full of sighs and swords, for
as in the still-existing marionette-drama of Sicily, there
were weeping maidens to be rescued and many duels to
be fought in the historical plays of that time. The
actor's dress is careless and disordered, his hair long
and tousled, for it was with an effort of the imagination that he projected himself among those pale wraiths
of the past, and, in fact, the artist who drew these
plates seems to have realised the anachronism of his

173

subject, and how nearly extinct was this class of play. So far was this life from reality, and so difficult to live up to against the incoming steam-engine, the sooty, funnel-like top-hat, and the wavering shadow of the crinoline under the complacent halo of gaslight, that we may put Chatterton or Berlioz in the place of that struggling actor, and imagine such an authentic hero as one of these preparing that last crusade of the mind against Stock Exchange and Money Market. Both these warriors of the imagination lived the hard and comfortless life of the soldier: Chatterton, whom we conceive as the L'Aiglon of the poetic world, dying what we can only consider as a soldier's death; while Berlioz, as we know from his autobiography, wandered about for days in fields and public gardens, and for some weeks only slept on two occasions, once on a restaurant table and once on the snow, during the days of his infatuation for Miss Harriet Smithson, the Shakespearean actress.

Or it is the actor in his uncomfortable garret, in bed this time, but still learning his part. He has got right up to the top of the house, among the rafters and tiles of the roof; indeed, there are so many beams and wooden buttresses that his room might be a cabin on board ship. The window is cracked and ill-fitting, so that his one candle burns fitfully in the draught, while the roof is in such bad repair that a bucket has been put in the middle of the room to collect the dropping water. In spite of poverty having driven him to the top of the house, he has a large box or two in his room, and a suit of armour hangs from a beam and is clanking gently in the wind. Various spangled suits lie about the room or are hung upon the walls, so that we may know this emaciate youth for the impersonator of every hero from Hector to Henry V. He is in the midst of this spectral arsenal, in the very act of evoking these ghosts.

A little later he is shown putting the last touches to his appearance before a mirror, that dumb witness of so many fictitious destinies. All round, in their various cells, we must imagine the other actors and actresses just disembodied from their own personalities, as they assume some one else's cloak or plumed hat. Then they gather in that waste, windy space behind, or edge up nearer into that tight, narrow passage between the proscenium and a canvas house or tree. Here he is in the course of a love-affair, which a turn of words interrupts and calls him before the audience, where in a moment he must continue it with a fictitious force over and above his genuine fire. A few dandified young men, who have been admitted behind the scenes, edge up as close as they can to watch this simulance, for at every spare minute their drawling voices protest their own shallow love for this actress. In the contest between present advantage, with its soft words and showered gifts, and future toil, we may conceive that the actor's anxiety gave his voice a shriller tone or made his hair more disarranged from a tragic bitterness which was no longer assumed. As soon as it is all over and these young men have lounged away arm-in-arm, we know that she will soothe him and dispel his jealousy, for a perpetual sprightliness the whole time she is not completely alone is an integral part of the soubrette's career, and if the actor's resentment is justified in appearance, it would yet be most unwise for those young men to attach any meaning whatever to her complaisance towards them. That sparkling and toothed smile is hedged-in by the most rigid boundaries, for, after all, every member of the audience cannot expect to be a participant in the favours of which it seems to be the prelude. At its best this mimed affection has a known depth and consistency, like the possibilities for self-expression that lie within a huge income. That is to say, it is measurable to a certain extent in its charm or prettiness, as of some one who has an income of thousands a year, compared with that other who has one of hundreds of thousands, but here the capabilities of enjoyment are exhausted and we must expect no more of it. In other words, real self-expression lies within the grasp, not of the rich man, but of some one who has creative power, and therefore, towards this particular gratification, we must envy the actor, should he prove to be fortunate, and not that individual young man who has wealth enough to overcome her scruples.

Every one else has gone away, the audience filing slowly, as out of church, and the musicians having bowed their heads and taken that last scrambling dive under the stage, not even waiting to put away their instruments, but dragging those green-baize covers with them in their haste. Out of that precipitate silence, the last door having slammed, our pair of players can walk away together through the rain, carrying the parcel of clothes that they do not like to risk leaving at the theatre, and this added weight makes the way longer and more tiring. The damp streets are very dark, and there are no lights, except in the top storeys of houses, and then only through a parsimonious crack in the shutters. There is no noise but the wind, and that same banging and flapping of notice-board or poster upon its wall, that I noticed myself. Very soon he has left her at her lodgings, and his own road home seems yet more silent and deserted, though now there is another creaking effect of solitude in the gentle grinding and grating of some loose portion of each oil lamp, high up on its post.

After all, it must be much the same now. The same walk home, only shorter in its extent, and with those identical noises that constitute of themselves a kind of proof of the real silence. Once through that swing-door, though, and within the dominion of that giant hall-porter, the burst of noise would sound awful and tremendous. The band was playing all the latest tunes from London, in a crescendo of loudness that showed their triumph in this piece of quick acquisition of what was most fashionable in the capital. They were bellowing it with a vulgar zest, like that in which a drunken man would welcome some new friend whom he was half-frightened of, and whom he was most anxious to impress with his bonhomie, his boon-companionship. Thus one school bully might welcome another. Of course all this forest of noise made concealment easy, if you shared in its spirit. On the other hand, against that loud background any dissentient voice could be heard. But there was none. Whenever the music lowered its violence for a moment, to gather breath for a fresh burst of strength, a hundred voices could be heard shouting in the key they had reached trying to talk against its force, and all that chatter and laughter expressed pleasure and a keen participation. It was a species of rhapsodised national anthem by that veteran ragtime composer, Irving Berlin, with a touch of patriotic intoxication in the presses of its brassy coils. I was able to personify the female side of this music in the shape of that person of whom I had come here in search. Her very young appearance, for I suppose she was little more than eighteen or nineteen years old, and the consequent audacity of that young body, poised against and interpreting that terrific din, as she had to

177

do night after night, made the greater part of her beauty for me. In spite of that complete simulation and that perfect expression of her purpose, she seemed at the same time to be that one dissentient voice which I have mentioned, by its very softness, as being capable of piercing and penetrating the whole body of noise. Her dancing, for she was an extremely beautiful dancer, was a sort of dazzling lightning-play out of that thunder, and this extraordinary perfection in little things must be, in great part, pure and unconscious talent. It was no use expecting her ever to be so happy in actual life as was her simulation, and all that freezing or fiery allurement was only to be practised under this consistent glare of the footlights. For this reason, one came to the point of never hoping for any clearer realisation than that offered one here, and had one ever wished for actual life to be as full as this of deep-breathed and burning moments, drawn out of a second's flashing life by those brakes and drags upon time, which her talent imposed, one could only have expected its continuation in the same conditions and under those identical lights. It would have meant, therefore, a lifetime passed between those electric forces, with nearly continual music and that uncomfortable permanence which actual existence upon the stage of a theatre would mean—a temporary hut, perhaps, or a canvas tent to keep away the draughts, and in the midst, therefore, of all those hanging suits and finery, among which we found our actor in his garret-bedroom.

It would be one perpetual false dawn, the strength of which could hardly be kept away by even the most quilted thickness of shade, and a Kirghiz tent, with all its muffled walls of rugs and felt blankets, would not suffice to fence out that insistent sunlight. It lay about outside with the consistency of water, so that as soon as she came out, the light had in a second entirely run over and drenched her body, just as you can thrust a piece of floating wood a little way under the surface, so that its whole extent is wetted and starts to sparkle, though now it is swimming again on the water, and most of it is dry once more. In fact, this electric brilliance turned even the skin into a species of gilded armour, so even and consistent was its shining smoothness, and legs and arms seemed beautifully encased by those clinging and thrown nets. Once they had caught her in this manner, and she was thus netted, as I have described, within a fraction of a second, they never left her again. The light lay as close to her body as the blue air which you can see clinging to the soft breasts or lips of the leaves, with not one empty space where it could climb down through the boughs. These nets enmeshed and clung to her, and they never overlapped from her, or trailed their fire towards any other object.

It is precisely in that particular quality that the difference lies between light and that other less yielding medium, water. Even, for instance, where you have a deep enough pool to hold some degree of colour in its depths, it has not such a mobile and swift beauty. Water, to these purposes, has the qualities of quicksilver; it is more obstinate, that is to say, and much less obedient to command. A body swimming has neither got quite its own life of colour or the actual blue substance of the water, but is sheathed in an opalescent glimmer of its own, and this very pale and half-hearted attempt is seen in all its weakness as soon as light has an opportunity of netting and holding a head or limb that has come above the surface. It is now an unequal contest, for water cannot advance beyond its own content, whereas light can throw all its armament of darts and spears and nets, and once these have caught their

prey, nothing can defeat them, save some substantial
and sharp enemy in wall, hill, or cloud. I chose light,
then, for my ladder of interpretation in preference to
water, and though one may imagine many dramas
under that pearled foam, and the tempting of many
bearded sea-gods by terrestrial nudities, who have their
smooth limbs to show against that scaled or scalloped
fineness, I found my preference lay in light, and that
this stretched an easy and unending ladder, out of the
rungs of which one could choose a point of attack.
From this selected position, anything you so desired
could be encompassed by the snares at your disposal
and shown with such a clearness that it seemed to be
drawn nearer to you. My headquarters were, therefore, in the heart of all this glamour, at the very tree-
foot of poetry, the boughs of which I am now shaking
for their dappled shade.

This fictitious life that one lived held as many ramifications as that tree had branches. In so far as art consists in interpretation, there was no point out of all
those boughs to which we could not climb.

Each one of those little sense-centres, of which music
consists, could be exploded and their content given.
They were little, hard mechanisms, with an unconscious
meaning behind their sliding movements, and this could
be detached and crushed out from them before they
were dead. It was a world, then, of true metamorphosis, where one thing changed into another as fast
as music would allow.

Outside the theatre, as all round this hotel, there
was mile upon mile of damp street, so that the lights
in shops and public-houses seemed to be reflected in
water. Here, where I was sitting, they had turned on
every electric light available, and there was not an
empty chair in the whole hall. It was like a full house

at the theatre. At any moment she might walk past with a lover, or, and this I should have preferred, with one of the comedians of the company. In the meanwhile one could do nothing but wait, for it was still too early to go to bed, and the band bridged time.

That world of metamorphosis through which I moved, while sitting alone and unknown to any one in the hotel lounge, was by its nature more suited, perhaps, to the cinema than to the theatre, so quick and drastic were its changes. In fact they needed either no background at all, or those properly fixed and appointed sets which only films with their universal and wordless diffusion can afford. Such a static and immovable frame as one of those realistic and recognisable scenes, a London street with all its shop signs, or a scene on board ship, came very seldom and had to be worked up to, so that they had irremediable purpose. In this life of poetry, in fact, they were equivalent to the lyrics, the final and quintessential moments of that existence. They must have a held and tense duration from which nothing could be taken away, so that if you cut out one movement in the dance, or one brick of the scene, the whole life and structure would collapse and fall into ruin.

The endless reaches of time were spaced and quickened in this manner out of their dragging slowness. Of course it seemed impossible that the one person expected should appear among this plethora of peoples and through and against the flow of cliché and image, by the aid of which one was telescoping time. Yet hundreds and hundreds of times during the last two months she must have walked through this hall, and it must have lost its strangeness and become usual, unnoticeable to her mind. Also, to some one whose life is spent in hotels, and whose livelihood depends upon enticing the public to a lesser permanency than a hotel, strangeness must soon vanish, and external coldness or aloofness cannot terrify for long. Theatre-seats have to be filled, and it is no use being frightened of the audience.

Then, suddenly it came about, just as one had expected and just as it had never seemed possible; she came from the top of the hall steps and walked quickly past, looking like almost any one else, and in the middle of a group of men whom one had no time to examine. She never looked my way, and was absolutely unaware that I was near. In a moment she was a long way in front, out of sight, and making most obviously for a lift, for in a few seconds the group that had been with her came into sight again, moving down diagonally to a far end of the hall where I could scarcely see them.

It all happened just as quietly and purposely as that. It was inevitable, like a war one has expected and cannot believe in, once it has started.

So all this waiting was over now, and time broke out of its measures. The numbered and unnoticed details of the room came into focus and were registered by the eyes. Before this, one had not dared to examine them for fear that their unimportance would drag out and intensify the moments. Now they burned like hot irons into the senses. The knotted ends of every instant of time struck one with searing, intolerable sadness.

Music fell out of the sky like lead, and its very weight made it meaningless. The other people in the room were as remote as a world of insects, but they had neither the communism nor the deadly hostility that makes one interested in insects. People were implacably polite, dangerously civil, and all the small idiotic jokes that were being gently exploded at table

182

after table were so many sharp stones in so many snow-balls. Words seemed a fanciful and ornate invention to hide such blunt meanings. Anyway words, and that other convention, manners—the brackets upon which conversation is supported—make a mean level, a common denominator, which reduces the strong and fortifies the weak.

These two alternatives, the strong and the weak, like those two social systems, the predatory and the communistic among insects, took on a spectacular importance that interposed between oneself and one's unhappiness. All these people became interesting again. Their background, the homeless permanence of the hotel, their own migration in and out through the rain, the insistent, false hilarity of the music, the conductor, so proud of his latest tunes from London, the waiters who were as much a colony from Italy as if they had settled on the shores of Hudson's Bay, all these components gave glamour and fascination. The heroes out of that cushioned world appeared armed with grossness and with a more oriental nose, or a more silver cigarette-case as their prerogative of victory. Softness and surrender were their objects, so that apparently the most dangerous were choosing the safest for their victims; on the other hand, the most yielding must think themselves flattered by the most insistent. Of course this mimic warfare had its own trumpets and alarms, and these were supplied by the band—as insistent as ever, now that one noticed it again.

All its false and momentary glamours came back once more, and each tune was a new language learned in its own abrupt or sliding intervals. There was nothing more to wait for. The peopling of all those different worlds had been a pastime while one lived the long moments down; now they were superfluous and wasted.

Where the stairs turned, the music became loud and mocking, muffled by those shining, white walls, and loud once more at a balcony in the landing. The passages led out like endless tunnels, and there was no relief from them. There was that terrible sameness, that identity of all details, with no wider space to stop in, and no end in sight. The turning of the key in the door opened out that dark hidden corner one had longed for; and the light, which sprang into life, was a steep, impenetrable wall that one could hide behind. Darkness, that one could produce by so simple an act out of the light, was a still safer refuge, but it seemed in a curious way to have crept up closer to danger, to be but a paper's breadth, thinner even than the wall's depth, from the armoured and shining hostility of hall and passage.

III

The Comedians at Luncheon

THE door was knocked upon, beaten almost, with a heavy thumping hand. The room poured into my eyes and the brass, unfamiliar bedstead broke into memory and made it move. I turned on the light and it was as pale and brassy as the bedstead.

A drizzling, sighing sound, blown to and fro in little pattering gusts, could be heard above the usual matutinal sounds of sweeping and hurrying, and as soon as I had drawn the curtain, I saw the damp court below, with the white, moist porcelain of its brick walls. There had been so much noise down beneath, all through the night, with people arriving and their luggage being banged about, that it had been very difficult to sleep, and I had determined to make them change my room. For this reason I wanted to get downstairs early so that I could make my request before all the rooms for the day were booked.

Everything had to be carried far down the passage, and this held in itself those contrasts of light and darkness that seem to shorten a journey. In places the corridor moved through utter darkness—where, that is to say, they had not made use of the electric light, while in corners where it burned, it did so with a coarse, diluted strength, that reminded one, somehow, of a cup of strong Indian tea—at other moments it was lit by windows that gave a fine view of the drenched court below. There was one particular point where it moved out from one projection in the courtyard to another,

185

and just before this, you could see through a window
that you were about to embark on one of a series of
bridges that lay above each other, and halved the circuit of the courtyard. There were windows on each
side of this bridge, and every time it was crossed, one
felt a few more minutes of the morning had been lived
through.

Down below lay the court, and it was difficult, looking on that wet, slippery gloom, to realise that it was
the roof of the Palm Court. This luxurious glass
lounge glittered with a false sunlight that shone upon
the baskets of flowers suspended from the ceiling, and
upon a whole forest of real palm trees that stood at
every corner the screens or sofas could contrive. From
this bridge it looked like the very dregs, the last
brackish mud in an old disused well.

After a number of these journeys, when everything
had been successfully carried from one room to the
other, I could examine the new refuge to which I had
fled. It had one window, and this looked out, not
upon the courtyard, but away from the station and on
to that blank space between the hotel and the first
houses of the town. There was a road, two or three
hundred yards in length, that was built over arches
and led at a gentle slope from the town to the station,
while both sides of this bridge were lined with hoardings. Their strident, querulous proclaim was like the
crowd of porters that swarm round you on arriving in a
foreign country. The posters had come as near to you
as they could, and were shouting out their wares in
chorus. But on the near side of that double line of
advertisements, and down below my window, was a
great blank space stretching away the length of the
arches, down to where the houses began, and this was
the scene of a permanent fair, which was always in

progress; indeed, I remembered looking down on it from the road even as a child. The steam-organs were continually grinding out their tunes, and there was an absolutely indescribable power of emotion to be gathered from that enclosed space. The hotel rose up in a blank, dark red mass, with tier after tier of windows, among which mine was simply a unit.

At this time of the morning there was not much going on down below. The fair did not open till the afternoon, and so some of the booths and the smaller roundabouts were still shrouded in their night-clothes —great sheets of mackintosh. Now and again some one would come down the steps of a caravan, now and again the flap of a tent would be lifted and some one would stoop and come out, but it was the sign of their morning inactivity that these two men, instead of being busily at work, would go deliberately towards each other and spend a long time in talk, the thin echoes of which were just audible at my window, though about as indistinct as the posters on the hoardings were difficult to read.

Many moments could be passed in this way at the window, but then a gnawing sense of uncertainty about what could be going on below sent one downstairs into the hall, and on an excursion into all the sitting-rooms. The tables were covered with papers, but they were motoring or financial magazines, with one or two curious and unheard-of Colonial gazettes, to none of which was it possible to devote more than a few seconds, while the absolute similarity of every chair in the room made it hopeless to sit down and try to gather one's thoughts, since identity was entirely submerged by that multiform likeness of leather back, leather arms, and wooden turned legs.

I was driven up into my room once more and con-

strained by the dampness of the window-sill, which
made it difficult to stay there long, to read once again
all the evening papers that I had brought with me in
the train. But in order not to achieve this too quickly,
I gave myself long intervals, in which I lay back in my
chair. It was now twelve o'clock, I discovered with a
shock, when the long moments had reduced me to that
act of surrender—looking at one's watch: it was twelve
o'clock, time to go down and wait events in the hall.
So I washed my hands, and in order to waste a few
more moments, let the water run in and out of the
basin more than once.

Downstairs it was just the same as before, and
despite the electric lights that burned everywhere, trying to get an answering glitter from each speck of
paint and every pane of glass or mirror, the hall was
so empty, there were so few people talking, that you
could hear the constant tread of the rain on that glass
roof above, a presage of time, or fate, which was surely
not intended by the management. It was beating in a
perpetual undertone beneath that built-up, terraced
comfort—it was there all the time, and not to be
ignored for ever.

Every few moments some one came in through the
hall and shook out his umbrella, or took off a dripping,
guttering hat and held it away from him. Everything
seemed mist-bound, rain-bound, and grey in colour
and substance. There was nothing but business and
commerce, commerce and business, and the very
thought of a painter or a musician was as bold a premise
upon facts as it would be to walk round a crowded
restaurant at the luncheon hour and beg subscriptions
for a statue to some poet, who, because he was not
Kipling, would be considered by the eaters never to
have existed. Meanwhile, the feasible moment for

such an adventure drew near, people began arriving in parties of two or three out of rich motors, and very soon there would be enough of them at lunch to be canvassed, had one possessed the courage.

This continual waiting seemed even more trying to the nerves when it had to be undertaken among a crowd of people than when the hotel was empty. All the new arrivals rushed into the restaurant as fast as their legs could carry them, so that the same people were never before one's eyes for more than a moment. Very soon I felt in disgrace, as though left outside in the corner, and forbidden to eat anything, for every one else who appeared in sight even for a second made that precipitous dash through the door and towards his or her table.

It was noon, the middle of the day, the positive water-shed of light, and from that steep slope it becomes transmuted into a broad-leaved faunal stillness and is diminished in gradual degrees, down to the drizzling and grey drabness of this empty North. Here they had not even an anticipation of its reality and were content with their false and perpetual summer. It was a stage-daylight of the senses, with every emotion changed and spirited away, just as music can alter them in a theatre, such being at least the intention, if not the effect, for it was as difficult to free oneself of a climatic depression as it is to be on a steamer and forget for many moments together that you are at sea. But once constrained to accept excuses, one had to admit that this substituted sunlight possessed its own scales and ranges of effect. It might rain as hard as it liked outside, but those hundreds of footfalls upon the glass roof made no difference to this perpetual summer within. Light was radiated forth in every direction without so much as a suspicion of shade to its violent brightness. This hard, diurnal permanence either flattered or exposed its victims; that is to say, it allowed no average but was insistent and bent on exaggeration, giving an accented form to every particularity it could notice.

A small table by a pillar that one could lean against seemed safe and comfortable in this bright bareness. It was better to have one's back against that hollow tubular falseness, for in the usual restaurant manner this pillar just stood there and did not support any weight, the steel girders being strong enough not to need this pretentious assistance; it was wise to have one's back against some kind of wall, however thin or feeble its protection. There was a little serving-table near by, like the traditional shield to one's left arm. Several waiters with a deeper degree of sartorial majesty were moving round from table to table, while, like doctors, they appeared to write out prescriptions and give orders to their subordinates about the care of these invalids, to whose number I had now attached myself. Needless to say that there was a large unoccupied table just on my right-hand side of an obvious import towards my day's happiness. Some time was to elapse before this emptiness became filled: meanwhile, old familiar faces that had impressed themselves on memory the night before in the lounge were disposed appropriately at every other table save this. In the shuddering white glare of electricity these various heads seemed golden or sallow if male, and dusted with a fine flour if female; but the insistent and dangerous red of a man's face near by who stared burningly into every other new face that appeared gave a kind of near focus to one's thoughts that might have strayed far away at the end of the room. One might hide behind that red and impertinent curiosity when this party that one had been waiting for came into the room and towards their table. In fact that red face completed my defences and left a clear field for investigation; it was a decoy of whose services I might avail myself, however unwittingly they were placed at my disposal. These different opportunities and advantages were a sheaf of arrows that I could fire out one after another towards my object, and I must use these little near-by tables, the moving screens made by the subordinate waiters with their white aprons, and the red face of my neighbour as so many auxiliaries to the campaign.

Here they were! and an incredible heaviness and lightness throbbed in the air. My sufferings were too intense to be borne, and I could have burst into a flood of tears, or been carried from the room in what would have been, I suppose, a pseudo-faint. Everything crumbled; all those little clichés on which one had survived so far were pricked and gone out. One existed on these pathetic and forlorn exceptions as though they constituted a kind of synthetic sandwich on which life could be supported, but now they were stale and useless; they were all shown up as shams. Poems, even the shortest and most lovely things one could imagine or remember, became old-fashioned and such a long way outside life that they were no part of it. They had about as much resemblance to being alive as the figures on a Greek vase have to a bicycle race, and one felt after this breaking-up of illusions as though the bicycle race meant more to one. The same with music—it simply went out like the flame of a candle, and even such tunes as those of Mozart became like clumsily built cardboard boxes, easily smashed and with nothing inside them. Nothing of all these had any importance or any more life than that of a dead leaf; they were no sooner thought of than spoilt for ever.

The whole aim of being alive became altered; one wished to work at it from a different end and narrow down every endeavour to the mere recording of one second of life. As long as one could give this single second some kind of permanence, there was nothing more with which ambition need play. All those fantastic and elaborate parallels which the imagination can build were now to be scrapped and thrown aside, being the easier destroyed because of the daring tenuity of their structure. Everything must be sharpened down to this one realistic plane, and all superstructures vanished or were erased as you would take the plume from your hat under an enemy's fire, or squeeze down the coloured handkerchief in your pocket. The poetical paraphernalia with which one had travelled up till now, taking it about with one much as a bag which can be unpacked in a strange hotel and will immediately surround you with the familiar accessories of home, all this vicarious baggage vanished at the sign of danger. There was nothing of it left.

Under this appalling inquisition of the nerves all previous escapes from reality were cut off and proved to lead nowhere. They were simply so much superfœtation of the senses, the fermentation of an idle hour spent in dwelling upon some subject beyond the poet's reach. The river Po, which Roberto Greene turned into the very stream of music, ran sluggish and muddy between its dyked banks. Only a day or two before it would have seemed a very different region, but now I had been driven and hurried out of this Paradise. His poetry, or that of Nashe and Marlowe, has always appealed more to me than the work of Keats or Shelley, because it is less occupied with spiritual recipes for remaining unhappy and misunderstood. The bold premises of these former men were

uttered without the hope of contradiction, and with a
surer eye and ear for beauty.

Listen to this madrigal by Roberto Greene, and I
will undertake not to quote poetry again in these pages:

"The swans, whose pens as white as ivory,
  eclipsing fair Endymion's silver love,
  floating like snow down by the banks of Po,
  ne'er tuned their notes, like Leda once forlorn,
  with more despairing sorts of madrigals,
  than I, whom wanton Love hath with his gad
  pricked to the Court of deep and restless thoughts."

This carries you, in the span of a tiny instant, to the
absolute fountain of poetry, and it is not necessary towards that objective to quote the madrigal in its
entirety; in fact, that these few lines from it should
have such a power of evocation, that they should survive without its being necessary to quote the closing
lines, is, perhaps, an evidence against their perfection.
They are not positively the last words, but almost the
first few syllables in the paradisiacal language of
poetry; but whatever may be their degree of merit,
they are unmistakably in the right dialect.

The river was gliding in a slow measure past those
low banks. The swans were drifting down the current
a little behind its force, for the water floated faster
than they did; but as the stream overtook one after
another of their snowy shapes, it passed them by like
the future, which is always drifting through the present
while it leaves the past to dwindle behind it as these
identical swans upon the river. It was this kind of air
that I had wanted, up till now, to breathe, and I had
longed to live upon the surface of such a sharp and
gelid current as this.

The banks must be, at this point, an unpeopled solitude without even a shepherd hearkening to the water-music. There was this peculiarity about life, that the very surface upon which one moved was itself moving visibly towards one definite direction, and this fact gave an excuse and a poignancy to one's own living. Sometimes a satyr, the presumed offspring of a shepherd and his flock, taking advantage of the ingenuity and the gymnastic power of both races, would contrive to reach down the banks to the water-face and to drink from his cupped hands. There was, then, that bearded, horned reflection, and at the same time, as an emblem of the bucolic deities, the horned halfmoon dipped itself deeply into the echoes and, although it was still broad daylight, shone right out of the middle of that answered sky. All the time the sun had a strong and violent life, so that any water dropping back from the hands or falling from a dipped leaf was turned to amber before it fell back into that continual gliding music. The absence of any shadows made all things seem hard, flat, and brilliant, so that the hills were like glass screens or slides over whose tops you could see the sky cut out and jagged by their edges but perfectly even in its colour up to the very point of contact with those abrupt blades. One or two shepherds, whose nakedness and young build made them into little machines beside their sheep or goats, were singing by a few sticks of fire, or were curved up inert and asleep.

A few more miles and the river had run out on to a shoal of sandy flats, long beaches parallel with the horizon, land-locked lagoons, and a hundred parted strands of the stream. It was as flat as an exercise-ground and wonderfully disposed for feats of the imagination. You could gallop down the horizon and almost take your quarry prisoner, while the long sanded bars were laid as if for an aeroplane to straddle the air from their terraces. It was like the Champ de Mars outside some unbelievably portentous Imperial capital, and against this agreeable greenhouse heat one must set the violent whips and fangs of winter and the locked, icy silence of the frost. But now the cruel rods had been taken out of their fleeced sheaths and the clouds lay still at anchor without a suggestion of their potential speed or of the force they could throw into their lines of rain.

At this river's mouth we were as far removed as could be from reality, or at least from its material application to life. Any voice that sounded from boat or sandbank would be carried out to us in a curving flight like that of a sea-bird; the sky was like pounded glass and glittered over its whole surface with that bright sharpness that you see in the leaves of a laurel or myrtle bush under the sun. This sparkle, as of sword and trumpet, had an universal diffusion over everything, so that the water was flat and hard and falling from one: it was so full of long reflections that you could not see down into it, and it seemed, therefore, to slope away from the sides of a boat as though this was at the apex of some tented ridge; it went quicker and quicker away from one to every side in anxiety to keep its reflections unruffled.

All the machinery of poetry, therefore, lay round one like the pens and ink on a writing-table. The water, so intent on its echoes, showed a determination not to be truthful in its revelations. Everything could be anywhere, or anywhere be everything. Whole woods of myrtle, whole groves of orange trees grew up as quick and abundant as the solitary mango that an Indian conjuror can force up in a few seconds. There were also gas-lit streets looked out on to by leaded

Baudelairean windows and peopled with those gar-
tered and white-stockinged beauties that the fancy can
collect from a hundred dim streets and place here under their hearse-like crinolines and with the coiled and
ringleted hair of that day. At other windows leaves
are leaning in like a delicate music played from the
dancing and chequered shade of sun and leaf, both of
them at a game of perpetual chess for their advantage
and both of them limited to some extent, as by the rules
of a game, as to the possible conquests that they can
make. The leaves, those fickle and volatile pawns
upon this chessboard, are continually crossing from one
camp to the other as they move from shadow into light
or tap against their own reflections in a pool of glass.
Lutes are rattling like young blades of grass, and about
everything there is a youngness and tenderness that
worry will soon lay siege to. Poetry, which here in its
primal condition has the force and tone of music, is
being declaimed with as much effect as a band of music
could make breathing suddenly out of the shadows, and
every group of trees is a grove sacred to some inspiration that is conjured up into life as easily as the blue
panes of air between the boughs which one can only
measure with the eyes by focussing upon the leaves that
border those unfathomable deeps. It is an improvisa-
tion that will flow into the most arbitrary of shapes,
dictating its own form as it continues, and achieving in
this manner a perfect freedom of expression.

Out at sea beyond the first salt-marshes there is
something perfectly unbelievable in the way of cities,
and we may regard those palace-quays as the mooring-
point of poetry, a destination beyond which there is no
reason to progress. You may lie at anchor with the
two elements of air and water between your ship and
the domes or towers that rise twice higher than your

masts, while there is no stretch or span of sail that can ever compare for whiteness or potential speed with the clouds that spread themselves at a breath of wind behind the marble masts and snowy rigging of this floating town. Even the elements of dress take on a transcendentalised air worthy of the occasion: the bridges, themselves like a high instep in the pride of their tall arches, are crossed by the red-haired women of the town who wear tall pattens, an adaptation of the noisy clogs of the sailors, and one well calculated to enhance the generous curves of their beauty; later on, if we can afford to annihilate the flow of time, a hovering appearance, as of beings half in air and half in water and without the help of trees as intermediaries between these elements, will be attained to, and the masks and dominoes of such disguise give a sardonic, but ethereal, pointedness to these various attributes; finally, there are at all times a host of Turks and Orientals in the turbans and silken robes of the bulbous East. A set of comedy characters who between them had the whole world to select from are playing in the squares, or on an anchored and brightly lit barge, a kind of mock harvest-wagon, at the start of the lagoons.

These little termini of the mimetic arts, these little rafts and barges at the extreme edge of familiar Europe, were drawn quickly back again into their boathouses or into the dark backwaters in which they were kept; they were hurriedly withdrawn like an unpopular piece at a theatre after one night's run, and in their stead the play was put on of which I was, myself, such a close witness, so near, indeed, as to be caught up in those bright toils which were fluttering out over the vulgar music like so many streamers of which one could catch hold, or, as I preferred to think of them, they were like the ropes you might throw from a ship to a drowning man. It was a rigging along the reaches of which one quickly climbed back into reality—into, in this case, a dining-room of common experience. The whole of the past had lain there to muffle and clog one's footsteps like the damp leaf-mould that lies heavily under the trees, but now it had been stamped down into a solid footpath that lasted a little way in front of one and promised a little safety. At the end of this track I found myself back again among the tablecloths, enmeshed, indeed, as though their folds were those of a winding-sheet, and yet at the same time fortified by their complexity and quiet enough in the senses to take note of what was going on round me.

The first thing I heard was that slight rain on the glass cupola not far above my head, like a perpetual tremolo in preparation for some new thematic development, and it entered into the whole atmosphere that I was breathing, it lay underneath it, so that this continual beat of rain became like the level rattlings, the planed hammerings, of the gipsy instrument that Liszt embodied into his Hungarian music. It was hinting continually at a climax, but these crises were more often resolved by modulations into another premonitory softness. This accompaniment to one's own nervous irresolution was a comfort when one noticed it, but no sooner had one of these gusts of loudness died away than one was away again towards a self-engendered climax and the beating of the rain passed unnoticed till this had in its turn subsided into nothingness. Time passed quickly, thrown in this manner between these two shuttles of consciousness, the being acutely aware, first of the agitation within oneself, and, a moment later, of that ceaseless external prelude to some sharp comedy of the nerves.

No extravagance of effort could now alter time out

of its new appointed measures; one could not get those long moments of waiting back again any more than retard the paper-thin present that tears so soon as it is breathed upon. Between these two torn edges one was left floundering as though in the black water between two sharp ice-floes, and it was a struggle in which nothing stood by to help. It was a perpetual pseudo-death by drowning, and every extreme of nervous horror lay rattling to the hand. Locked to each of these little centres of tension lay its equivalent in pleasure, so that the shifting of balance from one to the other was a matter of small degrees and quick accomplishment. First one and then another of these transmutations would be moved and perfected, although the return was as easily accomplished to the sharp, or dull, horror of before. Such a degree of nervous receptivity had been led up to bravely by the music and the yet louder silence of all this waiting, and the whole accumulation was there to be dissipated or charged with an even greater strength. This play of emotions may be best described as a crumbling glissando, a small sliding avalanche of nervous explosions, blowing one after the other into the fulness of their sudden strength and as rapidly dead and yielding place to the next. But out of the heart of all this confusion the eyes had still power to see their surroundings, and their more than camera-like perfection of machinery took in and registered every detail of environment. They were reigning in a quiet peace above that incessant subterranean turmoil, untroubled, even, by the dinning music. It was in their power to stifle down the storm of nerves and hush the drums and trumpets that preceded this military march of Time, so that out of the average of these confusions some true value of their reality might be deduced.

The actors were eating here before the eyes and seen
for the first time out of the pale fires of that element
in which they appeared to live, for they had seemed,
till now, to be in as great a dependence upon the regions of artificial light as are fishes upon their lakes
and seas, or birds upon the unencumbered air. They
seemed to live easily in this ordinary world, but with
an altogether slowed-down and diminished vigour, a
little staccato, even, in its movements, and a little reminiscent of the agonisings of a slow film moving only
just above the surface of a fixed and cataleptic calm.
Even so they were quick compared with the other people in the room and only slow in the comparison of
their present scale of speed with their action in the
liquid and fierce-lit regions of electricity.

After all, there were only four of them, not a
necessarily invincible battle-company, and three of
these possessing, so far as I was concerned, only the
reflected glamour of association and but this thin echo
of their original. They were at any rate the associates
of her own world, the other actors in her company,
and, as such, were free of some of the more bitter
trammels of jealousy that they might have incurred.
A great part of any quality that was theirs lay in their
awfulness, in the appalling quickness with which they
could open a cigarette-case and strike a match, and in
a kind of general smart snappiness of finish. They
looked a little at bay, too, towards the larger world outside them, but naturally no stare or attention could
unnerve them. A "light luncheon" was their meal, as
though always prepared to rise to their cues and enter
into the false summer of a matinée. How I longed
to join them at this dawning of a long hot afternoon,
engendered without a morning or a midday and passed
in the fictitious groves and pavilions of comedy!

Two of the four I did not know even by sight, but they belonged most obviously to the theatre, while the third man was her dancing partner, an unpleasant young man who appeared capriciously in the white flannels of a mock undergraduate or with blacked face, through which mask he perhaps saw himself approached nearer to ragtime, the throne of harmony and wealth. All three of them were on terms of equal friendship with her, though one hoped that the familiarity of such constant company must have barred out affection and kept simply to the laws of convenience. Having been longer in the hotel than anyone else and belonging, roughly speaking, as did the waiters, to the vagrant or migratory tribes of men, they were treated by the head waiter and his subordinates with an easy familiarity and a sympathetic degree of exertion to their needs, while they were also, there being only this one good theatre in the town, famous throughout the town, however transient their stay. They knew the Christian names of the waiters and were greeted in return by their own personal letters of identity, while the loudness of their voices made every one look at them. Also, one had only to read the local morning paper—it was a Monday—to see the description of her kicking off at a local football match on the Saturday afternoon, this being her contribution to charity as well as a sop for still greater popularity with the football crowd. This frail and feminine entrance into that fierce arena sounded as daring as though she had ventured, unarmed, in front of the toreadors and against the bull, that animal being transposed and multiplied in this instance into the roaring crowd that greeted her appearance. This was a far greater audience than any she had ever faced in a theatre, though its very size seemed to make it pliable, so that emotions ran through it with an incredible speed like a tongue of fire through paper. It was so large as to be quite beyond control, and the eddies of applause went rumbling on, one might imagine, like distant thunder, its voices never dying all in unison, but continuing from some far-off quarter of the field as though under a favourable wind to carry their echoes. I could picture all this clearly to myself and see the thousands of North-countrymen in their cloth caps, while if it was not actually raining one might be certain that the factory smoke lay anchored a little way above the roofs, as substantial as an iceberg.

Then there was the hotel to go back to, standing out brightly lit through the cold fog, with that damp courtyard above the winter-garden hidden behind its high cubical walls loopholed with these many windows; and there was the theatre, that perennial summer annexe for summer emotions and summer discontents; these two artificial and pathetic Paradises making up the whole of her life and constituting all that wealth or ambition could hope for out of the dreary winter wilderness where, besides these, only drink and prostitution walked the land, and indeed these two factors of gaiety may be said to have already marked down for their share at least half of the splendours of the hotel and theatre. In fact, they had set their foot so very firmly upon these two thresholds that hotel and theatre stand in the public estimation as the two safe harbours of prostitution, while, as for drink, hotel and theatre are at any rate safer resorts for the drunkard than his own home.

At that table in the dining-room of the hotel I now saw what, before, had seemed to me divinely inspired and animated statues come down, and standing in the shadow of their own pedestals with a harmless life bor-

202

dering on bathos after what I had expected of them. In this ordinary life—if any life is ordinary?—they were even at a disadvantage, thrown out of focus, perhaps, by the violence of their bad jokes or by the bathos of a continually repeated and ever-simulated love-story. They had fallen for once into their own emotions and found these even flatter and more plangent than the ones they mimed. At the same time they must be noisy and blatant to show their profession, and this they could not help. Soon they would finish their lunch and go off again to that gala oasis of the senses.

They had been eating a "mixed grill," a hurried— and can it be American?—excuse for plenty. This they followed up at once with coffee, spending that short interval among coils of cigarette smoke and with much striking and blowing out of matches. Still smoking, and having hardly given herself time to finish her coffee, she picked up her bag and walked with quick and birdlike steps out of the room into the hall outside. The three men followed her slowly, not so hurried, and delaying on the way for another joke or two.

This was all there was of it for the afternoon, and it had passed so quickly as to appear never to have happened. A moment later they were going down the long tiled passage from the hotel to the theatre, which was just across the road. They would be among the earliest members of the audience by the box-office and would then go through various dingy double-doors into the more secret recesses of the theatre, while winter changed into summer with the practising lights.

IV

The Winter Walk

BY the time I was on the stairs again on the way up to my room, for this method of getting there wasted more time on a wet day, the overture must have started bridging that little gulf of darkness between lowered lights and lighted curtain. It seemed to be dying down my corridor, so that by the time I reached my own door I had almost forgotten its lingering breath in the colder air from my open window. Even my own room seemed a desecrated tomb, cold and damp as are all vaults, and damper and colder from the opening that had been made. The cold water that I felt in the mood for ran from the tap not so much like falling water as like a solid, aching iron bar, and the strength of its smooth straightness was painful to the fingers and seemed to bruise their very bones. Then I arranged my shoes in a line and tidied the few things in the drawer, feeling my overcoat, meanwhile, to make sure it was not still damp from yesterday.

This was the early afternoon that should come just after the midday solstice of pulsing, ghostless heat. Indeed this hour was itself just as free from shades, for nothing save the aid of that trained dog electricity, barking so easily the moment it is alarmed, can produce any semblance of a shadow on wall or ceiling. Midday, that fine hour of normality, draws out all the shades to its own length, till, thinking of ghosts in regard to their origins, we may say that none of these

204

thin, flat statues is taller than its model. Against the myrtles that glitter like the sword and trumpet of war the warrior and his ghost show like the dark echoes of each other's steel. The lovers are no taller than those shallow beds they once made for themselves in the leaves with sharp green boughs for their bed-curtains; the mirror, that cave of echo, fills again with its own wind; the window hears those words again that the diamond, hard point of light for the millions of its brother raindrops, once carved there to lie across the sundrift or the fog of winter.

Here, I had to trust the electric light to run shadows for me across wall or ceiling; indeed at this very moment I write it follows me, dogging my right hand as I move the pen and lying still, pretending death, where my head and shoulders lean out across the page. In that cold hotel bedroom it would have done the same, had I allowed it, but I had no time, then, to play with other than my own ghosts, and these were most easily raised to music.

That winter afternoon, so like a sheet of green, dirty glass, could be broken this way into a thousand rainbow splinters gleaming with their sharp edges and refracted lights. Like fragments of glass, too, one must be careful in picking them up.

Ragtime tunes made the best vehicle imaginable for this kind of exploration. They are very primitive in their method, and, as do certain primitive dishes, they owe their quality to their want of refinement. A tune of this creation is like meat cooked on a skewer with the same sharp point running through the various clichés of seduction and being seduced. They reach, therefore, the complete end of these adventures with an extraordinary speed of attack and with but little doubt as to their precise degree of meaning. Such violent attacks down through the flesh into the heart must possess some of the primæval boldness of the matador matched against his bull, and where you would find the thin hips and the pointed cruel chin of these low-bred, or gipsy, Spaniards, here there is the Slav Jew who has fixed his claws into everything that has most marrow out of the big bones of Negro sentiment. In very fact the two best exponents of this noisy craft have been Russian Jews settled in America as children and who grew up in that busy, hard environment. Trained in the school of necessity, they have learnt to carve—I use the word in its surgical sense—with an adroit and wonderful speed; they separate flesh from bones in a second and can reach the sentiment, or flatter the senses, quicker than their more classical contemporaries.

That strong flavour, then, brought one back quickly into the alcoves to which these emotions play, and the short, vicarious journey was over and finished. Yes! it was the early afternoon, the very start of another desert of time. I went all through the chest of drawers again, counting the collars and handkerchiefs, and, even, to spend the moments, inventing a subtle game with my two ties, numbering first one and then the other as first or last in my count. But now with dreadful pathos it was borne in upon me that my Monday, this one great and free day of my life, was already half over, half-eaten by death, and that I had only its extremities left for my comfort. I had let that half of it slip by far too quickly: now I must waste no more of it, and spend the next hour or two in preparing to draw out the evening to eternal and spaceless limits.

My window-sill and a few patches of curtain were covered, I found, with what looked like a spilt egg upon a breakfast plate: it was the winter sun. So I opened the window as wide as possible, took my coat and hat, and went downstairs for a walk. On getting out of that swing-door into the open it was difficult to find from what quarter of the sky the sun was shining; it was so low in the heavens and the hotel behind me was so high. However, after going a little further, I could see it down at the end of a long straight street, not so very far above the houses: disposed there, so domestic was it in this nearness to human habitations, in its accessibility, even, like a workman's brazier when the road is taken up and they have to heat their tools or warm their hands; while, if this was the sun, that canvas hut which is always pitched near to the brazier must contain a cold and surly Almighty ungracefully minding this fire, and watching over the machinery of life that he has started and dare not stop. Let him keep it all going a little longer, I thought, so as to give me the whole of this evening I had won for myself!

And I started walking away from the hotel towards this refulgence.

There were none of the good shops along this road and I was glad to find that it led me into the poorer parts of the town. I walked along quickly, and, as though this had drawn me appreciably nearer to the heat, I felt warm from the exertion, although the sun kept just as far away as ever over the low roofs. I had to go through a great arch under the main line of the railway, going down and then up a little slope to accomplish this, for I found the street I had seen from the hotel door went steadily at a gentle pace uphill, and now I was far enough from the railway-line for these hammerings and hootings to die away, and for it to be possible to follow one's own thoughts, or take accurate note of the surroundings.

The sunlight as I went further became more yellow

and more exaggerated in its winter strangeness, and obviously the evening for which I had been longing could not be more than an hour or so ahead of me.

There was public-house after public-house; each in its own parish of slums. They were as important to their locality as are the churches in Catholic countries, where no one whom you ask will know the name of a church out of his or her immediate district, and the cathedral, as here it might be the chief drinking-bar in the town, is unknown and unheard-of among the parishioners. The public-houses offered the cheaper and more immediate Paradise, and so one cannot wonder at their being the only landmarks in these big Northern towns.

The gutters were choked with the rubbish from cheap sweets or fruit and were the chosen playground for dozens of small flaxen-haired children. They were all shouting out the same clatter of dispute as I passed them by and walked past the opening of street upon street of coffin-like houses, the front of each house having a door, as it might be a mouth, and windows arranged like the nose and eyes to this staring, senseless face. There must be some half-dozen of these children to each brick tomb, and I could in my mind see them pouring out at pale, twittering sunrise and playing first of all upon the doorstep and then on the drab threshold of the room as night turned cold and stern. These children had, for the most part, the long Danish skulls and the groundsel or bird-seed hair that I noticed in an early part of this book when describing the miners' families in Derbyshire who were looking for blackberries in the September hedges. The cheapness of their toys made them more pathetic than it is possible to imagine.

Noisy, clanking trams began here, their cable being

carried on a generous tangent and at a rakish angle to the final standard-post with some of the gesture to which we are treated with the last notes of a piano piece; and the road led along the side of a public park, or general refuse-ground for waste-paper, orange-peel, and old cigarette-boxes. I walked faster and faster; one always does if alone, and more especially when one's thoughts are interrupted, as were mine, by constant noise. I could see signs, on the faces of the passers-by, of a joke that I, myself, shared consciously with them; this being nothing less than my rather peculiar appearance in these mean streets shambling quickly along, very tall, and wearing an immensely long blue great-coat. No strangers, save commercial travellers, ever appear there, and so I must have struck them at as fresh and clear an angle as I possessed towards their unfamiliar world of fried-fish shops and football, or police papers.

There was a romantic tension in the cold afternoon air, and I was in a state of subdued excitement that it is painful to remember, holding in my nerves as if they were a team of galloping horses and at the same time feeling suffused with a strong and vital poetry that was quite out of my experience. I was softly singing one tune after another, and each of these called up an almost intolerably perfect atmosphere; everything, all the common things of life, walking, eating, sleeping, talking, moved in the idyllic measures of natural and true comedy: young, and never growing old, and at the same time living in a pretence which gives biting and painful beauty to every situation. In fact each one of these beauties burned and throbbed like an abscess that must be lanced, a simile which has, perhaps, psychological importance to these circumstances. I was already tired, before I knew about their workings, of those perfections which require weeks of preparation before they can live—fine writing, or skilfully played music—and here, with acting, there was something possessed of every artifice but apparently spontaneous, for it was difficult to believe that any one not twenty years old could have a technique born of years of practice.

So my thoughts were peopled and the waste spaces of the mind gave birth. These phantasies were born, and died, in fractions of time, living no longer than the distorted faces you can see in a nightmare.

The flowered verandahs of musical comedy were strung with beauties like apples on a bough, and their limbs, dimly seen between those brambles of "Dorothy Perkins" roses, had all the slenderness and the dewy freshness of branches and of young tree-stems. The shapes of face and hair suggested in so many instances the note of unimaginable bells of unknown metal. For example, fair hair would be like a golden bell, and the blue eyes in it with that strange and blinding innocence seemed like the melodious note, the sense, as it were, you could get out of the bell, while their virginity, for with this I credited them in my optimism, was the bell's potentiality to be cracked and spoilt. However, before this, there were all the tremblings and dallyings of love upon the brim of this breaking music, eternal afternoons of comedy summers.

Hair I conceived during this winter walk in a hundred notes and moulds of beauty. I could see it, as I have just described, in the terms of held notes of music, and I could imagine it in a hundred flower-shapes above that red fruit, the lips.

Nor was my mythology complete without Arcadian nudities, and my fancy flew away to the Titian I had seen in Madrid, one of the most lovely things in the world, I had thought it. Some one—and it does not matter whether we think of him as musician, the actual painter, or a poet, we may just credit him as being the male intelligence—is playing on a kind of dulcimer, or virginal, in a garden, while a naked Venus lies behind him, and he turns his head away from the music to her perfections of form. It is true that none of these theatrical beauties would have possessed that amplitude and full harmony of shape; but their very blemishes would add poignancy to the situation. Green afternoons, unbroken by a giggle, or by a too localised, and thereby earthbound, accent, could be disposed in the imagination with all the perfections that reality, making these scenes into a picnic, made impossible.

Other entrances came with fresh tunes into the mind. There were dances, again on the trembling brim of the bell of innocence, but so gay and young that no one could ever mind in the slightest what happened. The boards of the stage, that as you looked at them in the play of their edges with the bodies of the dancers flowed into and intermingled with each other, turned into boughs and branches that were leaped upon, and themselves swayed down under, to rise again, wavelike, beneath these bird-dancers in a wiry sunlight that followed them with a strange fidelity wherever they moved.

The loud trams, and the voices of people walking, acted like so many curtains, making a complete break between one scene and the next, so that each new tune began with even more than its real share of spontaneity. These theatrical figures moved in a ghostly fashion among the passers-by, so that one was dwelling between two equally real worlds of life, and no further removed from one than from the other. While the one kind of figure, that of live people, was continually passing or overtaking me, the other kind, those substantial shades that I saw in my fancy, lay for ever before me; and the more vivid my imagination the closer I got to them, but never near enough to touch them, and only with that tantalising proximity that one can purchase on going the second time to the play by buying more expensive seats nearer to the front.

A great brick building loomed to the right-hand side, and instinctively I walked through a gate and up one of the gravel horns of the drive, for this was the Somebody or other Institute, the local picture-gallery, and the only thing of interest to be seen in the neighbourhood. My stick was claimed and I spun through various turnstiles, past a melancholy atrium built round a gold-fish tank, and so into the gallery, which I found, as I had expected, to consist of the legacies of various manufacturers, all of whose collective instincts had been directed patriotically towards the works of what is known as the Early English School. Those treasures were under the eye of a sad, weedy custodian who bore traces with limp and scar of having played a part in some of England's wars.

So far as my own feelings were concerned, it was equivalent to spending the afternoon in a cistern, for I was so thoroughly drenched in my own thoughts that it was next to impossible to lift my head above these waters. When, and in so far as, this could be achieved, I found that anything I noticed round me sprang into some instant contact with my circumstances.

Of course they were "water-colour" galleries, for there were but few English artists of that time who were possessed of the temerity to advance into a bigger region. They contained, therefore, a characteristically national product, being what an optimist would call the bright side to the drab slums, or dreary winter fields, wet hedges, and wet houses. It would be needless, even if memory made it possible, to go into details of these records, and so I only recall particular contingencies.

They began with Rowlandson, but in too many instances the humour, as the drawing, was too blown out, as though the artist had access to a bicycle pump and had plied this feverishly in the knowledge that unless his figures were distended they would not be funny. Now and again a certain general largeness of scale brought these huge figures into proportion with their surroundings, so that they seemed really to belong to a world of giant ridicule. But too often they were diminished by their own fat inaccordance with the ordinary public-house or green field of convention.

With Cruikshank it was far different. In his early drawings before the time of Dickens and the steel engravers he lived in a continual Christmas with the pantomime giants never far round the corner. But before one came to his work, there was a whole room of Prout, and painters of the kind who went as far as Normandy or the Loire, and were staggered by this easy strangeness into something better than you might expect of them. They all gave drawing-lessons, I felt sure, and I could imagine them during their short holidays abroad walking as far as their feet would carry them into France, and drawing on chill mornings that pinched the hands and made the nose run. Then, having come back to London, they held an exhibition, argued with the publisher and the lithographers, produced the large coloured album that was designed for the drawing-room tables of the new stuccoed houses of London, and started their next term of lessons, while a piano from the floor above, or from the next house, stammered with a coldness appropriate to the morning.

It was a definite quickening of the senses to look,

213

after these, upon Cruikshank. The knotted thinness of
his figures made an appeal to one's sense of pity, while
he drew slum children with more understanding than
any one else has ever possessed. It was the start of the
Industrial Age, and the newly perfected horrors of
child-labour were superimposed upon Beer Street and
Gin Lane, and upon those squalors of the eighteenth
century that only Hogarth understood; while, towards
all this, the snuff-box and the fan, and Greuze and
Boucher, have assumed in the historical eye the part of
blind and curtain. That these horrors were true is
known to any one who has ever walked through the
slums of Naples, or Lyons, or Barcelona, where the
identical child is to be seen in hundreds who appals
us in Cruikshank when we think that he can never have
existed in London.

Between Naples and Pompeii there are fifteen miles
of the thinness, the spotted faces, the bad teeth, that
are to be seen in Cruikshank. A drive in a motor-car
on a wet day along this road is equivalent to being carried straight back to the London of a century ago.
There are the taller, bully children, possessed of mani-
acal grins and always on the look-out to steal from their
weaker fellows, or to pick up thrown-away cigarette-
ends from the gutter. Often they are munching hunks
of bread that are discoloured from being dropped in
the roads outside the various wine-factories, for this is
the centre of the trade in Neapolitan wines and these
are concocted no longer in the wine-press but in a factory. The pavements, therefore, are discoloured with
a red, vinous grit, so that bread dropped upon them
looks as though it had been rubbed on the rusty slag-
heaps of a colliery district. It is like Commercial
Road, or Mile End Road, but in the days before gaslight or the modern policeman had been invented.

Portici, Torre del Greco, Torre Annunziata, these
are the towns along that road from Naples, and these
are the places that those faint water-colours in the gallery called to mind. They had the thin colour, the
faded tones of a wet day, as seen from the swiftly moving windows of a motor-car. When I think of them
now, they remind me of nothing so much as of certain paintings by Picasso, dating, I believe, from his
very early career. There are the same wasted, fam-
ished figures sheltering in doorways from the cold and
damp; and sometimes a consumptive man and his wife
with their child, which, if it has not the brutal ugliness
of the other children it lives among, has, in any case,
its parents' consumption shrinking, as though in a perpetual laundry of the rain, what should have been
childish plumpness into the wasted form of a prisoner
undergoing a life-sentence. The genius of the painter
contrives, somehow, in all his works of this the so-
called "blue-period," to impart a slight suggestion of
the circus, hinting that this family, for example, are
travelling, nomad-fashion, from town to town, and if
this is not an actual clown in his everyday clothes it
must be some one sent ahead of the party to arrange the
details of their performance. Now and again he shows
us an actor in his actual chequered suit, with face innocent of grease-paint, because, perhaps, that false colour
would only accentuate his tragic pallor; while in, at any
rate, one picture I can remember we see the children in
their harlequin clothes, skin-tight, to show their dented
armour of bones.

There is no exaggeration in any of this. As for the
period of which I am speaking in connection with
Cruikshank, a novel, otherwise dreary and of too marine an interest to most minds, called *Redburn* and written by Herman Melville, contains towards its end some

215

sixty pages describing what Liverpool was like eighty years ago. Such, and so deep, were the horrors of that generation, the first of modern civilisation; while, if we want to see how bad it can be in our own day and how closely it can correspond to everything that was hideous in the days of Cruikshank no one need do more than take an afternoon walk in Sheffield. There, alone, he will find material enough to make a painter famous, if he will have the courage to set down what lies before his eyes.

So here I was back again in the Northern streets, though not of that particular town I have just named, using my eyes once more upon the water-colours and still looking at the Cruikshank collection.

A caricature of some cavalry officers caught my attention; their trousers were cut into an almost triangular shape, they had thin, foppish waists, hair like a pianist, and, by virtue of their profession, moustachios, for those were the days when only these paragons were allowed that adornment by a public tolerance that was only just recovering from the wigs and clean-shaven faces of a previous century, while the young Disraeli was in personal danger because he flaunted this ornament without the requisite authority. Even here, among these woollen heads, there seemed to be some latent germ of the future music-hall as it was to blossom into that half-century of fulness between the Crimean and the Boer Wars. That parrot-art of short snatches and slangy tunes meticulously learned seemed the only possible recreation to such figures as these, whom you could never expect to move freely about a ballroom.

A bright stab of sunlight, that kind which comes out of the void of winter to live for a few moments only and remind you of its summer potency, came down through the windows round the roof and brushed these artifices of fashion with a thin, dusty gold; for the caricatures of officers hung among no less remarkable travesties of the women's dress of the day, upon those fantastic enlargements on the Gothic or François Premier that they affected and which blew out their fulness into the shapes of tree or flower, and even seemed to make use of the bellying sail and the roping and rigging of the wind-borne ships that were now overdue to disappear at their moments of most forceful extravagance, as, for example, at a ball, or for a promenade in Hyde Park.

I could feel a familiar air blowing through those silken flowers and trees and through the satin sails, the same, indeed, if more gentle, as that among the triangular trousers and the laced coats and moustachios; there was always this same pantomime giant round the corner and hardly out of sight. My own bitter and fanged ghosts of music came back to me, but deprived, as always, of their evident cruelty, so that I derived nothing but pleasure from their play. And here, only a few inches away from the falsifications of fashion, lay exactly the thing I had set out in search of, one of those moments when Cruikshank actually ventured out of the wings. It was led up to by more than one preliminary of the actors talking a few inches away from their field of action, and of the damp garret-like dressing-rooms to which they were doomed. The pale, waxy flower, camellia, perhaps, or magnolia, of gaslight gave an even-edged hardness to all that was going on: it was a dull, aching light that never made good use of the spangles and sequins it lived among. It drew one by this very shortcoming to think of those same particularities seen under other conditions where their beauties received more fair treatment; for spangle

217

and sequin have the quality that is possessed by falling
water if you could isolate any one of its sequences and
at the same time keep the sparkling swiftness that is
the secret of its beauty. The facets of such a tumbling,
hurried light require, therefore, a more fiery and varied
treatment than that which can be given them by gaslight, for they must be allowed some variations of tone,
as of sun played into and broken by green tides of
leaves, or of electricity that can be heightened or lowered from its violence.

I suffered myself to be led away from this scene by
the harlequin who leaned against that painted house as
though he had knocked and was waiting for the door
to open. He took me down a grey perspective of
streets, lit only by the beacon windows of public-
houses, till we stood once more by a bed of yellow
flowers that I have described, and at the edge of an
asphalt path that wound away like a molten river
through the grass. That cropped lawn seemed to run
straight into the sky just a few feet in front of us, but
no sooner did we walk out upon it than the horizon
took a vast leap away from us beyond a huge surging
bay, a kind of immense amphitheatre in which we occupied the highest seats, while, below, the sea played to
us with a listless and tired enthusiasm.

At this highest point of grass, upon a bench which
was hot to touch and the brown woodwork of which
was blistered and swollen by the sun, sat Colonel Fantock, listening to the brave music from the band below;
but out upon the sands, and in front of the Spa and
the gardens on the cliff, there stood a box-like, open
booth, a small theatre upon trestles, with the cart and
horses waiting to take it away again when the tide advanced against the sand. The dimly seen figures there
were inaudible from above, and so we ran quickly down

the long flights of steps to get the noisy music of the band behind us as we came near to watch this open-air theatre. Colonel Fantock we left at the top of the cliff, agreeing to meet him in a tea-shop in an hour's time.

In a few moments we were treading on the sands, though just near the shore they were so crumbled and soft as to make walking heavy and difficult. As soon as they had enough solidity to keep a definite footmark they became crisp and delightful to walk upon, and they stretched right away down to the bottom of the bay, for the sea was very far out at low tide.

I was able to transfer myself with an extraordinary speed of the sensibilities from this picture-gallery where I was idling away a spare hour of that most precious day to the beach where I had played as a child some ten years before, and this journey of the spirit could never have been accomplished had not every atom of my receptive senses been awake during that long dead summer I have described in the opening sections of this book. I did not, then, enter upon these particular incidents because they established a contact which only now, in these later days, brought about its own fruition, so that I have reserved it till now for description.

Every day I used to go, as I was going again this afternoon, through the wall of Cruikshank in this gallery, to see that pierrot entertainment, and when the tide was too near in for them to play on the sands, or it was too windy, or began to rain, they gave their performance under the roof of the "Arcadia," where they always appeared at night during the hours I was sealed hermetically within doors. By this frequency I got to know them by sight and learned to appraise their differing degrees of "personality," a quality which can be present in the highest and fullest degree without in itself conferring any other excellence upon the performer. In fact it seems sometimes to drive away talent and grow by itself like a weed, so that you cannot ignore it and yet cannot call its potency an advantage. We may think of it in terms of a haunting, personal smell, of the same strength and certainty by which an animal can know when the hunter is near, or a rabbit sense the fox.

It was a thrilling experience to arrive down there before the afternoon performance had begun, for the different actors strolled casually towards their occupation, and the only sign of their profession lay in an almost too marked affectation of the ordinary, so that they appeared out of this excess with something peculiar to them. Grey felt or straw hat was too considerately brushed, suit too pressed, walking-stick too unused, while there was a haunting and mordant vulgarity about their voices.

There were ten or a dozen of them, and they were to be seen walking in the same couples, or trios; they lived, obviously, according to this very grouping, in the same theatrical lodgings. I can never forget on these fine days seeing them coming along some quarter of a mile away down the sands that were as fresh and virginal as any island shore of which you could possibly dream. The lighting was admirable: there is never such a background for character, we know from Jacques Callot, as the actual boards of the theatre built with their cross-bars along the body, right up the limbs, and above the head. On summer mornings the sun had prepared just such a setting as this for their approach, and where his light was so perfect that every detail could be seen without the necessity of some other measure to give it scale, he had dispensed himself of the actual board-marks, rubbing out all those parallel lines in the sand and giving us just the lion-coloured sea-floor for foreground, wings, and background. It gave the effect of that casual entrance upon the stage which is one of the most perfectly finished products of theatrical technique.

A virtuoso who drew pictures on the sand with his toes was at work, as if upon the wings, of this scene. I do not think they are to be found anywhere else save in England, these developments of the pavement artist into something that approaches the feats of Hokusai; on this particular day it was Lord Roberts in a garland of victory over the savage Boers, and to see a comedian walking past the huge twists of that moustache, or by a blaze of medals, was in itself an experience of stage possibilities. Of course since the artist was at work a great square like the lines of a football field were scratched upon the sand, and he addressed indignant reproaches to any one who endangered his picture by walking within its borders.

Just a few feet away, and nearer to where I stood, lay another of his sketches which had been more than half-destroyed by yesterday's high tide, though you could still distinguish Russians and Japanese, while every sporting instinct of our race was centred upon Admiral Togo. This scene, since it was old and done with, could be walked right through and its details knocked about or kicked with shoe or walking-stick. The bright sunlight lived again for me, magnifying itself from the wintry, sad fires that came down for a moment, as I have described, to give me light to look into every intricacy of Cruikshank's theatre-haunted mind. It lived again for me, burning into an admirable clearness so that I could recognise these friends of mine who were divided from me only by that thin glass wall which I could never climb over, or get through, and which was the space of air between my seat and their small world of activity.

The rest of their walk to the partitioned hut behind the stage led them past a photographer or two who held his tripod and black hood ready as though for a feat of necromancy; while the most considerable among them owned a primitive tin-built, pseudo-motor-car into which parties could climb to be photographed. More humble vendors stood by with baskets of beautifully coloured sea-shells, and trays of those strange marine creatures who seem to be half hedgehog and half doughnut. These last they would put for you as a final temptation into a pail of water, where they blossomed into a strange and glossy beauty.

A few moments later, when a whistle had been blown, the curtain was raised to show these actors in a strange mixture of character; for while the only two women were dressed in the conventional pierrot dress, half the men—like that variety of sea-shell?—were pierrots, and half, naval officers. It soon became apparent that only those members of the company who were not credited with being funny, and who relied upon a "straight" song or recitation for their success, had adopted this latter excuse to favour. They stood at the salute, while their brothers and sisters remained rigid, hands to sides, when the curtain rose and till the piano had begun that inevitable doggerel song, a kind of musical legend of the company's activity. This, in itself, had a conventional horror which completely captured the attention. It seared and burned itself into memory, to remain there for ever.

That glass wall was built, then, and the secrets of its visible and inviolate strength were to occupy my thoughts for a long period from that day.

There was this violent, biting attraction in something so near, and yet so far away, and in an art which advanced to such a distance from so humble a threshold. It had extremes of haunting beauty and mordant vulgarity, with hundreds of intermediate phases, each one containing a whole complete world of interpretation.

As I thought of it from my picture-gallery, almost so it seemed to me, from the end of time, there came moments when I had to hold my breath in order not to breathe upon that shallow mirror echoing all my memories. A fidget from the custodian in the room, or my own shifting of position from one drawing to another, was sufficient to obscure some of the details of the scene; and so I sat down on a long, leather settee where I could be as still and quiet as possible.

The melancholy of being alone, alone with one's own far-distant memories, and close to what seemed such a vital part of one's own future, while this very thing was so near as to be almost the hot-blooded, palpitating present, kept me spellbound in that cold gallery. All this was before me, all that lay behind me; and, as for the present, I could conceive of it as nothing else than some kind of a live animal I was riding, for it moved and breathed under me, devouring the future and digesting it into the past at the same speed as I did myself. We were moving together in the high, green fields and leaving a track behind us as we advanced; we could look back on what we had destroyed, as on what lay before us, but we could neither revive what we had killed or get at once to some distant spot in front without passing over and destroying what lay between us and that knoll of tufted, summer heads. This particular day we were moving through a very tall har-

223

vest, for I have seldom known past and future to be so near, one to the other.

I wonder what has become of them, I thought to myself, feeling certain that the chief man of the company, dressed appropriately to his position as a naval captain, must have been killed in the war, where I could imagine so well the easy transition from stage-officer to real, enabling him to play that part in a hastily raised regiment long before the others had grown into what was expected of them; but, then, remembering his imperturbable calm, I could well imagine that he went straight through the obvious and actually into the Navy. He may be still alive, if such was his choice, and at that moment, when I wondered where he could be playing now, the horror of this telescopic vision into the past broke upon my mind, for I realised that this man, who must in those days have been forty years old, was now, if alive, between fifty and sixty and must, therefore, have resigned his fictitious commission. Whatever becomes of them when they are that age? Where do they retire to—and where from?

And all the others? The two soubrettes, who would be, by now, well over the half-way line to eighty? And the fat, agreeably ruffed pierrot at the piano? Those powdered faces with a black patch or two put into that whitened mask much as you put in a few stars to show you are drawing the night! The dangling eyeglass, the black dancing-shoes, that peculiar tension of the look, when his or her part required one of the company to look in the eyes of another! What degrees of bored indifference, of real or simulated love, of private jokes breaking through the thin skins of those intended for the public!

The audience on their folding wooden chairs laughed as stupidly as ever; the pierrot at the piano played with lodging-house tone but with more than lodging-house pace. The rest of the company sit still, while through those draped curtains at the back of the stage a premonitory and powdered hand emerges, followed in a second by the whole figure of their "lead," a young man with the calibre of cracked voice that would have enrolled him among the Sultan's private bodyguard, though those emasculate notes were really the result of a too premature appearance upon the stage with the strain of late hours and the effort of singing out above cheap and noisy music. Both his parents were stage people, I expect, so that this tone of voice may even have been inherited, if one can inherit from a parent some quality which has been accidental in its origin, a tendency to melancholy, for instance, or a disposition to cry when you hear music. Despite all this, I remember such a performance as his for its gaiety— this young man had some inborn tricks and devices of the stage which made his acting professional and not amateur—and he contrived in a few seconds to evoke the whole "seaside," as it exists to the Anglo-Saxon mind.

Mile upon mile of iron railing, on which to straddle facing the lodging-houses with your back to the sea, sucking, meanwhile, the handle of your summer walking-stick, this shall be our background, with sea and sky running into each other in shades of Oxford and Cambridge blue, respectively, at this regatta of a few limp clouds. We must imagine some great eating-houses with such notices in their windows as Three Courses 1/9; or Cut from the Joint. Two Veg: Cheese. Bread. 1/6,—these providing the fortification to so much pleasantry of the spirit, and there is a line of cinemas, each of them flanked by sweet-shops with a fearful machine in their windows spinning out and weaving the local peppermint rock. To invite to these delights, since feasting alone is no banquet, numbers of young girls are wandering on a few days' holiday from shop or factory, and their spirits, like the summer weather, lie between the two hysterias of tears and laughter, their balance moving easily to either extreme at the slightest provocation. Anyway, they are free to make friends and to share these deleterious pleasures.

Turn off that troubled sunlight and switch the night down upon these long promenades, and this must be done as in moments of sentiment the full glare of electricity in the theatre can be lowered into a secret and pathetic gloom! But even this is lit in chosen places, and cones of whitish light fall from the electric standards on to the pavement, recalling by their shape and consistency the cones of ice-cream that you buy from the "hokey-pokey" man. Light streams out of the cinemas and shops, in fact it is spilt from their doors and windows so that they stand in their own puddles like a spilling tea-cup in its saucer. Where bands in café or cinema are not heard, the mouth-organ and the Jew's harp make themselves felt, while, eventually, beginning little by little and growing steadily louder as its volume increases, you can hear shutters being lowered, chairs being carried inside, platforms being taken down and packed away; it is as if a gipsy encampment is being broken up in a cold dawn. Soon the very nomads who trade upon these crowds have vanished, and only the cries of revellers with an occasional drowned giggle break the stillness: it is another day of holiday over and finished, another dawn nearer the factory siren blown at six o'clock, summer and winter.

All of this could be attributed to those cracked notes and a great deal besides, but even such a voyage as this has its limits, and no sooner had the piano glided into another measure, than, as though pulled in on a leash, one's thoughts returned to this threshold of destiny on its little stilts above the sands. All this time, with a sudden realisation of what lay before me, of its immeasurable importance compared with these dim origins of my present state of mind, I tugged at my own strings so sharply that they drew me out of that quiet summer afternoon back into the gallery where I was waiting in a kind of numbed silence of memories.

Every year those figures would fade further and further in my mind; their voices would go first, then their faces, at last their very personality must leave me, and I should only have an empty cell with nothing to put in it, remembering that there had been something, but not what it was. The very music to which these ghosts had danced might leave me last of all, forgotten, perhaps, for great spans of years and then recalled suddenly in the middle of the night, when these scenes were too far off for me to fit them to figures. They would have a thin spectral life, always just on the point of blossoming into its fulness, and each time I sang it over they might seem to be nearer to this miracle, but it would never come to pass, and by the time I was awake again next morning the whole thing would have left me, so that no threat or bribe could bring it back to me.

I kept still for a few moments while my thoughts climbed heavily laden out of the past, and till their balance, from having sunk too much to that one side, reached the present, and then drooped and fell to what lay before me.

While on the kind of watershed between these two extremities of thought I realised that those pale beams which had helped me to this recollection were quite extinguished and that the gallery was colder and darker than before; in fact, my watch told me it was nearly four o'clock, the hour at which the collection closed, and so I walked once more round the walls, taking a last look at the drawings that had stretched out such a distance for me through their opaque water-colour. Like marionettes that are hung from a line of hooks after their performance is over, all these figures I had remembered, moved their limbs convulsively; they might have been bodies dangling from so many scaffolds, and kicking their limbs out in that terrible struggle with the rope that was round their necks and throttling them. It was, indeed, a fight between life and death; and all these memories were wriggling and writhing so as to try to survive through this perspective I was building. As part of my own private and personal legend I was as anxious as they were that these things should last in the mind, and certainly their convulsions cut the sharpest kind of shadow against my windows.

They blew into a shrill and exaggerated life for one moment more, and it was as if one had blown upon red embers till some resemblance of flame came out of that dying struggle. I heard the loudly rattling piano again and felt that glass wall of air between my world and theirs. Everything was hurried in the last few minutes of their performance: and why? Because the sea, glittering all over its huge mass, was slowly creeping towards them over the crackling sands, which, themselves, shone with such a transparent fire under the sun's eyes that you could readily believe how important an ingredient sand might be towards the making of glass.

The turn of tide one did not notice, but over a great stretch of what had not long ago been sand, the blue

228

sea now shook and played in its tidal strength. It would besiege one rock after another, running back again so as to have the pleasure of once more surrounding and taking it. The actual shelves of sand it ran down as quick as wind bends the corn, but even this easy conquest it repeated again for its pleasure. It was shaking a thousand cymbals, rattling a thousand silver coins in each wave that broke; and this slighter music came out above those tumbling, sleepy moves of its great mass.

There was now but room for people to walk abreast between the first plumes of foam left by the waves and the back of the stage where horses and carts stood in readiness. Even before the traditional seventh wave had time to raise its head, this narrow space was gone and a thin film of water lay in its place; it broke in little gurgling rings against the wheels of the carts, the horses' legs, and even, though this was the limit to its advance, ran below the trestles on which the stage was supported. Further than this, and among the audience, the sea was forbidden access by the traditions of high tide, according to which there must always be a few feet of rough, shuffled sand between water and shore.

These ghosts faded out of my mind to a rattling piano played above the sea's great mass, and the tunes fought bravely for life, that premonitory and powdered hand hung once more on to the curtain, though this was but a straw to hold to and the actor never came forth from his thin cloud. In place of that, I leave them there as I best remember them, in a waning afternoon when the tide upon the sands put an end to their performance. Nothing could well be more melancholy than dying to this kind of hour-glass, that, at the same time, made them remove and rubbed out the signs of

229

their livelihood; but, in spite of this, we can picture the next morning's fresh sand lying there agreeably to their stage and to the feet of the sand-artist. It lay there like the clean sheet of paper of the lightning-sketch artist when he tears away and crumbles that old calendar of his work.

They still haunted me after I had gone down the last wall and finished the whole series; they gave me no peace until I had walked through the turnstile and taken my coat and walking-stick. Then, the evening and the cold air claimed some attention and contrived to dispel those forms of smoke.

The public park was quite deserted; it stretched out cold and misty through the high railings that one had not noticed much on the way here, so noisy were the children and so green the grass between these black bars, however thickly strewn with orange-peel and waste-paper. As for the road, it was as long as ever, and perhaps even noisier than in daytime with its clanking trams.

I was now safely out of those memories and becoming acutely aware of the present and of the small rest of the day which I could already just see before me, like your own hand which is the furthest you can see on a foggy night. Beyond that, I neither wanted, nor was able, to prolong my vision. For the moment I was contented that all I wanted should be at arm's length.

The long straight street was so noisy, now that the park lay invisible and there was nothing there to distract the attention from its clamour, that I turned away to explore some of the side-streets. By keeping more or less at a parallel I was sure of my direction and was able to waste a few more minutes of my spare time.

These side-streets lay up-hill, and as the houses stood further from this long road of the trams they seemed to increase in comfort and prosperity, so that, towards the top, from being real slum dwellings, they had become good brick houses, not quite at the status of standing separately, but in any case strung together in pairs.

This very degree of difference had something terrible in it, for the dwellers in such houses were far enough from the slums to be at a good focus towards those pinched and wasted lives, and were yet, themselves, far from secure against a possible descent into these regions, did anything go wrong with their livelihood. Doctors, music-teachers, bank-officials, insurance-agents, were the kind of persons who lived in these roads, for these were roads, emphatically, and not streets. The huge, black town lay below them in a kind of crater of its own smoke and filth; and in the other direction, if you walked some half-mile farther, you passed the newest and most red-bricked houses and came out on to the bleak moors that were as desolate as the wildest parts of Spain and without enough scale in their hills and slopes to give them any degree of magnificence. The best to be hoped for was that these same moors might one day be worked for coal and iron to bring more prosperity to the town, and sandwich these better roads of houses between the slums below and the new rows of houses that would rise in lines, with a line of lavatories back to back between each pair of rows, on the gaunt slopes above them.

Just here, the roads were too proud to have shops, too refined to have public-houses, so that either instinct of food or drink was satisfied with difficulty, and as if with a certain shame attached to its gratification. This very reluctance must mean the presence of religion, which always condemns the animal in man, and, sure enough, there was a parish church at one of the corners with dwarf Salisbury spire, and walls of that peculiar flint which suggests primitive guns and the earliest form of match-box. The Wesleyans, the Baptists, the Methodists, had not allowed this competition to pass unchallenged, and their more squat, square temples rose near at hand, each with a vicarage standing aloof up a small stretch of gravelled drive. The fact that these places of worship with the houses among which they stood were all on a slope affected one with a slight, but definite, vertigo, as though the brick and stone with their occupants were sliding perceptibly into the black abyss of smoke below their affected gentility. The laurels bordering the short vicarage drive had their speckled leaves dusted with a fine black grit which stained the fingers like ink; and thinking of this same omnipotent smoke one wondered what almond tree or laburnum would look like when they came into a short life and hung little pink flames and yellow tongues of fire before the clergy windows. At the moment, the pair of them looked drooped and sopping as though they had lain for weeks in a fish-pond full of weed, and one wondered how tree or flower ever summoned up enough confidence to prepare for their short burst of life in a winter that showed so little hope as this. It must simply be instinct working automatically without the power to question its own traditions, for the slightest curiosity or enquiry on the part of tree or flower would hush them into an eternal death unbroken by the most pale of springs.

Equally pathetic were similar attempts on the part of human beings, for if the real slum-dwellers below had abandoned, had never even entertained a hope, these people here who had lifted themselves a few inches out of the mud and smoke must have a shade of ambition in their procreation. Child-bearing in the slums is like a bruise in a football match, something unavoidable and neither quite an agony nor entirely a source of pride; it flows in a rhythm with the passing years, and its pains are considered generally worth the price, the small lupercalia of Saturday and Sunday, and the supposed support that children should render to their parents, when old, in payment for these pangs and delights. Children cost little, if anything, after they are fifteen years old; while, in the semi-detached brick houses where we are walking, this very same age is a kind of apex, a climacteric, a point where everything possible has to be collected and put like a price upon the child's head, so that he can buy himself a place in one of the lesser slaveries. To this end many years of saving and scraping may go, so that we can think of the children in such a neighbourhood as this in terms of hope and ambition: they may "become" something, and not merely "be" anything.

To a cranking, slightly wheezing rattle a kind of home-made sledge of wooden boxes mounted on a roller and two little iron wheels came round the corner and ran some hundred yards down the slope. Then, the two children working this toy got out and pulled it with strings up the road again towards their starting-point, and passed me half-way up their run.

They were of that same long-headed flaxen type, but sharper and finer in this thinness, and they must have been four and six years old respectively. Perhaps the most singular feature of their pathos was their being alone, not surrounded as they would have been in the slums below by a whole mob of other children. In this they reminded me inevitably of myself, for I never had any other children but my brother and sister to play with. They did not talk much, either, and seemed to be playing together rather mechanically, as if they

233

knew that when you are a child you are supposed to play, and that when grown-up you would be sorry if you had not done so. If this was their only motive they must have been most sensible of its force, for although they were not vociferous they showed no slackening in their game.

Most children, rich or poor, are credited with wanting to be an engine-driver, a chauffeur, a soldier, or something of the sort; but it was my opinion that these two I was watching had already seen through this fallacy and were content to be what they were. I think the fact that they still played, despite of this usual child-incentive to games not being in them, showed that they realised something more than this, the fact that they would grow up, inevitably, into some profession they hated; and that, therefore, as I have suggested, they were playing because this was the only time for play.

This was the point of their life from which every ghost starts, and I wondered whether they were having, that evening, one of those peculiar realisations of time that I have noted in the early part of this book, when you know that you will remember all the rest of your days some apparently trivial circumstance that you fasten upon as being of supreme future importance to your life. It is just such a meaningless break in time, as this, that is remembered: some winter evening as the mists close in like sleep so that you only remember this much and no more out of their intervals, as it might be smoke of a bonfire, a lighted sweet-shop window, or a particular tea-time under the hard nursery lamplight.

Whether this took place in their minds, or not, the sight of them seemed to me like a central point in my life up to that day, like a watershed between the two slopes of being young oneself and in the process of growth, and what, in contrast to that mental and physical climb, we can only think of as a descent. I had begun coming down, and my zenith had been reached, as should be all the Alps of experience, in a land of fog and mist.

It was my own curtain ringing down, but neither for the first nor the last time.

These two little children affected me with a terrible self-pity, for I found myself continually filling their rôles with my own ghost. But whilst crediting them with my own feeling, I made that mistake which is the trap or snare which hides in pity, that is to say I gave them my own personality and fitted it to their circumstances. This is imperfect acting, for you should either take a part written specially for you, or throw yourself into a character and fit its clothes and manners so exactly that there is no shade of your own personality left outside its new habitation. The misfit, so to speak, in this impersonation had some advantage, though, for it gave me room to move about in those clothes and in those minds, and since I could stand at some angle to them I was afforded a perspective of their lives which a too complete identification with them would have made impossible.

I could see their hazards, their little, strange chances, lying out before them like the few poor effects of a soldier at a barrack-room parade of his kit. A photograph or two, enough room for a little gardening, a pretty child, seats at the cinema, surely these were sufficient baits for their ambition. But then it seemed to me that those thin, pale faces might presage some higher if more bitter future; just think, for instance, if one of these two children might elect to be a poet, or musician; worse still, that rare and incredible phenomenon, a good one.

At this thought, the form into which I had poured my ghost affected me with so dull and aching a pain of pity that I could hardly still my sufferings to think of such a possibility. How could any one climb out of this black quicksand of ugliness and poverty; how could they find foothold; even for a moment, in this sliding horror of hopelessness!

The idea of these children having any kind of personal possession of their own—a few sweets, toys, a book of fairy-stories, anything, gave me an acute misery. Even the idea that they would think the slum children from the town dirty and not fit for them to play with was an anguish, because this argued that they must see themselves as something apart and of a higher life than those urchins of the street-corners. To be brought up in any belief about yourself that is based on such tenuous defences as a weekly wage is so near to the precipice edge as to give one vertigo and an insensate longing to fall over; this seemed to me to be as close to the abyss as it is possible to stand balanced. Those thin bird-features through whose childish curves of chin and wrist I fancied I could see a profitable sadness, as of some latent talent, made me think of hundreds of failures, of hundreds of attempts only just foiled by ill-fortune. I could not bear to think of them playing along this road and apparently already conscious of the pains and anxieties that lay before them: I would sooner they were ignorant, and by that much more fitted for danger.

Then, thinking from them, to all I had remembered and wandered over in the afternoon, I could see all acting as a brave and dangerous playing with fire, or, to use my former comparison, as an elaborate dance upon the chasm edge. To have to execute this, carrying the weight of other people's spirits as well as your own, must require one of those two alternative ingredients of bravery, either no nerves at all or an iron courage.

Once more I could see that powdered and premonitory hand upon the curtain and hear that rattling piano above the thin creeping waters. His little staccato notes came bravely forth, the banality of his words being almost a comfort, and they sounded sharper and more ghost-like than ever before, so completely did the two ghosts, his own personality and the part he was acting, tally in their particularity. The rest of the company I leave silent on the chairs listening to their spokesman, for he is fighting for them all in that soft and shadowy armour, and no wonder he holds to the curtain, for when this falls and the lights die he is, himself, dead again, as are all ghosts at cockcrow.

Walking away into the town in his grey suit, carrying wash-leather gloves, a silver-topped walking-stick, a parcel from shopping:—isn't he alive, then? Or walking in the morning past a band that may play his own airs—which of his two lives is that? I see the ridiculous little farded embryo at first one shop-window and then another, moved like a pawn upon a chessboard by his small wants or idle curiosity.

And then, from inventing a real day for his shadow-life, or carrying sunlight and open, uncaged music upon the stage, and playing thus a subtle game across alternations of light and dark between this choice of spectres, never knowing which of the two was the more unhappy and wanted his spirit laying before the other, I came back to the problem that was to occupy all the rest of my day. Something admirable and lovely seen through and across the glass wall between stage and audience; was this impression of beauty spoilt or unspoilt, when the convent-wall was scaled and the gardens of Thelema reached under unabashed and banal music?

But by now I had reached the nether slope; in a moment I was back again in the long road of the trams. The station, with every thing and person coming or going away, and, if delayed, only kept a few hours as though on purpose to annoy and aggravate, howled and hooted and roared at my ears. As if in last reminder of my thoughts I found myself in that short space between hotel and station besieged by a rabble of small children. These were so vociferous, and so pale and starved, that it was impossible to believe one was in England; they were of all ages up to fifteen, the oldest and tallest among them showing incipient moustaches and long hairs on the face that wanted a razor. They were all shoeless, hatless, and in rags, and they made a gaunt and horrifying file, like one limb of a guard of honour, while I went through the swing-door of the hotel on my way to the groves and pavilions of comedy.

V

The Winter Walk (continued)

NO sooner did the curtain go up than one was lifted
right out of one's bones and carried beyond time
and space, for the tideless summer of comedy began,
in the provincial manner, at half-past six, so that there
had only been time to eat a sandwich before it started.
Even the poorest kind of stock jokes from the comedians seemed funny, because that ludicrous world in
which they could be thought amusing was carried down
so far in the adverse balance against certain extravagant
beauties that the angle each took up to the other gave
an obtuse interest, even to that far end of its tangent.
They seemed like fat, ugly creatures laughing at the
bottom of a pit, with frog jokes and frog laughter; but
this deep, muddied pool might well be the source of a
fountain, the hole into which you stretch your hand to
turn a tap and start the leaping jet.   Anyway, I would
not have the one without the other, or a Latin church
without its beggars at the porch.

At moments, because the clock in spite of my feelings had gone at the same rate as ever that day, I was
reminded by some phrase of music, or by a turn of
words, of the primitive theatre I had been remembering most of the afternoon.   Those tunes were still fresh
in my mind—it was such a short time ago that I had
sung them over to myself; and it dawned on me what
a violent and abrupt difference had come over the
phrases, the very words of music.   At that earlier time
—it was some four or five years before the War—the

same school of music lived that had been started in the
'Sixties and 'Seventies of last century; those were the
days of "Champagne Charlie," the "Lion Comique,"
and the turgid memories of the "Winning Post." It
had been continued down to my own day by Vesta
Tilley; but an Indian Love Lyric, a song by Guy
d'Hardelot, a stage-gentleman like Sir Gerald du Mau-
rier tapping his cigarette-case, these different elements
may be said to have ruined that tradition. In its place
there was this new American music that grew in the
course of the War into its full and blatant strength;
and it needs no description because it is younger and
stronger than ever.

Numbers of things I should have been trying to remember slipped away from me before I could retain
them, because, in my excitement, I would concentrate
upon one detail and ignore the rest. In this way, just
when I had determined to learn some particular tune
at all costs, a painted face against a painted branch, or
some haunting and mordant vulgarity in limb or movement, took me away from my task until it was too late,
and I recovered just as the last notes of this dying language were dead. I kept hoping to hear it played over
again during one of the intervals, but even when these
came one tune followed another so quickly and they
were all played in so truncated a version that it was
impossible to identify the correct one out of this parade
of cliché. Everything glided continuously into the
next thing, and one did not dare to stop this flow in
the mind for fear of missing both the new thing in
progress and the old thing one wished to remember.

But here I find myself falling into the very fault I
have mentioned, for the curtain rose to show the stage
in darkness and we had quite half the overture in this
double night. It was equivalent to being introduced to

every one at a party the moment one has arrived at the house, for the tunes kept tumbling in on each other's heels and there was little hope of remembering them all. Their intervals were joined by hardly so much as a flourish of notes, like a hurried introduction where one cannot catch the person's name.

Any tunes possessed of some atmosphere to their short lives were obviously what are called "extra numbers," that is to say, they were written by some greater expert than the person responsible for the rest of this music, and they had been roughly and stubbornly included in the play. They came in with even a shade of the compiler's jealousy to their presentation, for of course he would be conscious of their merit and perhaps lamented, as he joined them up, that he was only an English, and not an American, Jew. This matrix into which they were embedded was a mass of sentimental catches, some of them with a certain degree of liveliness to their embrace. They had all been tried out, in the beginning of the autumn, at the "wakes," those great fairs of the North of England and, particularly, Lancashire; for these act as sorting-house to the Christmas tunes. They are submitted to the crowds of mill-workers, being roared out to them continuously by loud-speaker or steam-organ, and those which in a day or two are not being universally whistled and hummed are summarily rejected. This kind of choice by plébiscite neglects, obviously, the subtler banalities, so that there is nothing very difficult to understand in what is left. Even so, there are many different colours in vulgarity, and more than one hint of something a little better than its full blatancy.

Where, oh where, do these chameleons derive their inspiration? I refer by this term to the lizard-like composers of these catches, who, with Hebrew astute-

241

ness, manage to colour their product with the exact tones of both their original and their audience, matching each with each as though the public wrote their own tunes, were their own tunes, and played their own tunes.

Is it a yellow pier in a flapping seaside wind? or some quieter retreat, a penny chair behind a Corporation hedge, and in the shadow of the Great Wheel? We can trust the sun, that placid and mocking parent of so much loud brightness, to effect any introductions simply by his soft balsam to the senses, that we must think of as bruised and overwrought by so many whirring belts and screws, beating hammers, and by the steam-siren, that new kind of dawn bugle. These are, surely, the situations by which this talent profits; and so long as Mother or Granny are left out of it we can trust the international interpreters, the chameleons of our holiday colours, to turn our feelings into suitable words with music nicely mated to our shades of meaning.

Such, sure enough, was the scene which displayed itself in a huge blaze, a concentration of light, some few minutes later. The Great Wheel of Blackpool, dangerously near, loomed straight above our heads on the back-cloth, but certain improvements improbable even in that wealthy town had been effected in this travesty before our eyes. The sea, of a Mediterranean blue, was covered with yachts tacking about in what we may imagine as the winds of music, while the stage threw all its electric violence of light upon the young face and the beautifully thin legs of a girl who waited on one of the penny seats I have mentioned. Presently this reasoned delay became explicable when a cracked-voiced young man, recognisable at once as one of her lunch companions, was wafted in on the tune's breeze. It was really quite indescribable; though I knew that

had I been a painter it would have been worth many
months of my life to capture and put upon canvas the
gaiety and innocence of their dancing, so easily interpreted, too, as the very opposite to these moods. This
change from lyrical to elegiac seemed ever to be near
but it never came to the actual break, and I listened for
this transition through that parched harlequin throat,
and from the farded lips that moved like cherries to
the green tree of music, but neither faltered, neither
moved towards the edges of sunlight, and the tune sang
easily from the boughs, moving their limbs to its measures.

It was the same sort of Harlequin that I had remembered early in the afternoon at the seaside of ten
years before: it might have been his brother, and I felt
sorry for the little creature while my pathological instinct told me I had no reason to be jealous of him.
He moved at times, by one of the secrets of English
eccentric dancing, never lifting his toes but appearing
to glide on level feet across the stage, and this he did
to a ghost-like interpretation of the music's spirit in a
parody of its wanton and careless air. This difficult
feat was done without one sound from his shoes, so
that the two comedians who waited in the wings heard
their private jokes cut off and lifted from them as will
happen at a concert when the orchestra stops for a moment and the stupidist members of the audience are
caught out shouting their banalities at each other.

All this time, for the moment was drawn out to much
more than its true length, she waited for him at one
side of the stage near the footlights and the sharpest
pitch of the music. She followed that ghost upon his
tight-rope with a continual smile, while she swayed
very slightly to the tune like the gentlest blowing of a
flower when wind, as here it might be the brilliant lights,

played round her limbs and body. She moved her ankles and feet apart and then together again to this rhythm in a manner which I can only describe as the whole epitome of seduction, for it seemed to banish care with so quick and free a gesture. At a particular accent, a certain turn of the tune, when she appeared to be so much in the absolute heart of the light as to be encased and entirely rolled round in its golden cloths, she would lift up her green eyes and then cast them down again as though the weight of delights that these lifted was too great for more than a moment's lasting. These were her methods of spending that long moment of time till he came to her side.

As soon as he had reached to where she stood, and stumbled from the end of that tight-rope dance on to the flat of his feet again, they both moved to the chorus; before this it had been the verse to which he had danced and which led back by a curious and sharp joint into the burden of the tune. She lifted her beautiful legs into the air like a fountain-foot that springs suddenly into its own curves of grace and from that moment seemed determined, like the fountain, only to touch the earth again in spray. Perhaps the hot boards of the theatre burned and stung her feet, making her reluctant to do more than touch their surface; in any case her dancing seemed to lie almost entirely in the lower reaches of the air, among the lowermost branches of the scenery. Her limbs were seen, there, in their true perspective of beauty, not hedged at the knees' mean level. Had those been real apples upon the simulated boughs, they would have fallen in a pattering rain upon the tune's thin walls, thrown down by her dancing, for they hung, as upon the oldest orchard trees, but three or four feet from the ground and well within her reach.

By this time the verse had come round again, and this necessitated a new movement nearer to the ground so that they could gather strength and breath for the last minute of their dance. So she remained at the same height, lifted there this time by his seemingly puny arms, the apparent weakness of which only served to point her extreme lightness. Sometimes, out of his arms, she would do what is called, I believe, in the technique of dancing, an "entrechat"; that is to say, she struck her feet together so that they quivered and trembled her entire legs, and before that plucking or rattling was over she repeated it again, this time high in air so that she shook and trembled down the length of his arms till the points of her toes touched the boards for an instant and stilled their shaking. One would have imagined this to be the breaking of the wave, the actual touch of exhaustion where the senses are scattered, but she rose again in an instant to his full arms' length, and the petals of her dress were gathered up and crumpled in his strained embrace so that the twin stems of her legs could be seen joined and growing into the flower-body above. This was for but an instant, and then the joint of those two thin stems was hidden once more while she came fluttering and quivering down his body to the ground, hovering just over the boards as though never to touch them.

She balanced on one point for a flying moment and was at fountain height again with her flashing harlequin, whose colours changed as he danced like the water falling in bright spray, for this was the chorus, the burden of the tune come back, and they interpreted its springs and curves with as many leaps of their own through the mock sunlight. The more I realised how near to its end the tune was, the quicker its last moments seemed to go, and before I had time to take another breath they had glided like a pair of ghosts into the wings. They walked back a moment later to bow to the applause in rather a flat-footed fashion, it seemed to me, in comparison with their dancing, but, after all, you do not expect a boxer to bow and shake hands gracefully. She had a quick, rather jerky walk like a bird upon a lawn; then, the band, to hurry matters on, began another verse.

The next few moments seemed still-born, dead before they had ever come alive, and I remember nothing of them. But, gradually, if I noticed nothing round me, at any rate my thoughts began to stir out of their numbed silence, and I remembered that this was the first of her rather few appearances in the piece and that I must collect myself to remember what happened next.

The cracked, eunuch voice of the harlequin was a comfort to my depressed spirits; it was as if I were poor and dreaded living among the hard rich, and had now found equally poor neighbours for my solace. On gramophone records of ragtimes you can sometimes hear an identical voice to this singing the trashy words, and they sound, in their thin tone, above the virile and complex instruments of the band, just as strange as this cracked voice did against the happy colours of the scenery.

Next it was a swinging song. They both came in carried on a kind of bracket of music, for the introduction to this new tune took them just on to the stage and no more. So she had to jump with a high, wanton leap among the branches from which the swing was hung and into that narrow seat. The music had a saturnine childishness of air suitable to suburban gardens —you might see this from a train window—or to the most haunted of woods. At its crises it became plangent and threadbare, but was saved, time and again, by some extraordinary ornament on saxophone or piano. He held first one rope and then the other, as though tolling out the summer hours. She went to and fro among the leaves, followed in her swinging by the prying lights that moved with her, and which fell now and again upon his body till that suburban tennis-shirt was ribbed and chequered with colour.

At the lowermost point of her flight her face and head showed out with deep intensity of meaning; the other dancer, against her body and looking into her eyes, was seen by us from his back like one plate held at an angle to another plate. They were in a flat relief against each other and they moved in and out of each other's orbits in a beautiful and involuntary dance. Her green eyes and her smile, in this strongest area of light, reached to the very point of irritating loveliness, making you feel you would like to scratch your own eyes to relieve their pleasure. But this little space was so quickly crossed that seizing it was like trying to follow particular drops of a waterfall with the eyes, and your vision pursued her up again into the branches. You could see her thin waist admirably as she moved towards that apex of her flight, and once more you could watch her beautifully curved legs thrown into the air as if she were dancing and shown in all their loveliness up to the joining of the body. Just at that moment, at the very summit of this fountain throw, she came down again on her flight, passed through the strongest field of light, and moved up into the far back of the stage, though the whole of the movement was not directly facing the audience but moved diagonally to where they were sitting, so that you could always see her partly in side-face, and saw her outlined and not foreshortened against the backcloth at this second summit of her dance.

247

men with whiskies or beer, hundreds of women with
glasses of lemonade or cups of tea, thousands of children with oranges or boxes of sweets. Some of them
noisily whistled tags of the different tunes, but before
one had quite finished a second cigarette and still felt
in a numbed silence from the noise, first of the stage,
and then of the audience, an alarm-bell rang and
everybody started to scurry back to his seat.

The band was already playing. They were at the
start of a new ragtime by some good composer of the
species whose work was always international and
reached to all corners of the earth as though broadcast
in some kind of Esperanto of the senses which was understood by all nations and in all tongues. It was a
work of the most subtle carpentry, fitting in old clichés
with those newly discovered and foisted into a fresh
activity wherever it sagged by a great glissando, a
scroll from the wind instruments, or by a Spanish throb-
bing and thrumming of the strings. Every care and
concern was kept at arm's length for the two minutes it
lasted: in this space of time it broke into that kind of
universe of expression to which a picture attains in the
same span of time after you have set eyes upon it. It
was so clear-cut and bold in its self-enjoyment that one
could not help admiring the courage of the man who
launched out so readily upon the waste seas of romance; he traversed that great space with such an ease
and returned so quickly and successfully from his
voyage.

Because it constituted the sort of gaiety in which one
could never share this music affected one, beyond the
keenest appreciation of its qualities, with a deep melancholy. For this reason it was a relief to see its interpretation in the hands of people not too secure, themselves,
from the rags and crusts of chance. These hazards

only made them more determined to enjoy themselves, and they were not stale and placid at their pleasure, like those whom wealth has made safe. Their zest made me think that the lights and the music must be very different from the grim theatrical lodgings in which they were passing the winter, introducing, probably, a few cheap comforts into those drab rooms, some framed photographs, a bedspread, a spirit-lamp for hot cocoa and tea. It was just the same little superfluous cares that they changed into a deeper note of carelessness to the loud music among those cheaply glittering lights; a kind of bonus that you paid back to yourself out of the proceeds of your profession, and then spent on an outlay that helped your employer more than yourself by its raising of your spirits.

Ten o'clock, only another three-quarters of an hour of the performance, and then the curtain would come down and I should never see any of them again. I had often sat in a train for much longer than this, for a whole day and a night, and at the end of an hour from the finish of the journey I had forgotten all my fellow-passengers. Here, after a much briefer acquaintance, I had got to know these people far better but without speaking to them and only seeing them in one half of their lives; but their very number, and the fact that I was particularly interested in one individual among them, meant that by a few minutes after the fall of the curtain I should forget everything of importance about them, even trying to banish from my mind such details as I could recall in order that these should not clash with and obscure that one set of memories for which I searched.

Music, for which I have always had a better ear than I have an eye for recalling things I have seen, I found to be my best aid in this direction. Already, in a lull between two tunes, when some silly jokes were in progress, I found that by remembering one particular tune the figures that had moved to it came back into the mind, as though the notes of music were the strings to which these skeletons had danced, and now by dint of a little thinking I found I could clothe these bones with flesh. In this manner I had chosen my system before the real time for its working had arrived, and I found myself folding it away so that its first endeavours should not interfere with what still lay before me.

It was difficult not to turn, in the imagination, every banality into that quality to which it lay opposite, being in effect nearer to its alternation when it seemed farthest and most removed. They were so many trips through the looking-glass, as though, in order to scale that thin, high wall I have so often mentioned, I had recourse to the tallest of mirrors and, turned Archimedes by the force of my curiosity, had contrived this magic glass that showed me everything I wished to see, fired it into a reciprocal feeling, and then fulfilled all my ambitions by a distortion of the actual into the desirable. This latter kind of food for the mind is more easily digested for the lightness of its substance, and it runs, therefore, within much wider boundaries.

They were dancing again, and the simple white curtain that was their background, together with the fact that this same barrier did not allow of their going farther away than some ten feet from the front of the stage, made it all the easier to travel with the music to a long distance, since there was no imprisoning detail forced upon the attention.

We were transported easily from those Elysian fields, I mean that little, narrow space turned by the bright lights and the gentle winds of music into the most smooth and golden of lawns, and found ourselves among the possibilities that lay behind its sharp borders.

Every conceivable delight grew up near enough to one just to give that added pleasure of its capture. Music, itself, turned into solid forms, so that listening to its strains was as much a feat of physical strength as the playing of it. We had to break through huge blue waves, spangling them with their own blown spray; there were cliffs, high as castle walls, up which we were carried with a fabulous ease and swiftness; all the elastic contacts of perspective were stretched or drawn in, for their dramatic importance; we lived through every fulfilled or unfulfilled love-story; and the sounds of mimic war shook the leaves of the glade to their glitter of sword and trumpet.

In this perpetual false dawn I found myself living with her in an uncomfortable permanence upon the stage of the theatre. This was the only means by which I could make my life as full as this of deep-breathed and burning moments drawn out of a second's flashing life by the brakes and drags upon time that her talent imposed. I could only expect its continuation in the same conditions and under those identical lights, and so I had come to live in this hut, this canvas tent, to keep away the draughts, and in the midst, therefore, of all those hanging suits, the finery, and the dangling armour, among which we once found our actor in his garret-bedroom.

The wired windows of the dairy shook and darkened with the leaves blown against them; the wings of birds that hovered there tapped, bat-like, on the wiring; the sun walked in his woods of shade and his huge voice fell hushed upon the darkened panes. Cream for the sweet summer berries was being skimmed from the wooden pails of milk, and Pyramus and Thisbe were under the dark thatch when these various shadows

253

moved in the room. We must have a bucolic music
for this, with the distant flail, the lowing of cows
blown over the woods by slight summer winds, grass
or yellow corn bowed one way to its purring voice, and
the calls of reapers. The symposium of a summer
afternoon must be broken, now and then, by a bell tolling a long way off, or by the threatening hunter's horn;
for we should mime every possible menace, every conceivable danger to their trysting.

They can come out from the dairy and sit under a
hedge in the very heart of these sounds. The long
drifts of cloud overhead are parodied by the cows
wandering home, apparently of their own will, but
really shepherded by a dog or a tiny child. Presently
the reapers pile their sickles and climb through the
stubble of their battlefield on to a beaten path; where
the corn remains uncut it stands up like a golden honeycomb unbroken; on the hillside the grapes upon their
thin canes are like clots of black grass, distilled, perhaps, like a kind of sugar from their canes and leaves.

Then they walk out from their hedge-side to the
crops below, for this is their first meeting away from
that loose stone in the garden wall which fell to show
them to each other for the first time, such a meeting
being at least as probable as the scene I described a
little way back, at a swing which, as I said, might be
seen from any train window in any suburban garden.
The rôles are most admirably adapted; Pyramus,
pinched and innocent, and Thisbe, her name like the
sound of lips, guileless, but willing to profit by the
fallen stone.

Every sound is ominously hushed as evening falls.
The labourers have gone over the crests of the hills
and all the animals of the farm are in their folds and
pens. So they sit down against a corn-sheaf leaning

their backs against those tied prisoners and whispering to each other in the soft stillness. But a sudden terrible leaping runs through the uncut corn at their back and those hundreds of bearded, chattering heads bow one way, and are crushed by a great sunset wind, being the chill of darkness that runs over the earth at the moment of sundown. That simulation of a yellow body leaping down the field towards their cover turns in their eyes into a yellow lion ranging the hillside; Pyramus dies at its mane of yellow corn lifted above his chest, and Thisbe takes her lover's sword and runs its point into her heart.

By this time, and under that facile encouragement, we may think of the convent-wall as being successfully scaled, but this sacred subject I could only conceive of in terms of herself alone, without the aid of her wan and hazardous partner. The strong moonlight makes a thick black bar of shadow run by the side of the wall, a kind of closed corridor along which we can creep; but the moment comes when we have to leave its security and go across a space of violent whiteness into the mouth of a passage. This is immensely long and leads out at the end into a cloister which is filled like a pool with moonlight and is clearer and sharper than day, save for the extreme blackness of the shadow that its pillars cast; they break at that point where wall joins ceiling, and their twisted shadows, together with the pillars themselves, make a slanted arcading, a kind of running cage, within the cloister itself. We have to move down two long sides of this before we can throw up the rope-ladder pointed with a fine hook, which will pin itself into the wood of her window-sill; all this time there is a distant bee-like droning, as of insects in a summer wood, from the nuns who pray every two hours through the night.

It is a continual busy murmur like that of voices in a market-place, and now and again one individual drone asserts itself above the others. This midday in the most plangent of summers seemed to be buzzing and humming under the high trees; we were walking along the very wall of the chapel, so that its white-washed surface was steeped and soaked in the noise, and the little temple built over the well-head in the centre of the cloister lay in a stark, white midday of light, so strong was the moon.

The climb was easy enough, but backing out of the window on to the dangerous rungs was like coming down a ship's side on to the heaved and tumbling waves beneath, though, in this particular glare of midnight, it was more like a perilous climb from cloud to cloud with the whiteness of their unsubstantial bodies still more accentuated by the blinding light of the spaces between them. All the time there was that continual droning in progress which seemed never to pause for breath but to be independent of that function of the body, like a cat's purring or the scraping of a grass-hopper. It made, in any case, a good background for the detection of any other sound, and under its cover we came safely down into the latticed shadows and into that dark well-mouth, the long straight passage.

At the end of this the moonlight played with a slanted theatrical effect over the roofs on to the high wall we had to climb. Although it still kept that black bar of shadow under and along the wall, it contrived to pick out the figures and the very clothes of any one standing within its blackness, so that it followed all our movements like the spotlight on a dancer's body and made that poise of the body upon the wall's edge and the disappearance of limbs, head, and then hands, into a real theatrical exit under its violent brightness.

After this we may imagine, as we please, the rumble of a coach and its horses whipped into a gallop, or the dipped oar and the steel nose of the gondola, that is thrust into the corner of each fresh canal like the trophy of his armour borne before a warrior's ghost.

These journeys were accomplished on the light wings of this comedy music, for the whole beauty of music lies in the arbitrary nature of its meaning, in the fact that any one can fit his own interpretation to its mysterious clichés. I had forsaken the actual for the fanciful, and the knowledge that time was running out, that the performance was nearly finished, compressed and still further accentuated my efforts to escape beyond the bounds of realism. Here, in this cheaper kind of music, I had fallen, luckily for my purposes, into a world where everything that failed to be good had, at any rate, the merit of falling away from that standard at a slope whose very angle towards real downright badness was thrilling in its desperate attack upon the black heart of misery and illness.

The actual blew like a disturbing draught of wind upon the fanciful; whenever I became conscious of a particular scene, or some individual expression of face or pose of figure, these seemed irrelevant and like a distraction from what was in progress. There was no power I could exert against the flow of time, and I found that all I was doing tended only to make that endless passage a little shorter in this division of its length.

I found my mood beginning to change, ever so slightly, in its direction. That this evening was a unique experience, that it would never be repeated, and that, so far as anything more than the mere power of eyesight was concerned, I could have no contact with anything the other side of that sharp hedge of music, began to turn, from being a grievance, into constituting the whole mystery and the whole delight of the situation. I looked forward more than I could say in words to my night in the hotel spent on the same passage as these five or six principals in the piece, while I should go away next morning never to come back again. For a few hours I should be right in the heart of their memories and their plans for the future, as close to them in my circumstances of the moment as if we were all prisoners together waiting trial in the cells. I felt an absorbing interest in their movements, their thoughts, their ambitions; they had none in mine, and this alone sent me at a kind of tangent against their personalities. I should go away early next morning, and this gave me a "take-off" from my contact with them that built, once more, a dizzy perspective for my thoughts.

I fell out of that near future with a considerable shock into the present and found myself dashed up against the drums and trumpets of an emotional crisis. It was a plangency in which I could not participate, so curled and brassy were its coils, but I sat in safety behind that bed of sunflowers; and I thus particularise those sentiments because of their florid openness and their gilt and rayed ornament to so large and simple a centre.

Above and round me as I sat a new and sliding measure began to spread itself. It was another dance tune with the same springing and elastic shape; if ever in its fine energy it was carried out of exact form by a stress or ornament, however much this might point and emphasise its outline, the tune was carried back into its mould by just the method by which two dancers will steady their rhythm after too wild a leap with the headlong music; they move with a glissando of little steps,

in beat like a heart slowing suddenly after some
nervous shock, back into the burden of the tune; and
this main body of the music itself moves a little forward to catch the curving-back of its own ornament,
for this must never be thrown off from the parent
unless it leads back again and flows into some progression of the main body. This daring economy of effort
made one travel boldly with the music, for one felt
confident of its support beneath one.

The end was coming nearer and nearer; it was a few
handfuls of minutes in front of me. Every possible
metamorphosis of the spirit accomplished its changes
visibly, as if before my eyes.

A sprig of little bell-like notes, blown, for it seemed
impossible that they should be the work of a wooden
hammer, upon a peal of metal pipes, brought up in my
mind all the refinements upon rain, running water,
fountains. This particular run of bells was like the
raindrops on a dead winter branch, or like one of those
dried memorials of the autumn, a little branch of currants dipped in sugar and crystallised all over its ragged
cluster of fruit. Then, as if fired by that taste of sun,
I went right into the heart of these changes and muta-
tions.

Outside this bounded and finite world of the imagination the things that had an existence led their lives
with a bitter truth that I enjoyed just as much as the
false sweets of the fancy. I was now actually pleased
that I should never see her or her companions again,
and I felt it was time I turned my attention to something else, though all the time I should be spurred on
towards this new thing, whatever it might be, by the
store of energy I had directed towards this and then
discharged in some other direction.

They were going, going, slipping away from me,

and yet never nearer to me than in these last moments of their life. My receptive senses, like those currants dipped in sugar that we have just mentioned, must have been steeped in the frosty air during my afternoon walk, for inside this hot vault of the theatre they registered every detail and kept them for me as if preserved in the music to which they had lived and moved.

The threadbare theatrical wardrobe, which never holds a hundredth part of its possibilities of expression and is therefore a poor arsenal from which to fit out expeditions, had been ransacked and its darkest corners had been searched for resources. There was little left for the imagination to play with now that every stream had sung between its banks to lifted oars that chimed like chains of bells; to lifted water falling back from cupped hands through the sunlight on to the river-neck in drops of yellow amber; and to limbs half hidden in its blue, cool hair. The springs that had risen in the steep woods had been curbed in pipes until they leaped high into the air like dancers at the appointed fountain-mouth; rain had been made to fall through sunlight like a golden shower into castle windows at the greenest height of trees; and the sea had been made use of in all its changes, from its surges that turn like a sleeper in his dreams to the wildest battery of its winds, and back again to the ragged hours after the storm, when the waves toss and churn and the sharp edges of wind play like a penny trumpet and rattle at doors and windows.

The dented armour that dangled from the hooks had been used, as I have said, to impersonate every hero from Hector to Henry V. It had gleamed in sun or moon by the fountain-foot, among the reeds at the blue lake-edge, and at every cliché of fortification or rampart. These masculine heroics are fitted easily into the male elements of even such a cracked-voiced tyro of the gladiator-age as he who danced with her, throwing those trashy and spangled words into the troubled air above the music. Sometimes, when he had not yet made his entrance, her music seemed to carry a kind of trophy of his achievements before him like the helmet, the sword, and the breastplate they used to carry before a hero's corpse, and carve on his tomb before his body. In the same way her dalliance with time and her annihilation, for a few moments, of its consequences, were foreshadowed in his music.

We were now at the steepest part of the slope, and so near to the end of the whole piece that everything about it, the music, the words, and all the movements, were being taken at an exaggerated pace like the last minutes of a film. There was no time to remember, or to improve on anything, and one had to accept things as they came in order to recall the bare bones of their outline.

It was too late, now; I should never see her again alone upon the stage, and had only the half-satisfaction in prospect that she was sure to appear for the very last minute of the piece with the whole company on the stage. This came with a terrible, shuddering rush of destruction before I had quite expected its precipitate fall. All the actors were out from the wings in a moment and taking their places of precedence in long ranks. There was such a din of music and voices, such a galaxy of lights turned on to burn in their hardest glare, that though I recognised her, I could hardly take note of her appearance or attach the particular importance that I had intended to her movements. And then the curtain fell down from either side and was caught and held together in its folds by two stage-hands, while the music still went on and you could hear them singing from the other side of this rampart of wool and cotton.

Everybody was already standing and holding his hat as best might be, while struggling into the twisted arms of an overcoat; and then, just at that difficult point where my whole intentions were in peril, the turn of the tune came back again and I realised they were going to play it through once more.

The curtain went up and I had this one more opportunity of seeing the whole of what might well have been an entire summer spent in the groves and pavilions of comedy. By that reversal of the laws of nature which we notice when we are close up against its rules, it was as if I was a drowning man, and, far from myself rising to the surface three times, the sea, here a huge billowing curtain to the tides of music, made three distinct and definite attempts at my destruction. It fell and then raised itself for another fall three times, till, hardly conscious after its last descent, I was aware of that particular situation I had longed to see.

Just as the tune had curved back from its final scrolls and flourishes, the curtain, after a longer fall than before, rose to show them standing together on the empty stage. All the others had gone to their dressing-rooms to get ready for the wet streets outside. This was exactly the sort of encore one likes to extract by the imagination out of an imperfect memory; it has the sort of illusive truth that there is in a picture or in a fine page of history. Thus should things be and happen, though but rarely are they to be seen in these trappings of poetry.

They were rather too late for the applause: the theatre was already half empty; and the band, after a little fidgeting with their instruments, started on a fast, careless tune that was designed to empty the theatre by making the audience move quicker to its pace out of the hot vault. And so the curtain fell for the last time, and had I waited another moment while the attendants put dust-covers on the chairs and picked up chocolate-boxes and old programmes, I should have heard the rain falling through the open doors. But I was already steeped in that wet mist, and the only door under which figures still came out into the rain was at the back of the theatre. Once they had crossed that threshold into the damp night outside, they had crossed that transition from one half of their lives into the other; they had come through that glass wall by which I had been so intrigued and puzzled, and were back again out of the lights into the black, drab realism of one side of its transparent hardness. And so we all walked home through the rain, together, and yet apart.

VI

Finale

MY hotel, like the Pyramids of Egypt after a shower of rain or a hotter day than usual, stood there just the same as before. I came back to it like a mouse to its hole in the woodwork without the satisfaction of feeling that I had done more than to scratch the glass wall I had set out to shatter into fragments; in fact I had hoped to climb through its rainbow splinters into the strange world that lay behind, and if I had failed it was because I lacked the vulgar resolution to launch myself correctly upon this adventure. I held no one to blame but myself, and this very diminishment of my self-importance was made more pointed still by the imperturbable bulk of the hotel, to move which with the force of my own personality I might as well have set off in a rowing-boat to tow an Atlantic liner behind me.

Once I had come out from the revolving cage of the door I found myself caught up by a loud tune the hotel band was playing and put back by this into my old cells of thought, just as though these two bands, of the theatre and the hotel, had thrown me from one to the other so that I had been hurled away from the theatre music and caught in the strained meshes of the hotel. I found this new cradle resilient and yielding to the imagination, and I passed quickly through its haunted lobbies to the cold corridors above; cold, though, to the eye alone, for they were overheated to a fearful degree by long lines of hot pipes, and these steel rods hammered and beat one into a fever with their sullen fire. Behind these boiled and tortured elements, for one must acknowledge that both the water and its pipes are tormented for our comfort, my bedroom was cold and dank, its windows sponged with a thin mist at the contrast of a cold outside yet more intense than that within.

I had landed on the shores of this strange country for but little more than the space of time between two trains; I arrived one evening, and I was to leave, not the following morning, but the next time this same train was to run after that. Although by now, as one does always before a journey, I seemed to have left my present surroundings and, yet, not to have arrived back again in my old familiar environment, I felt in the mood for calls in front of the curtain, and therefore I made up my mind to come downstairs again for a little and look for the last time upon those marble halls and their sparse palm-groves. My last minutes in the theatre had given me a fondness for these recalls, and, at any rate in this set of circumstances, I was able to manage my own curtain and could control the number and force of my farewells.

I am approaching, too, at about this point, the last pages of the book, and if I have attributed so much force of emotion and such a plethora of memories to the events, though nothing happened, of what was little more than twenty-four hours in its extent of time, I do so of a special purpose, for in the only other book I have written I can with justice be accused of hanging too much to facts of history and art. For this once I have determined to do without these supports, and like Ulysses I have crawled into the ogre's cave hanging to sheep's wool, which makes but a weak steed for my purpose, and indeed I cannot now remember whether

Ulysses crawled in or out of the Cyclop's cave by this stratagem, and I must leave my doubt as to the direction of his crawling as the criterion for whether I have myself succeeded or not in the object I set out to achieve. I hope to get back safely from that hot vault, whether it be the ogre's cave or the lit theatre, by quickness of resource and a subtlety in choosing my means of escape.

Having arrived to this point with my present personnel of characters, it is now too late to introduce any others, and I must be content with the few I chose at the outset. For this reason I may have cause to return to some of the figures in the first part of this book, but such themes will be developed and brought to a conclusion in their due place.

Sometimes I wish I had the white staring gaslight for patron, since that particular sun-god would give me harder edges and a more even distribution of light. Its shadows are by contrast blacker and heavier than those thrown by electricity, and, like the posing of portraits for the early daguerreotypes, any person or thing seen in gaslight assumes a solemn and hieratic stillness; a family murder under the gas-chandelier would be turned at once to a wax-work scene with the blood running bright and hard like its waxen counterpart; two lovers in each other's arms seem as stiff and rigid as in a living-picture tableau, determined to keep their attitude and not to enjoy their kisses: they are like a clumsy stage-photograph in which the figures have the sort of monumental importance that grave-sculpture in wax would have where stone or wood were not to be procured and wax was the only material available to the sculptor's hand. Some one coming in through a door is invested with a mighty importance; this dull, thick, heavy body impends slowly under the architec-

266

tural frame, the pulpy, wax-like flesh has been pinched or swollen into features in the only place where it is visible except the hands; for the rest, the body is covered with a striped or checked cloth that arches or sags along the limbs and above the chest and stomach. Every movement is heavy, as though the pockets were weighted with lead, for gaslight lies heavily round the figures that it shines upon so that they appear to be wading through a stiff, yellow water of its own distillation.

Here, with electricity, my colours are altogether brisker and more keen. The Eighteenth Century we must conceive of, so far as a third or half of each day is concerned, in terms of candle-light. A Mozartean delicacy and sureness of detail plays around any figures in drawings of the time that reach to some degree of a social reality. In the fashion-plates of Moreau le jeune there is an incessant trembling and silky candle-light that burns in a soft and hesitating glow in and around the very figures themselves; and these effects are more certainly nearer to what I desire to achieve than the livid and staring details of gaslight. Yet with the electric light one misses some of the more plangent and slangy effects of cheap music.

Heard in little bursts and gusts through the open door of my bedroom any music that lived to as far down the corridor as where I was waiting seemed to be possessed of peculiar evocatory powers. Knowing, as I did, that everything I wished to see and discover lay round me in this passage, or, at furthest, lay down below in the hall, I would far sooner have heard music blown along the passage by a draught than have listened to it through the boughs of summer trees. I was actually in the dead of winter in one of the most bleak of Northern towns, but my surroundings turned to summer at a touch of these curved and sliding coils.

It had been a most wonderful day for me, and the ascent and gradual decline of its light had built a sloping roof for a whole treasure-house of my mythology; inside this, the artificially lit hours of the evening were like a sacred room to be unlocked by the most-hard-found of keys, its delicate machinery only to be set in motion when I could remember music, movement, and all the atmosphere of the moment.

That was the whole end of the day, but in the meantime there had been my vigil of the previous evening in the hall of the hotel, various cold moments at my window while I killed time by idly watching the sleepy fair below, not yet stirring to its afternoon work, and finally my own afternoon walk and those various drawings that had acted as so many frameworks to the peepshow that my memories projected through them. Now I was about to call all my emotions before the curtain in order to take a last adieu of these strange things that had possessed so potent an interest for me.

I was now able to pierce at any rate one of the curtains of convention and could from my observation of them in the hotel think of the different characters in their profane hours, at rest, that is to say, from what we might term their sacred activities. Making use of my own preference, I kept on placing her at different perspectives towards the false scenery or the sham reality of either kind of life. For the moment I preferred that which lay nearer to my hand and found myself walking, as if with slow and drugged deliberation, through, perhaps, a crowded room where no one whose idea of her was not strengthened through having seen her in her other kind of life could have any conception of the transcendental qualities now lying dormant and invisible. Indeed there were those traces

268

of flat and clumsy convention about her everyday life which any one else would betray if asked to act and thrown without much preparation upon the stage. With this neat and complicated machinery at my side I felt like a magician with his automaton, and the unavoidable sense of luxury from the possession of such a being became still more accentuated when I thought that the workings of this miracle were impossible of achievement without such difficult and expensive aids as a theatre, a big orchestra, and certain devices of scenery and lighting. There are few people who can drink Tokay without having their appreciation of its flavour and coolness increased by thinking of the huge Hungarian plain in which it is produced, and of the silver scissors with which the clusters are cut, the silver baskets in which they are heaped and carried, and of the virginity of the grapes from the touch of human hand until they have been crushed out of their clusters into a liquid and perfumed amber. In just this manner was my appreciation of her increased by thinking that her qualities could not be called into action until music had opened to her interpretation a whole fresh world of simile and metamorphosis. But then it was the affair of a second, and there was hardly time for a leaf to turn in the breath of the brass instruments before the trees had broken into blossom, all the seasons were set into motion in a world where they had been asleep and waiting for this signal, every emotion sprang into life, and one lived through every turn and phase of experience in the time it takes to walk down a long hotel corridor or play a gramophone record. All the time, in the play of these violent alternations of emotion, what I described in the case of the grape-clusters as their virginity from the touch of human hand was preserved by her in the manner with which she floated in, and yet outside and above, the strains of this plebeian music; so that while she seemed to deliver herself into your hands with their support and instigation, she yet recovered herself from this dangerous angle and was outside both your interference and that of the music, except in so far as this latter guided or ruled her movements.

Certain tunes were possessed of a brazen daring like the most hardened—in its human aspect—of sea-fronts. At other moments one was carried to the native regions from which these tunes sprang, where the hot air was so burdened with tropical leaf and flower that its very sweetness became thickened into a hoarse and rasping languor. The cooling draught that nature has perfected for those lands, the West Indian lime, has that same grating and husky quality as the air, and is, like the breezes that blow there, at the same time sharp and tiring, salt and spiced. We must imagine no more sign of the white man than his blood in a gentle diffusion among their daughters, where its effect has been to straighten their features and fill their limbs to a more subtle mould of beauty. We must carry back our fantasies for them to some remote and bucolic valley away from motor-car and tram, and place outside the leaf-thatched houses a whole multitude of naked children and some white-haired patriarchs of their race who may have heard from their own grandparents of the African mangrove swamps in which the raiders made them slaves. One of these old men will be thrown by the violent sun into some re-birth in sleep of his old tribal activities; he will seize his spear, long and thin as a fishing-pole, and go stalking beneath the shadows of the neighbouring groves as if about to offer combat to a cannibal knight. But he will soon come back again and put up his spear in its hiding-place among the high eaves of the house.

No one who has seen Florence Mills can deny the most extraordinary tragical and pathetic qualities to the heavy-lidded negress eyes and their jutting lips, while these talismans of so many wars of the emotions are carried still further in their fierce potency by the loveliness of their smooth shoulders and the savage suppleness of their backs. These superlatives upon everything that should be most beautiful in a European are here intensified into a tragical emotion to which it is impossible to attain among the usual chorus faces of a white theatre. We can think of the simplest parallel to these conditions in the difference between white and brown bread and the altogether disproportionate interest and satisfaction of the latter compared with the insipid and commercialised ordinariness of the former. The bird-like lightness of their feet, their faces cast in both a more lovable and a more tragic mould than those to which we are accustomed, and the line of their bodies which have never been constrained into the tightness of modern clothes, all these different factors combine into tightening their possibilities of expression into a scale of notes the conceivable melodies from which we are as yet scarcely able to grasp in the imagination.

The smooth cool flesh of the cactus grows from every rock in their valley, it is pointed and burning as a star at the spikes that guard those flat green blades; the aloes grow in great masses with a terrible ape-like air about their lopped and twisted limbs; they seem like an attempt at a vegetable man which has been manufactured by the million and cast aside as soon as finished; their piece-made limbs have been assembled and strung together with a mechanical heartlessness of in-

vention; their limbs are covered with coarse spiky
points like those the clown exposes when he pulls up
his trouser and shows the calf of the leg sprouting with
a thick noisy hair in one of the frightful demoniacal
jokes of the circus; his boots, below that horror, are as
large as the cactus-roots and splayed out at their ends
to show the gnarled toes that writhe convulsively in
socks that show each toe separate as would a glove.
But though cast aside by their maker as useless, as so
much waste rubbish, the cactuses have been invested
with a formidable fertility and they increase and thrive
among the most parched of rocks and in the most desolate Thebaids of the hills.

Trees and low bushes burn to every point imaginable
of their native green and lie at every height from the
lowest human hand to that of the tallest tower built
by man. The most huge among them turn their heavy
boughs of leaves in the wind like a wave rolling over
and breaking, so loud and rushing is their turmoil as
one stands beneath them. Some of the lower trees
have leaves of the strangest colours, like those you can
see on calm water when there is a film of oil over its
surface, or like the hues of the dying dolphin who runs
every gamut of colour through his tortured flukes as
though a certain blue, once attained to, would bring
back an untroubled sunny sea, or a particular green
some glaucous, safe level of the depths.

One came back swiftly and easily from those glades
at the dying of the tune, and was in the hotel once
more, shutting the bedroom door and about to start
down the passage towards the hall. The commonplaces of that geography seemed as familiar as the objects in one's bedroom at home, but they were hardly a
day old in the memory and were to be seen again but
once after that night—in the cold drab light of early

morning as one started off with bag and overcoat to catch the train. So from the very moment my door shut the farewells, the calls before the curtain, had begun.

The stairs were so many shallow steps into the full tide of music and one was back again in all the old surroundings of the previous evening. The little tables round the walls were occupied as before, but several of them by one person alone, and there were not so many people circulating about from group to group. It was a Monday, and the return of the business men to their work had left a greater part of these women without their relays of friends, so that there was some degree of lifelessness about the room, the dog-days of summer had come back for a day into the winter week. Out of this listlessness the essentially summer music preserved all its qualities of sparkle and life, and since it did not move many people to dance to its measures the workings of that admirable machinery were more audible and visible than usual, as though the hood or lid of an engine had been taken off so that you could see the beating pistons and flying wheels of its working.

I should never again be turned to that particular pitch of emotion by circumstances so simple in their origin. I was at just exactly that age where these things most impress themselves upon the imagination, and I entered into every conceivable delight or depression that was hinted at in the music, or in the air and atmosphere of the people sitting round me. I found that all these things, even those which were sad in import, were beginning to yield me the most intense pleasure from their association in my mind with some form or other of an expression of their meaning, so that while I preferred for my own personal enjoyment those circumstances which were happy or optimistic, I was at the same time forced to admit to myself that those things which were dreary and full of gloom had greater and more permanent possibilities in them.

I wondered whether the women sitting round me at the different tables ever took a holiday, and whether, since their present occupation was work, rest from labour meant a few days at the seaside with one of the more wealthy of their patrons, or the same thing in company with some friendly member of their profession. Why indeed was any holiday necessary where dalliance and all the other associations of idleness were the commonplaces of life? But this very reflection led one on to another: if the theatre was your livelihood, could you, on a holiday from work, spend the evening with any pleasure seeing the same kind of tricks and effects put into working by others while you watched and did not take part and saw everything from an unfamiliar external point of view? If all the workings of your life were towards preparing yourself for that dangerous intangible attraction of effecting a ravishment of the senses through the theatre lights and the nets of music, what must be your feelings towards these humbler and perhaps more immediately successful rivals to your art, and who practised it without the aids of music or special lighting effects?

Several of those faces had burned their lineaments into memory so that they could never be forgotten, and lay there to be called up easily before the eyes during a feverish night, in a railway train, or at some interminable wait when time stands still and none of the next set of scenes will build itself up into the level of touch. I can see their faces, now, one after another, each neatly framed in its hat and hair, and as visibly, tangently, there before my eyes as the heads of saints you can see sometimes in a Spanish church, each one writhing with an expression suitable to the method by which his death was effected, and all of them lying side by side in their glass cases on the sacristy shelf or cupboard.

These are the first encores, then, out of my short span of hours, and I can dangle these heads before me, remembering even some scraps of the talk that came from their lips, a little discussion of clothes, an anecdote or two, and the names of a few of their men friends bandied about among themselves as though these were the coupons for so many free meals, packets of cigarettes, or rides in motor-cars. There was only this much of warfare in their careers, that savoured in all things other than this of peace, or at any rate of the recreation, of idleness, and that was the nature of the alarm most likely to give them their cue for retirement from these cushioned halls and hired alcoves, for it is unlikely that anything save an illness would bring you to the point of feeling you had better abandon this gay but dangerous dreariness for a drab and profitless monotone of life, without much value, except as a kind of clock for time to mark its passage by a disintegration of all your fine hereditaments of hair or skin.

Returning to that life after the interval of a year or two in order to revisit your friends or your old haunts must be among the most peculiar experiences possible to human beings, for it must give your own decaying sensibilities a kind of jealous immortality to see your place filled so rapidly and easily by some one who might well be yourself, reborn into flesh and health. Everything would be altered, while remaining, in all its essentials, exactly the same. The same hotel building, only with a freshly darkening coat of paint and perhaps new carpets and sofa-covers, and with the band playing another set of tunes that, though new and unfamiliar, were with difficulty to be distinguished from the old. Clerks and people in shops have their position filled as easily out of the plethora of human beings, once they are gone, but it is no part of their lives to pretend that even a simulated gaiety is required from them in the hours of work.

Towards these pathetic tones of gaiety any one who had actually worked himself, or herself, into a permanence on the theatre boards could not possibly help feeling both a compassion and a deep degree of interest, like that we feel on discovering some trait typical of Europeans among the natives of the Congo, or the Amazon, which emotion has its sort of return boomerang of sentiment in the platitude about our all being brothers and sisters. So must doctors of true medical science regard the witch-doctors of the Zulus, or members of the Meteorological Office the native rain-makers.

A kind of repressed and constipated hysteria in need of a perpetual laxative must be one of the motives that drive people into what are really, in these kinds of cases, but different conditions of the same profession, for you cannot be forced to go upon the stage any more than you can be driven by necessity into an immediately successful livelihood from the streets. There is a nicely graded road into the fully fledged condition of both these ways of life, and along this people cannot be propelled who have not some innate yearning towards the more dangerous degrees of comfort. I suppose that nearly all these women are the children of mothers who have suffered the same constraints of necessity and predisposition.

In the case of the person I had come here to admire the circumstances were different. She was obviously— and I knew it to be so from reliable sources—the daughter of stage-people, and the most rigorously guarded walls of virtue always surround such as her. If she ever favoured one of her lovers, he would almost certainly be some actor in her company or whom she had known from childhood. Perhaps their near angle to the audience allows them to appreciate the silliness of so many rows of admirers, for as a rule they keep to themselves in their spare hours and are not tempted into the enemy's ranks by anything except the very excess of wealth. Yet the mere conditions of life in such people as this, passed hurriedly for several generations from place to place, and in every place near to the glamours of surrender, have given them a kind of innate knowledge and an extraordinary power to simulate these leanings over the precipice edge.

Safe above its sudden break, they can rehearse every subtlety of danger above the absolute brink of virtue, and their movements are so clear and transparent in the intense and studied light that the only hedge between us is that glass wall I have spoken of, behind whose tangible but invisible barrier they can be seen in every movement.

It stood there higher and stronger than ever; impossible to climb across or to get through, and it seemed that the only policy was to enjoy this clear frame which showed to such advantage everything that was in progress on the other side of its safe strength. That pleasant fruit which seemed for ever about to fall into one's arms was really held up on to its bough by some mysterious agency the wind, perhaps, from all this music below, and it would never tumble through the space of air between us, however much this very wind might blow it out towards us over the fronds of these same tunes.

These necessary ingredients, the music, the haunting vulgarity, all the hazards of this life, in the attraction that shot out its summer flames towards me, blew upon all these short moments and fanned them into a perpetual summer heat, so that both at the time and ever afterwards, if I think of them, I see these little inconsequential hours lying out of the winter in a brief summer of their own making.

This space is quite circumscribed with lights, so that I had mimic suns to choose from and could have my sunlight sifted through the summer boughs, or let his red spikes, his cock's-comb, stay out of sight while the indisputable light, as if you were sitting at a window and felt his heat but could not see his precise post in the clouds, fell on everything round and was obviously waiting for some one particular moment of concentration.

Inside this radiance everything lived with a remarkable freedom of movement and seemed cool and refreshed by its force. There were none of the pinched waists or fortressed skirts that gave the theatre to certain minds in a peculiar atmosphere of artifice, when its banal vulgarities were encased in a more solidified stiffness of dress than any Spanish Infanta ever suffered. We can see the can-can dancers, in drawings of Constantin Guys, flounced in curtain thicknesses of material and with their long white-stockinged legs thrown high into the air like spindles. The audience in their high hats and huge plaid checks, their faces covered with long whiskers, seem as heated under the tiring gaslight as do the dancers. These later summers in the artificial light have been broken of that hardness which gave them their point; their moments of energy are less staccato in tone, and the science of light has been developed into a kind of idealised weather control, as

will be the climatic conditions when science has made
mankind master of the seasons.

I was beginning, now, to learn the rules of this warfare; I had already taught myself to have no regrets
and to leave no sentiment over from the moment; to
put it all, that is to say, into what pleasures there were
to be deduced from sharp curves and sliding scales in
the music, or from violent prettiness in the sort of concentration of light that a surgeon would like thrown
upon his victim on the operating-table.

After all, in a few months, a few weeks, even, this
whole set of characters and all the tunes to which they
were put into motion would be dead and useless, they
would have no more purpose left in them than the
scenes against which they had been posed, while their
places would be taken easily and instantly by some
other false family whose lives would be unfolded with
the same accessories of painted canvas and music, all
of them alike doomed to perish at the end of a very
few weeks of life.

In fact, one succeeded to the other and was as difficult to distinguish from its predecessors and successors
as the crowd of confederates that I have described
sitting in the halls of the hotel. I should be wrong,
therefore, in taking a particular, as against a general interest in these scenes; and yet my bias drew me into an
indescribable degree of emotion at what I knew to be
only the type, the sort of crystallised spirit of this background. It was the very strength of this embodied
ghost that appealed to me, the solidity of its thin
shadow and its life-like steps that were the embodiment
of so much of which I was ignorant.

They all came from their tombs at the band's harsh
breath; they lived again one after another to its measures. I could not help thinking how the very spirit of

their evocation tallied with that system of convention
by which we divide the indivisible body of time; for
these tunes were being played over as they would be
for some few dozens of evenings, after which, the following winter, an almost identical set of tunes when
played would evoke a nearly similar caparison of
ghosts, so that while the machinery of their production
and the general impression of their appearance were
the same, the whole process had in reality moved one
entire circle nearer to its end like the clock which
traverses an exactly similar path in its working and yet
advances you, everything connected with you, and all
the externals of life, one step nearer to whatever chasm
it is that lies in front of you.

The clock had advanced to well within the boundaries of one march of its path; the band had played for
some half-hour, and the whole machinery of time and
place was in motion. So far as I was concerned it was
the last cycle they were to describe, for it was already
my day of departure and, even now, were I to go upstairs to bed I should have under six hours of sleep
before it was time to get up and prepare for the station. In order to ensure a deeper profundity of sleep
it seemed as well to stay up a little while longer.

Then I looked up from my watch and saw them
coming downstairs into the hall and making straight
for the empty table opposite to me by one of those
torments prepared for us by whatever evil chance lies
round us watching its fortune. In order to beat back
its attack I stood my ground and remained stolidly behind the rampart of my table. They seemed to be a
little tired themselves after the play, but had obviously
had supper and were now coming in to sit still a little
in order not to go to bed too soon after their meal.
They talked in low voices and looked round curiously

on the people near them, for they must have grown
familiar with all the usual inhabitants of this hall and
could recognise a newcomer as soon as they set eyes
on him.   Simply because I was opposite to them they
looked in my direction last, having registered some one
at the nearest table to them but being more interested
to see what was going on in distant corners of the room.

Then they all turned their eyes towards me and I
could see that there was a general discussion as to who
I could be and for what purpose I had come there,
since, without undue vanity, I may at any rate assume
that they could not have mistaken me for a commercial
traveller.   I was too young to be in the town on business, and no one ever stayed there for pleasure.

This ordeal lasted for several minutes, and I wondered at times whether she had any inkling, even a
passing suspicion, of the truth; if only I had possessed
the boldness to cross the carpet and go to their table, all
my difficulties would have been ended, and I should
not, I can see now, have been received with that coldness I anticipated, in fact the very informality of such
an approach would have disposed them towards me.
If I had only said quite simply why I had come there,
I should have been greeted with nothing worse than
gentle laughter.

Now, indeed, I come to the whole climax of this
adventure, and it is my legitimate right to examine
the alternatives to what did actually occur just as no
one can read of the battle of Waterloo without thinking, for a moment, of Napoleon as victor, and of what
the developments from his success might have been.
Towards the events of one's own life one must also, at
times, try to take the impartial attitude of an observer, and this questioning of possibilities leads very
far from the path life has actually taken.

The concentration of my whole emotion and all my senses did, undeniably, make some impression upon her sensibility, but it may so well have been, as will happen in these moments of urgency, a message quite different from that I sought to convey. The battery of nerves with which one is equipped can in its agonies produce an effect upon the nervous senses of other people, but the very aiming of all these shafts towards one point, instead of their leaving the body like a sheaf of rays or arrows, causes them very often to just miss their mark, passing sadly near to it but failing to do more than disturb it with the wind of their passage.

I was travelling perfectly straight in the direction of the romantic country I wished to arrive at, and it was as if some bribed pointsman had deliberately switched my train at the critical moment on to the wrong line. A moment later we were getting further and further apart, and now every single day I live takes me into reaches of life more remote from that possibility. In fact, what never took place has become part of my own antiquity, a kind of legend growing out of some cranny of my memory to which I cannot climb. I can see the branches growing from this tree, I can even examine many of the leaves, but it is difficult for me to authenticate the strength of the stem that supports them, since I cannot vouch for the soil from which it springs.

I can see many lingering days passed in this environment of hall and corridor, till long moments in each evening at the theatre seemed to be loaded with lead, and till the pantomime jokes exploded night after night seared into one's flesh like the explosive darts the Spaniards throw into the backs of slow bulls. Perhaps her very complacency towards all this monotony would have enraged one at the end, but stretched out of those last evenings, from the last week of performances, I can see the summer groves and pavilions of comedy prolonged into the real circumstances of life for a space, as, at some gala performance in the great age of theatrical staging, they would take out the back of the theatre and extend the scene from sham trees to real, and from painted fountains to those flowing with water.

Here I divert even the Thames into my service, for it has been the scene of river parties since the days of Henry the Eighth and Elizabeth, and its slow stream would seem inseparable from this particular summer diversion. To the accompaniment of many nasal gramophones I can imagine ourselves floating past the villa lights and out of those glassy fires into the dark shades beyond. The slowly gliding water beneath our boat is an unpleasant reminder that, however fast or slow we ourselves move, there is another speed, whose pace we cannot brake, and upon whose surface we can only describe a kind of zig-zag motion against its swifter and deeper progress. Those beautiful, over-arching trees stand back into a whole hanging wood above the river-bank, and all round, wherever there are lights, the houses, if you can flash the sunlight upon them just for a moment out of the summer night, seem like the exact embodiment in life of those rooms we have been watching at the theatre. Moreover, they are filled, like the stage of that theatre is in the evening, during only certain hours of each week, and these are towards its end, as, in the theatre, it is the last hours of each day that come alive.

I am certain we should have travelled abroad once, probably to Venice, and that I should have been at great pains to explain antiquity to some one who had never seen anything old before—except her own grandparents. All the different stages of decay were, therefore, fused in her mind into one long season, out of which they had declined all at once like the leaves falling off the trees. Nevertheless, that endless water-carnival of everyday life did not fail to fascinate her, for it made the ordinary events of life as strange and different from what they are generally as they become when interpreted, like they were in her profession, to strains of music.

I come up sharply against the most vivid foreground at this point, for I can see ourselves, with the most extraordinary degree of realism, standing in the Banqueting-Hall of the Labia Palace, and my watching the effect upon her of Tiepolo's frescoes of Anthony and Cleopatra. The romantic precision of the painted architecture impressed her because of its likeness to scenery, and she was delighted by the size of the pearl that Cleopatra was about to dissolve in a glass of wine. And then it suddenly broke upon me, as it does now whenever I think of it, how dead that whole painted world was, though I could see that its twin in mortality was her own sham world of verandah and suburban house, and of the two, granted that both were dead, there was no doubt which was the better embalmed and the more likely to keep its beauty.

I found it easier, and I still find it so, to walk about in that world, which, if painted, has at any rate attained to some kind of permanence, and I now felt the necessity of cutting myself adrift from this other realm of possibility, resolving, meanwhile, to enjoy its contemplation still more from my negation of it, and whenever in years to come I came close to its groves and pavilions to take my pleasure from them in deeper measure than ever because I had never really attained to them, had never set foot inside them; the glass wall

I have so often mentioned having acted as a permanent and impassable frontier to my advance.

And so I determined that this must be my last moment on that threshold, and I sat there not wanting to breathe, or move, till those few seconds I had allowed myself were dead. In that time I ran through my whole associations of the hours I had spent there and found them distended to what seemed a whole lifetime, while their rapid flowing in, one upon another, was like what a drowning man must experience in his last breath of life. Indeed these memories so wholly occupied my attention that I am quite unconscious of what else was in progress during that moment, and as to whether I was still the object of their thoughts or had by now given place to some other person they found more interesting.

I moved mechanically and with leaden feet out of the room and was so depressed in spirit that I found the very exhaustion of walking upstairs a kind of solace from its making one too out of breath to realise much else than the day's fatigue. Counting the doors along my corridor was another palliative, a drug against thinking, and I found myself at that now familiar door-handle and back again in the dark room, which I must confess sprang into some degree of liveliness with the electric light.

The process of undressing broke itself into different stages divided by such acts as the taking off of one's shoes, the cleaning of one's teeth, and the arrangement of tie and collar on the dressing-table. These little busy divisions of time acted, again, as so many distractions from the intolerable sadness that I felt, if still for a single moment.

Unfortunately that moment could not be much longer delayed, and it arrived before I quite expected it, drawing me in my slippers and dressing-gown to the window, where it forced me to draw up the blind and look out through the drizzling rain upon what I had thought would be the sleeping fair below. But here again the evil providence that watches its opportunities to torment us and harrow our feelings waited for me and threw its darts.

One of the roundabouts must have been out of repair all that evening, and I dare say they shrouded it with sheets of tarpaulin to hide those animals of the Zodiac which were the steeds to bear you round, and that they kept the groaning, asthmatic voice of the steam-organ silent until they had time to attend to it.

Through the misty window, which was now more clouded still with my own breath, I could hear them shouting down below and hammering inside the halo of lights which was thrown by this one solitary roundabout, for all the others were in darkness. Presently, after their blows on its machinery had reached to a climax, I saw them standing aside out of the way of its passage, and I realised they were going to try it through once before they threw up their work and went to bed.

It was in perfect order, and it started out of a complete silence to play just that one tune which was most calculated to carry me back out of the kind of island I had built for myself in this bedroom with my personal belongings into the groves and pavilions I had resolved to desert. I was taken up and entirely carried away from the breathless tension of the nerves in which I was listening, and I found myself travelling to its fiery measures as though I had the freedom of all its boundaries and should never again come out of those summer evenings into the realities of winter street and frost-bound country. But the tune was now but a line

286

or two from its end, and I was thrown back into the midnight fog with its death and the simultaneous turning out of all the lights to which it travelled.

Luckily I was too young to sleep badly as a result of the disruptions I had undergone, and I fell out of a hopeless effort to feel this kind of happiness once more into a deep and entirely dreamless sleep, out of which I never properly awakened till I found myself back in the train and leaving the suburbs of that town for the ice-locked countryside.

The very next morning I left London to go abroad, and we stayed the first night at Boulogne, in a hotel which was reached by a long, curving drive from the harbour, so that it lay just opposite the piers and had a narrow strip of public garden between it and the sea. I went to bed very soon after dinner, because I felt so tired and depressed.

No sooner had I got into bed than music started again, but a kind of sacred inertia kept me from discovering whether it came from a bandstand outside the hotel or from a concert-hall which I had seen some few yards down the road. This time it did not do what I had grown to expect of it, but the very difference of its strains from those to which I had been listening two nights before led me into a terrible poignancy of the spirit.

I could see all the lights of that other world burning out feverishly, those tunes born one after another into their fulness of expression, and every single thing to which I attached any sentiment lay and breathed in the summer air that I should never see again. They were living and thriving without me, and it was my own fault, and not theirs, that I had not joined them. This band, which would keep on insinuating its difference of spirit between my situation and my attempts to regain, if only in thought, the world which I had lost two days before, I forced into helping my memories more and more by its contrast to their kind of life. When I attained to a complete birth, to the real actuality of any of these thoughts, the painful contrast from the groves and pavilions in which I found myself to the situation in which I lay made me want to die and not live. However, the very sweetness of the light summer gales which carried such lively music on their wings palliated my depression, for I realised that I could make these blow upon and cool me whenever I liked, and that they waited in the summer air to do my bidding, if ever I wanted the real winter frost to be broken for a moment, or the authentic, faunal summer wind to be cooled with music.